The Ecology of City Policymaking

The Ecology
of City Policymaking

Robert J. Waste

California State University, Chico

New York   Oxford
OXFORD UNIVERSITY PRESS
1989

Oxford University Press

Oxford New York Toronto
Delhi Bombay Calcutta Madras Karachi
Petaling Jaya Singapore Hong Kong Tokyo
Nairobi Dar es Salaam Cape Town
Melbourne Auckland

and associated companies in
Berlin Ibadan

Library of Congress Cataloging-in-Publication Data
Waste, Robert J.
   The ecology of city policymaking/Robert J. Waste.
      p. cm. Bibliography: p. Includes index.
   ISBN 0-19-504313-8   ISBN 0-19-504314-6 (pbk.)
   1. Municipal government—United States. 2. Urban policy—United States.
I. Title. II. Title: Ecology of city policymaking.
JS341.W379 1989   352'.0072'0973—dc19   88-9716   CIP

9 8 7 6 5 4 3 2

Printed in the United States of America
on acid-free paper

To Kathrine

Preface

My sole intent in this small volume is to produce a clear and easily readable "map" of the city policymaking process—a map of use to both new and experienced students of local politics and policymaking. I have attempted to distill the basic elements of this process into a coherent model, one designed to facilitate both description and analysis of city policymaking. The thesis of this work is fairly straightforward. I argue that city policymaking progresses through a life cycle common to all cities, a process which helps explain why policymaking is exceedingly fragile in most American cities. In addition, I suggest that one must consider ten interrelated factors that collectively comprise the ecological system in which city policymaking takes place. Paul Peterson is correct in insisting that city governments have limits, and that these limits weaken the ability of cities to deal with urban problems.* In fact, one of the key problems facing American cities is the very weakness of city government itself. The ten-part ecological model and the policy life cycle are used to explain how and why cities are weak policymakers. I have referred to this problem as the fragility of city policymaking. The ecological model used in this book is designed to illustrate the limitations and weaknesses of the local policymaking process.

In many respects city problems and city policymaking are hopelessly mismatched. If these unequal forces were viewed as a boxing match, most states would probably refuse to grant the event a license. Such major city problems as poverty, homelessness, racism, decaying core areas, violent crime, rampant "leapfrog development" of suburban and/or environmentally sensitive areas, gridlocked high-

---

City Limits (Chicago: University of Chicago Press, 1981).

ways, and literally mounting garbage disposal problems are so huge in scale and so apparently intractable that pitting them against the policymakers and policy processes of American cities seems cruel indeed. Of course, irrespective of the odds, not to attempt the fight would be unthinkable. This volume provides a map of the city policymaking process in the hope that knowledge of the terrain will better the odds, even if only slightly.

Chico, Calif.   R.J.W.
December 1988

Acknowledgments

Having incurred several debts in the course of this study, I am pleased to be able to acknowledge them. I am particularly grateful to the following scholars, who read earlier drafts of one or more chapters: David Ames of the University of Delaware; Roger Cobb of Brown University; Bryan Jones of Texas A & M University; Paul Peterson of the Brookings Institution; David Tabb of San Francisco State University; and Aaron Wildavsky of the University of California at Berkeley. I wish especially to thank two exceedingly helpful outside readers for Oxford University Press: Paul N. Hirsch of Georgia State University, and Robert F. Percorella of Saint John's University.

In addition, while they did not read drafts of this manuscript, I have benefited greatly over the past several years from discussions of local policymaking with several colleagues. My debt in this category extends to my former jogging partner, Arnold B. Ajello, of *The Providence Journal,* as well as the following scholars: Roger W. Caves of San Diego State University; Robert A. Dahl of Yale University; G. William Domhoff of the University of California at Santa Cruz; Thomas R. Dye of Florida State University; Byron Jackson of California State University, Chico; Woodrow L. Jones, Jr., of Texas A & M University; Dale Rogers Marshall of Wellesley College; Kenneth Ornstein of The Providence Foundation; Robert S. Ross of California State University, Chico; Alvin D. Sokolow of the University of California at Davis; Glen W. Sparrow of San Diego State University; Clarence N. Stone of the University of Maryland; and Larry L. Wade of the University of California at Davis.

Chapter 3 represents a revised version of "The Early Years in the Life Cycle of a City Council: A Downsian Analysis," which appeared in *Urban Studies* 20 (1983):73–81.

I would like to thank Valerie Aubry, Social Science Editor at Oxford University Press, for her numerous substantive and stylistic suggestions. Whatever clarity the book possesses owes much to the rigor with which she reviewed the manuscript and the tact displayed in communicating her valuable suggestions. Thanks are also due to Niko Pfund, Editorial Assistant, and Henry Krawitz, Associate Editor, at Oxford for their many kindnesses, which greatly eased the burden of checking the manuscript at the editing stage.

I also owe a debt of thanks to my longtime colleague and friend Michael Goulding for his advice and support, and for the abuse which his printer and computer frequently suffered so that this project might be completed in a timely fashion.

Finally, I am grateful to my wife, Kathrine Lemke Waste, for believing both in this book and in me. I am also grateful to my son, John Jackson Waste (aged three), who interrupted the writing of the book countless times and, in so doing, improved it immeasurably. Surely Aristotle was correct in arguing that the city draws its strength—and we our understanding of the city—from the family.

Contents

List of Figures

List of Tables

The Ecology of City Policymaking

1

The Ecology of City Policymaking

Cities are both remarkably different and remarkably similar. Both the differences and the similarities have important consequences for local policymaking—and for the study of local policymaking. Differences among American cities vary from the obvious to the extremely subtle. For example, obvious differences among cities include region (sunbelt or frostbelt), location (central city, fringe city, suburban city, or isolated independent city), size (megacities of one million plus or smaller cities), and age (newly incorporated cities or cities such as Boston or New York, which are older than the American national government). Cities also differ in more subtle ways, such as political culture (conservative or liberal), rate of growth (fast, slow, or no growth), psychological attitudes (statesmen, conservers, climbers, zealots, or advocates), and leadership styles (entrepreneurs, crusaders, bosses, or brokers) of elected officials.

Despite this wide range of differences among cities in America, all U.S. cities are similar in two important respects. First, as we shall argue, policy is enacted in the same way, and goes through the same "life cycle" in every American city. Second, all cities share a policymaking environment, or "policy ecology," comprising ten key elements. These include: (1) age, (2) locale, (3) the growth process and rate of growth, (4) the local political culture, (5) the personality of key elected and appointed policymakers in the city, (6) the presence or absence of political scandals or reform efforts, (7) the types of policy conflict that occur in American cities, (8) the types of policies enacted in American cities, (9) the presence and strength of regulatory activity in the city, and (10) exogenous factors subsumed under the heading "intergovernmental relations."

While the local mix of these ten elements often varies greatly from locale to locale—Berkeley, for example, differs greatly from both neighboring Oakland and from faraway Boston—the basic process of local policymaking follows the same pattern, or "life cycle." The present book uses the policy life cycle model and the ten-part "policy ecology" of cities to explain policymaking in American cities.[1] My argument, in brief, is that policymaking in American cities is best viewed as the result of the policy cycle of a city interacting with, and affected by, ten internal and external variables in accordance with routinized laws that govern the behavior of local governmental bodies and assign advantages and disadvantages to various players and policy alternatives. To greatly simplify my argument, city policy is not caused or determined but is greatly influenced by ten identifiable ecological factors that affect the policy life cycle in differing degrees in all American cities. This process is illustrated in Figure 1.1.

Thus city policymaking is the result of a discernable life cycle merging with ecological variables to produce a specific outcome; the result of a process, as Bryan Jones has described it, of "wheels within wheels."[2] I do not claim that the life cycle view is a causal model. Instead, the life cycle model is presented as a way of better understanding and explaining policy, especially in terms of explaining why one city might respond to an issue and a second city not. In chapter 4, for example, we discuss why New York City addressed the problem of the homeless long before Santa Barbara, and why Santa Barbara eventually was pressured into adopting a more humane position toward the homeless in that city. Chapter 4 also attempts to answer an equally puzzling question, namely, why wide policy variations exist not only between cities such as New York and Santa Barbara but within a single city. Why will some cities succeed in making policy to solve one set of problems but fail to enact policy to solve a second set of equally or even more pressing policy problems? Chapter 4 examines policymaking in the San Diego region, where policymakers successfully enacted two complex growth-control ordinances to deal with the problems created by rapid growth in the third-fastest-growing metropolitan region in America but could not decide where to situate a futuristic trash-to-energy power plant. Before turn-

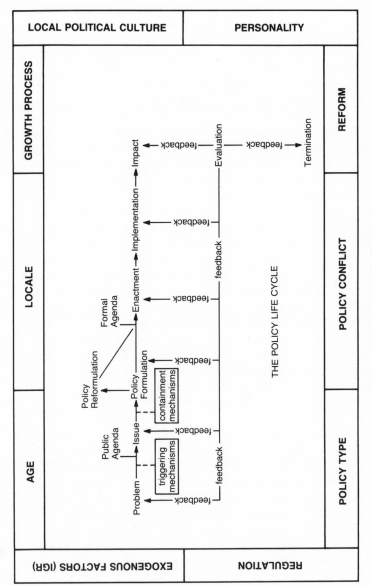

Figure 1.1 The Ecology of City Policymaking

ing to a consideration of these questions and case studies, however, it is necessary to sketch out in greater detail some of the basic elements in the ecology of city policymaking, an ecology which, as I shall argue in the final chapter, is exceedingly fragile.

The Local Community as an Ecology

As Thomas Dye has observed, a model is "an abstraction or representation of political life ... an attempt to simplify, clarify and understand what is really important about politics."[3] The ecological perspective and the life cycle model are used to distill the essence of city policymaking, to simplify a complex process, and to present the basic ingredients of that process in a systematic fashion. It is significant that although the model itself is systematic and rational, city policymaking frequently is not. Instead, city policymaking combines elements of episodic, reactive, incremental, reflexive, comprehensive, rational, substantive, and symbolic policymaking. The life cycle model abstracts this process and describes important steps or elements in the city policymaking process.

Norton Long once argued that local communities could be thought of as "an ecology of games."[4] In the same article he reasoned, "Looked at in this way, in the territorial system there is a political game, a banking game, a contracting game, a newspaper game, a civic organization game, an ecclesiastical game, and many others."[5] The argument of the present book differs from Long's depiction of cities as an aggregation of the games within it. Instead, I argue that the communal policy process consists of interrelated factors that differently affect the local policy life cycle. Nevertheless, there are some similarities between my view and Long's depiction of communities as an ecology of games. Many of the points that Long made about games in the community are applicable to my discussion of the role of life cycles in the city policy process. As Long notes, both the policy life cycle and the ecological factors of a given city share a "common field" or "territory." He explains that "the local territorial system accomplishes unplanned but largely functional results. [The ecologies] and their players mesh in their particular pursuits, to bring about overall results; the territorial system is fed and ordered. Its inhabitants are rational within limited areas and, pursuing the ends of these areas, accomplish socially functional ends." Furthermore, the ecology of a given city will often "provide the players with a set of goals that give them a sense of success or failure. They provide them determinate roles and calculable strategies and tactics."[6]

Thus city policymaking may be thought of as taking place within a given set of boundaries—a territory or policy "ecology." This territory or ecology of city policymaking, illustrated in Figure 1.1, has ten basic environmental elements. While the ten parts of the municipal policy ecology affecting the policy life cycle—(1) age, (2) locale, (3) the growth process of city councils, (4) policy types, (5) policy conflict levels, (6) reform activity, (7) regulatory activity, (8) external factors, (9) personality factors, and (10) local political culture factors—are the same for all cities, the composition and strength of the ecological factors will vary from city to city, producing a differential set of impacts, demands, cues, advantages, disadvantages, and incentives for actors in the policymaking life cycle of any given city. A description of the policy life cycle and the first eight environmental elements of the ecology of cities follows. In addition, a lengthy discussion of two of these ecological variables—the personality factor and the local political culture factor—will be found in chapter 5.

The City Ecology Model: A Brief Overview

The *life cycle of city policymaking*—the key element in the city ecology perspective on policymaking in American cities—is the process or circuit by which policy must travel in order to be enacted and implemented in local government. The life cycle—which spans the distance from the shift of a potential issue from a community "condition" to a community "problem," and through enactment and implementation to evaluation and feedback or termination—is a unique way to understand the life span of city policymaking and the crucial stages of that life span. In addition, triggering mechanisms and containment activities and strategies are central elements in explaining the success or failure of issues in successfully completing the policy life cycle circuit. The policy life cycle is analyzed in depth in chapter 2.

The *age, growth process, and locale factors* account for many variations in city policymaking. Included in this dimension of city policymaking are the effects of zealots and voluntarism, the density and spatial location of the city, the differences between councils that tend toward one of four main orientations (economic boosters, amenity providers, caretakers, or arbiters), and the impact of geographic regionalism upon local policymaking. The affect of these environmental factors on policymaking is examined in chapter 3.

The *policy types and policy conflict level factors,* including the policy conflict typology contained in chapter 4, provide a way of understanding and anticipating the general pattern of political conflict associated with policymaking in American cities, as well as a way to explain deviations from the general pattern in local policymaking. In general, I agree with prominent scholars who argue that issues determine politics. Chapter 4 introduces a new typology of local policymaking. It argues that local issues can be subdivided into five issue sets—allocational, collective goods, mixed goods, social welfare issues, or collective bads—which produce, in turn, (unless deflected by mediating influences) what we have labeled in chapter 4 as autonomous, pork barrel, conventional, redistributive, or intrusive policy politics.

The *reform, regulatory activity and external factors,* described in chapter 5 are key components in the ecology of the city policymaking process, interfering in the policymaking life cycle at irregular intervals as they ebb and flow, at times affecting the operations of the local policy life cycle greatly, and at other times affecting it very little, if at all. Chapter 6 contains conclusions regarding the life cycle model, the ecology of cities, and the fragility of city policymaking.

For the purposes of this book, the ecology of city policymaking is presented as the model depicted in Figure 1.1. Thus in order to understand, for example, how policy X unfolds in a given city, it is necessary to understand the context in which X was constructed and implemented—in short, the life cycle of policy X. In this sense, understanding policymaking in cities is a study in ecology, a study not just of public decisions but of the environmental forces that helped shape those decisions. In the Preface I listed several urban issues (e.g., violent crime, decaying core areas, gridlocked highways, homelessness, racism, rampant growth, and an inability to cope with mounting trash and garbage problems) that will be considered in this work. Chapter 2 considers the problems of violent crime and the controversy surrounding an attempt by San Francisco to enact a gun-control ordinance. Chapters 3 and 4 discuss how the problems of decaying core areas and development are being attacked by modern American cities. Chapters 1, 3, and 4 also briefly consider such celebrated efforts to revive center city areas as Boston's Quincy Market, New York City's South Street Seaport, and San Diego's Horton Plaza. Chapter 4 contains case studies of highway policymaking in San Francisco, policymaking on the homeless in New York City and Santa Barbara, controlled growth policies to prevent overbuilding in San Diego, and a case study of the still controversial use of "trash-to-energy" conversion plants in urban areas. The rest of chapter 1 introduces a few necessary technical terms and, in doing so, touches briefly on two key urban problems, namely racism and violent crime. Racism, I maintain, can be seen in the willingness of many American cities to prefer symbolic over substantive efforts to help nonwhite city residents. Violence in urban areas, as the discussion of "choke-holds" illustrates, sometimes appears to come not from the people arrested by the police, but also from the police itself.

Defining Terms

In addition to demonstrating the effectiveness of the life cycle model for understanding the local policy process, a second aim of this work is to apply many of the findings and terms used in the larger public policy field to the specific area of city policymaking. Many of these terms have been widely used for years in the fields of public policy, public administration, or American politics. My intent in the current study is to show how these terms may profitably be applied to the study of policymaking in local communities.

Defining City Policy

David Easton once defined politics as the "authoritative allocation of values."[7] With some important modifications, Easton's definition of politics is the definition of policy that I shall use in this book. The authority of city officials, whether exercised formally or informally, *de jure* or *de facto,* substantively or symbolically, is the prime focus for students of city policymaking. City policy is, as Larry Gerston has noted more generally of public policy, "the combination of basic decisions, commitments, and actions made by those who hold or affect government positions of authority."[8] Thus for our purposes, city policies are actions, commitments, and decisions taken by persons in authority in local government, and involving the allocation of the symbolic and/or substantive resources of government.

Policy Ingredients

In order to be effective, city policies must have three ingredients: an objective, a strategy to reach that objective, and the means to carry out the strategy.[9] Put somewhat differently by Bryan Jones, city policies must have four components: (1) cooperation leading up to a policy decision; (2) a goal that the policy is directed toward fulfilling; (3) resources, including "money or obvious effort committed by the government to achieve the announced goal"; and (4) a branch of local government, ranging from the mayor's office to municipal courts to local mosquito abatement control districts, to carry out the policy.[10]

Types of Policy

Policy scholars have identified several different types of policies. Murray Edelman has distinguished between substantive policies involving tangible rewards, such as large expenditures of money or resources, and symbolic policy involving the less expensive but equally important use of assurances and the orchestration of values and authoritative symbols by government.[11] Viewed in this light, construction of a freeway or airport by a community is an act of substantive policy. However, naming a freeway or an airport after Martin Luther King, Jr., for example, is an act of symbolic policymaking;

little real expenditure of capital is involved but the act may still be an important use of the authority of local government. The action may reassure constituent groups that *something* is being done by the city, that the influence of civil rights groups or the wishes of the relatively less powerful groups in the community are being taken into consideration in the highest councils of city government. But, such symbolic policymaking may be confusing or even insidious in character, as in the case of cities willing to name freeways or airports for Martin Luther King, Jr., but unwilling to commit the funds (i.e., enact substantive policy) to improve the conditions of generally inferior inner-city neighborhoods or schools. In such cases, as Michael Lipsky has noted, "symbolic dispensations may not only serve to reassure unorganized political group interests, but may also contribute to reducing the anxiety level of organized interests and wider publics which are only tangentially involved in the issues."[12] Regrettably, this is often a successful policy strategy by city policymakers. As Lipsky's study of protest activity in several American cities concluded, "symbolic reassurances are dispensed in large measure because these are the public policy outcomes and actions desired by the constituencies to which public officials are most responsive. Satisfying these wider publics, city officials can avoid pressures toward other policies placed upon them by protest organizations."[13]

Large-Scale Policymaking

Paul Schulman has recently drawn a sharp distinction between policymaking involving large projects and policymaking on a smaller scale.[14] Schulman's study focuses on extremely large projects of the national government, including the manned space exploration program, the war on poverty, and cancer research. Schulman argues that such large projects are different in character from smaller policy spheres in several important ways. The large projects are primarily differentiated by their "go/no go" nature, their requirement of vast outlays of public resources, their resistance to the traditional democratic processes of negotiation, interest accommodation, and compromise, and by the fact that such projects pose grave dangers for public accountability and democratic control.

Several of these considerations are applicable to city policymaking, although admittedly what is meant by "large" projects and policy spheres for cities is understandably less than it is for the federal government. Even so, the percentage of a city budget allocated for such major undertakings as redevelopment projects (e.g., Quincy Market in Boston, Harborfront Square in Baltimore, South Street Seaport in New York City, the Moscone Convention Center or Ghiradelli Square in San Francisco, or Horton Plaza in San Diego) may be equal to or exceed the percentage of the federal budget allocated to programs such as NASA.

Unlike most *nonmandated city programs,* the projects or policy options of large-scale city projects, as with federal programs, are frequently presented as go/no go in nature. That is, the city is going to build a convention center, to develop the downtown, or it isn't. The choice is between A and not A. It is not between part of A and part of, say, option C. In the NASA case it is easy to understand that it is ludicrous to speak of sending an astronaut halfway to the moon, or to build half an orbiting space station. Policymaking in such scenarios is not subject to the normal tug and pull of competing policy options and interests. Policymakers decide either to do or not do the given project.

However, Schulman probably makes too much of this point. As the 1986 space shuttle *Challenger* disaster illustrated, even NASA policymakers compromise and trade off efficiency for economy— which in the case of the *Challenger* resulted in the tragic choice to use less expensive multiple-piece instead of single-piece external fuel tanks and the decision to yield to bureaucratic pressure to maintain an overly ambitious launch schedule. Nevertheless, there is much to be gained by applying Schulman's argument to city policymaking. Cities are frequently engaged in large-scale projects, such as downtown redevelopment programs in which only one or two developers can put up the necessary capital. A city council or planning commission, in cases involving huge sums of money and very few major policy players, make their decisions based less on give and take than go/no go. Furthermore, with only a few players involved in the negotiations, the entire policy area raises serious questions of accountability and democratic control. Indeed, in some cities the projects proposed are so vast and the proposed developers so few in number that these large-scale projects may pose for urban policymakers much the same problems that such major contractors as General Dynamics,

Convair, or United Technologies provide for the Pentagon. City policymakers may be able to extract considerations from the few players, but in the end, if they wish the large-scale project to be built, they will have to deal with one of a very few actors with the knowledge and capital to construct such a large-scale project.[15]

Reflexive and Incremental Policymaking

Most policy, even large-scale go/no go policy, is bargainable ("divisible") and incremental to some degree—at least after it is adopted. Thus we may elect to send three instead of five astronauts to the moon, or build a two-block instead of four-block city redevelopment project. The project itself may be zero-sum in nature (either a policy body decides to support or refuse to support a project), but the scale and the conduct of the project are subject to compromise, and the increment finally selected as the preferred policy option eventually provides a precedent for future projects. Thus a freeway or a school decision is both reflexive and incremental. Reflexive policies are those that allow for the possibility of future consequences—a two-lane freeway may later be extended to four lanes, a magnet school pilot program may later be adopted systemwide. Incremental policies, as Charles Lindblom and Aaron Wildavsky have noted, are policies that may build on precedent or past policies and allow for further modification or change as experience or public pressure warrants.[16] Thus a policy such as use of the controversial "chokehold," which has been adopted by several metropolitan police departments, may be, as it is in San Diego, an example of incremental decision making at work. In the case of San Diego, the policy on choke-holds, a restraint measure used by officers to subdue persons suspected of presenting a danger to the officer in the field, is a compromise, a halfway measure between the use of no restraints at all and the far more dangerous options presented by the use of a baton or firearm by the arresting officer. San Diego adopted the use of the choke-hold in 1985 for a two- to three-year period; it was not the best rational policy choice before the city, but it provided an interim measure that would allow the city police force to "muddle through" until all the officers on the force were trained in superior self-defense methods.[17] Much of city policymaking is incremental in nature, aimed at muddling through or "satisficing" in a given context rather than achieving a perfectly rational or comprehensive policy decision.[18]

Yehezkel Dror has written of the more rational or "rational-comprehensive" side of policymaking.[19] This involves policy areas where most of the imponderables are known and knowable, where past policies do not serve as precedent or guide, time constraints do not force a rapid decision, the city is free to act in an unrestrained fashion, political compromises do not detract from the rational nature of the policy decision, and "unanticipated consequences" do not arise and present insurmountable obstacles to rational decision making. Within the purview of relatively small noncontroversial projects or policy spheres where sufficient funding exists, city policymakers can engage in small, discrete examples of rational-comprehensive policymaking. This usually occurs in those areas with little or no policy history or precedents, such as the formation of a new agency (e.g., a consumer affairs agency or a tourism promotion board) or a new project (such as the construction of a general plan in a newly incorporated city). Planning is the only large-scale policy sphere that is likely to be determined by rational-comprehensive policymaking in most American cities. This tendency, however, is complicated by the observations previously made about the nature of large-scale policymaking in local communities.

The Political Culture and Ethos of Local Communities

Local communities tend to share distinct sets of beliefs, ideas, and historical experiences that characterize a given locale. Thus we can speak of the rapidly growing but politically conservative sunbelt cities, the slowly growing frostbelt cities of the industrial northern United States, the politically liberal communities of San Francisco (which spent city money to warn citizens of the dangers of nuclear war) and Berkeley (which, for a short time, refused to conduct the pledge of allegiance to the American flag at city council meetings and, on another occasion, instituted a rent-control policy that it later successfully defended before the U.S. Supreme Court), and, equally unique, the small town that enacted a city ordinance *requiring* citizens to possess a firearm. Each of these communities has a set of beliefs and a common history (collectively referred to as the political culture) that helps to shape community ideas and policy. Political culture is not neutral; it assigns advantages and disadvantages. Thus a liberal proposal has a much better prospect of enactment in a town with a liberal political culture than it would in a community with a far more conservative political culture. Recent municipal policies declaring cities to be "nuclear free zones" or "sanctuary cities" are cases in point. The policies were aided or hindered by the political culture of the various communities. Not surprisingly, city government, in favor of a nuclear freeze or in favor of declaring the city to be a nuclear free zone were far more prevalent in cities with a liberal political ideology, just as resistance to the civil rights movement of the 1960s was greater (although not exclusively so) in cities with a conservative political ideology.

Another way to think of the political culture variable is to refer to the ethos, or orientation toward local government, held by people living in a given locale. As Banfield and Wilson, as well as Wolfinger and Field, have noted, city residents living east of the Mississippi River tend to be "private-regarding," that is, such city dwellers prefer a "strong mayor" form of government, a partisan election system, wards instead of at-large council elections, small rather than large council districts, and a patronage system of employment for city employees. Westerners and many Midwesterners, on the other hand, tend to be "public-regarding," meaning that they prefer a "mayor–council–manager" form of government, nonpartisan elections, at-large council elections, large council districts, and a large civil service–based system of city employment. In addition, Westerners tend to favor the reform institutions of *initiative, referendum,* and *recall elections* at the local level.[20] Initiatives, increasingly popular in the West, are measures placed on local or state ballots after a sufficient number of registered voters sign a petition supporting the measure.

There are several drawbacks to the political ethos concept that should be briefly catalogued here. The concept itself is inherently vague. Few studies on local political ethos exist, and even the studies on the national ethos that Americans may be said to hold in common are vague and, in places, contradictory.[21]

Interest Groups in City Policymaking

Local communities may be viewed as not simply a collection of
beliefs but also of interest groups. Organized groups that share similar attitudes and that are willing, as Ray Wolfinger has noted, "to
make claims on government on the basis of a shared attitude," are
defined as interest groups or pressure groups.[22] Such groups must
have members who are conscious of belonging to the group (e.g., a
labor union, a neighborhood-based community group, a group of
builders or developers) and who have a claim to make to city policymakers. Significantly, community groups differ in their degree of
influence or political power and in the degree to which they are able
to achieve effective access[23] to the political decision-making
machinery of local communities. The resources, social standing, and
influence of interest groups in local communities varies from group
to group and (as I shall argue in chapter 4) frequently varies from
issue to issue. If groups, as Robert Dahl has recently asserted,[24] are
unequal in their resources, they can be expected to have unequal—
or at least different—routes or patterns by which they advance their
claims in the local policy process. Finally, it is probably accurate to
assume that in most cities, as Michael Lipsky has noted, not "all
groups which make noises will receive responses from public
officials."[25]

Political "Power" in Local Communities

The ways in which community groups advance claims or "make
noise" also varies, depending on the group and the situation. Still,
some useful generalizations about group power in local communities
and the routes they follow in attempting to influence local policymakers are possible. In a *Primer for Social Dynamics,* Kenneth
Boulding distinguished three types of power exercised by interest
groups; coercive, exchange, and symbolic power.[26] Furthermore, they
could exercise these powers in either a potential or actual manner,
that is groups can threaten to use their power, or actually use it. Coercive power is the use or threatened use of punishments. In the local
political arena this might include active opposition to a candidate,

perhaps by endorsing a rival candidate, spending money to advertise against candidates or proposed policies, and so forth. Exchange power involves trading rewards, such as campaign contributions or precinct workers, in exchange for support. Symbolic power involves the lending or bestowing of legitimacy in exchange for support. Thus an interest group such as a civil rights group, an environmental group, or the local chamber of commerce which has a high status in the community and is associated with "good government" or "reform government" may lend its support to a community issue or candidate. In this fashion, local interest groups that may not have large amounts of money to spend in local politics may still be able to bestow legitimacy on a candidate or policy of their choice.

For the purposes of this book, I will distinguish among the three types of power held by interest groups and players in the local policy process; power itself is defined in terms of "ecological power." Clarence Stone has written that "ecological power is a competitive advantage in modifying conditions over which no one has complete control or full understanding. It is the capacity to make adjustments that are not mutually desired, though many of those affected are simply nonparticipants in the process of ecological adjustment."[27]

Effective Access to Community Decision Makers

Because community interest groups have varying degrees of resources and power, they will also differ in what David Truman has called their "effective access" to policymakers.[28] Truman noted that the access that groups have to policymakers depends on three factors: the "strategic position" of the group in the community, the resources of the group, and the American system of federalism which provides "multiple points of access" to interest groups. Airline pilots, for example, will have an advantageous and strategic position in discussions of whether or not a city should extend one or more runways at the municipal airport. Planning professors at local universities, on the other hand, may play a similar role in downtown redevelopment decisions, as may local neighborhood groups, builders, and bankers. Generally speaking, the higher the socioeconomic status (income, educational level, and occupational prestige level) of the interest group members, the greater their influence is likely to be in the local community. There are, however, enough exceptions to this rule of thumb to make it far from a predictable or inevitable iron law of local decision making.[29]

Slack Resources

Groups vary greatly in terms of resources, including status in the community, skilled leadership, size of membership, discipline or group cohesion, skill in using the local media to gain publicity and promote group aims, or experience in local policymaking.[30] But local policy outcomes are not simply a matter of the group with the greatest amount of resources defeating the others. Resource-poor groups may sometimes win because they are willing to spend their comparatively fewer resources in a cohesive and strategic way, bringing all their available resources to bear on policymakers.[31] While this is no guarantee of success, the use of *slack resources* by a low-resource interest group that feels strongly about a community issue may turn around what appeared on the surface to be a struggle against overwhelming odds. Thus, a group that is willing to use all its available resources—pulling out all the slack—may defeat a group that has more resources but is unwilling or unable to bring its slack resources into play.

Multiple Points of Access

As Figure 1.2 illustrates, the American governmental system of federalism in which power is subdivided into national and local centers of power, and further subdivided into executive, legislative, and judicial branches, provides "multiple points of access" or leverage points that groups may use to influence the local policy process.[32] Thus an environmental group such as the Sierra Club, which wishes to stop development and building in a section of the city they consider environmentally endangered, may do battle with a group of builders that wishes to build condominiums or an office complex in a scenic area

	Executive	Legislative	Judicial
National	President	Congress	Courts
State	Governor	Legislature	Courts
Local	Mayor	City Council	Courts

Figure 1.2 Schematic Depiction of Federalism

of the community. As large campaign contributors, the builders may have direct access to members of the council or the mayor, while the lower resourced environmental group may seek to testify at council and planning commission hearings and, later, sue in court.

There are, of course, several other possible points of local access in city policymaking. As Figure 1.3 illustrates, cities in the United States usually have one of five main types of governmental structures: (1) *strong mayor–council,* (2) *weak mayor–council,* (3) *mayor–council–city manager,* (4) *commission government,* or (5) *New England town meeting government.* In a strong mayor form of city government, mayors have many options not available to "weak mayors." Typically, strong mayors have the authority to hire and fire department heads, the ability to veto legislation passed by the city council, the power to appoint council members as members or chairs of key city council committees, and in some patronage cities the ability to hire hundreds of city employees, many of whom supported the mayor in his or her election. In cities with a weak mayoral system, department heads are selected by both the mayor and council members, the mayor cannot veto council legislation, and the hiring of city employees in weak mayor cities (as well as in council–manager cities, and commission cities) is usually based on civil service procedures rather than patronage or the spoils system.

The mayor–council–city manager form of government is typical of American cities west of the Mississippi River. These cities are often referred to as "reform cities" because the mayor–council–man-

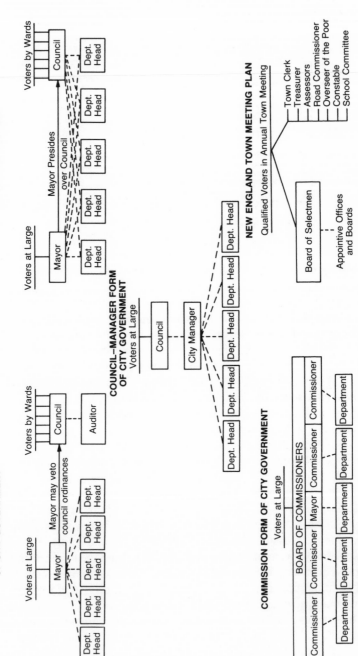

STRONG MAYOR–COUNCIL FORM
OF CITY GOVERNMENT

Voters at Large

Mayor may veto
council ordinances

Voters by Wards

Council

Auditor

Dept. Head
Dept. Head
Dept. Head
Dept. Head
Dept. Head

WEAK MAYOR–COUNCIL FORM
OF CITY GOVERNMENT

Voters at Large

Mayor

Mayor Presides
over Council

Voters by Wards

Council

Dept. Head
Dept. Head
Dept. Head
Dept. Head
Dept. Head
Dept. Head

COUNCIL–MANAGER FORM
OF CITY GOVERNMENT

Voters at Large

Council

City Manager

Dept. Head
Dept. Head
Dept. Head
Dept. Head

COMMISSION FORM OF CITY GOVERNMENT

Voters at Large

BOARD OF COMMISSIONERS

Commissioner
Commissioner
Mayor
Commissioner
Commissioner

Department
Department
Department
Department

NEW ENGLAND TOWN MEETING PLAN

Qualified Voters in Annual Town Meeting

Board of Selectmen

Appointive Offices
and Boards

Town Clerk
Treasurer
Assessors
Road Commissioner
Overseer of the Poor
Constable
School Committee

SOURCE: George S. Blair, *Government at the Grass-Roots*, 4th ed. (Pacific Palisades, Calif.: Palisades Publishers, 1986), 125–35.

ager form of government was adopted in response to the problems
of corruption and ward politics associated with such administrations
as the "Boss Tweed" Tammany Hall scandal in New York City. In
mayor–council–manager cities, council members are elected at-large
instead of from wards or districts, and one of the council members
is selected by the council to serve a short two- to three-year term as
mayor. In this system, mayoral power is supposed to be limited to
avoid the possibility of corruption. Thus mayors serve brief terms,
are selected by their peers on the council, have no veto, and cannot
hire either city employees or department heads. In fact, a public
administration professional, a city manager, is hired by the council
to run the day-to-day operations of the city. These city managers are
empowered to select and remove department heads, and they generally supervise the civil service process of hiring city employees.
Typically, a city manager will have worked in increasingly responsible positions as an administrative aide, a department head, and an
assistant city manager for several cities before he or she is hired as a
city manager. City managers spend an average of about five years in
that position, then move on to a more attractive opportunity (unless
forced out of their job due to council displeasure). In cities with a
commission form of government, a common form of municipal government in both Texas and Oregon, each council member is responsible for managing one or more city departments.

Each of these governmental forms offers different routes for groups
seeking direct access to city policymakers. In cities with a strong
mayor system, interest groups may seek to gain the ear of the mayor
or, conversely, to play off the mayor and council members against
each other. In weak mayor–council cities, interest groups will frequently bypass the mayor and seek direct access to the council itself.
Many mayor–council–manager reform cities allow citizens additional access to policymakers by providing the possibility of initiative, referenda, and recall elections. Also, groups in cities with city
managers may seek to gain the support of department heads or the
city manager for their requests before presenting them to the mayor
and members of the city council. In cities with a commission type of
government, interest groups may seek to influence only the council
member that directs the day-to-day operations of the planning
department, or the police department. Finally, groups in smaller
New England communities may choose to wait for the annual town

meeting (or to call a special town meeting) to present their demands
before city policymakers.

Local Federalism: The Impact of
Multiple Governments in One Region

The multiple points of access available to local interest groups are
different from one community to another. Other aspects of metropolitan government (see Figure 1.4) affecting access to policymaking
bodies include whether or not the city shares policymaking authority
with neighborhood or borough governments, or shares authority
with regional governmental policymaking bodies, such as county
governments, special districts, or areawide Councils of Governments
(COGs). In some cases, for example San Francisco and Miami, city
policymaking structures are more difficult for interest groups to pen-
etrate because the city and county governments are consolidated,
resulting in fewer points of direct access to policymaking bodies. It
should be noted, however, that the two consolidated governments of
these cities differ greatly. San Francisco has eliminated the city council but retained the mayor, resulting in a consolidated mayor–board
of supervisors as the governmental unit. Dade County voters

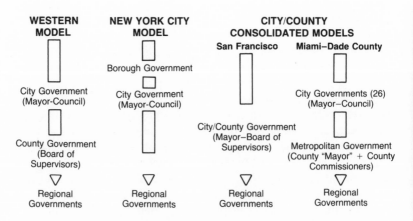

Figure 1.4 Local Federalism: The Multiple Points of Access

adopted a charter in 1957 that established a two-tier governmental system which left the twenty-six city councils in Dade County intact but strengthened the Dade County Commission (the county government). The Commission was redesigned by the charter to serve as a "metropolitan government" and assigned certain areawide powers. Some tasks are shared by both city councils and the metropolitan government of Dade County; however the metro government was authorized to establish minimum public service standards county-wide. If cities fail to meet these standards, the charter authorizes the metropolitan commission to take over the delivery of services in those cities. The charter also removed the county commissioners from direct control over departments and vested that responsibility with an appointed county administrator, the county manager. Under the 1957 charter, the county does have a mayor elected at-large to the commission, but the actual executive functions of the county are assigned to the county manager.

Independent and Dependent Local Iron Triangles

Douglas Cater once described the national policymaking process as an "iron triangle"—an informal three-way relationship of dependency, support, and information that exists among key legislative committees with their powerful committee chairmen, executive agencies whose operating budgets are supervised by these commit-tees, and interest group clienteles with a vested interest in the poli-cies enacted by the legislature and the programs implemented by the administrative agency.[33] To a certain degree, as Figure 1.5 illustrates, iron triangles may be said to exist in the local policy process. Thus it may appear to an outsider at a meeting of the city planning com-mission, for example, that policymaking in the commission is a three-ring circus,[34] featuring the commission members and staff, the city planning department, and prominent builders, with little room left over for irregular players to intervene successfully in the process. Indeed, as Hugh Heclo has noted, a mayoral appointee or a neigh-borhood interest group "may occasionally try to muscle in, but few people doubt the capacity of these subgovernments to thwart outsid-ers in the long run."[35]

Independent: A Hypothetical Example   **Dependent: A Hypothetical Example**

► Indicates policy routes: the route or path of influence and interaction among
partners in the iron triangle policymaking relationship.

Figure 1.5 Subgovernments in the Local Policy Process:
Independent and Dependent Iron Triangles

Iron triangles can describe certain local policy scenarios in one of
two ways. First, there may be an *independent* iron triangle in which
a city policy body, such as the planning commission, is influenced
by and, in turn, influences two other partners, including the city
planning department and a large association of area builders (for
example, the local Building Industry Association [BIA]). In such
cases, each of the partners needs the support and information the
others can (if willing) provide. The triangle is thus based on a symbiotic relationship among all parties. The second type of local triangles are *dependent* in character. In this scenario, while all the partners still need each other to some degree, one of the three partners
needs the others to a much greater degree. An example is the relationship among welfare clients, welfare agencies, and city councils,
or the relationship among homeless people in urban areas, the area
agencies for them, and the legislative body responsible for programs
and policy on the homeless. In such cases, typically involving low-
income or low-resource community members such as welfare recipients, occupants of low-income housing projects, or the homeless,
one of the legs of the triangles depends on the other two legs for both
material existence and policy advocacy. Frequently such groups are
unsuccessful players at the iron triangle policy game and are unable
to achieve direct access to policymakers. In such cases, these groups
may well resort to indirect access techniques, including protest activity and the use of third-party intermediaries, to argue their point with
local policymakers.

There are a few difficulties with the iron triangles concept. First, there may be far more (or far less) than three players in the policy relationship. For example, in cases involving the city planning commission, the BIA, and the city planning department, environmental groups, neighborhood groups, good government groups, the chamber of commerce, and other business groups will all be involved in attempting to influence policy formation. Thus a more realistic picture of the policy relationship is not a triangle but a *polygon,* what Hugh Heclo has called "issue networks."[36] Heclo is correct when he notes that "[t]he iron triangle concept is not so much wrong as it is disastrously incomplete. And the conventional view is especially inappropriate for understanding changes in politics and administration during recent years. . . . Looking for the closed triangles of control, we tend to miss the fairly open networks of people that increasingly impinge upon government."[37] And we also miss, I might add, the less open networks—as the one-legged iron triangle that Robert Moses constituted for years in the planning and growth policies of New York City.[38] Local policy players unable to compete in the rarified high-resource and high-visibility atmosphere of iron triangles often pursue indirect routes in attempting to influence local government.

Indirect Routes of Access to Local Policymakers

During the Progressive Era, several American cities adopted the use of initiative, referendum, and recall elections as ways of limiting the power of urban political machines and reforming local government. Groups unable to gain direct access to city policymakers or which lost an earlier round of the local policy game may attempt to use initiatives to reverse the earlier policy decision. Increasingly in western cities, citizens discouraged with the planning and environmental policy decisions of local city councils have taken such issues directly to the voters in initiative measures. This manner of planning, prevalent in several cities in the West, has been described as "ballot-box planning."[39]

Many community groups lack the resources to participate in the iron triangles style of direct access to policymakers or to mount a successful initiative, referendum, or recall election campaign. Such groups—typically but not exclusively the less affluent or minority groups—must resort to third-party intervention to achieve their aims in the local policy process. These interest groups may still achieve indirect access to policymakers by activating "reference publics."[40] Michael Lipsky has described the process of protest politics in which the demands of low-resource groups are brought to the attention of the policymakers on city councils, even when the council members may not at first hear or ignore the demands of such groups. Low-income groups may, for example, dramatize their grievances with landlords who provide inadequate heating, water, or repairs by a rent strike or by providing a "photo opportunity" for local television stations, taking reporters on a guided tour of a tenement in the dead of winter, allowing them to film graphic footage of children and senior citizens living in squalid circumstances. Often such media coverage may be a necessary but insufficient condition for scoring an impact on the local policy arena. In such cases, "reference publics"— persons who respond to such coverage and who are in a position to make policy or influence those who make policy—may be activated by media coverage of the protest activities of the low-resource group to intervene in their behalf. According to Lipsky, reference publics (such as the League of Women Voters, the American Civil Liberties Union, the chamber of commerce, or various service clubs or community notables) do so because they are genuinely motivated to do good in the local community and because doing so provides them with symbolic rewards such as prestige, media exposure, and recognition as a community "mover." In other cases, coverage by the news media may be all that is necessary for low-resource groups to have an impact on local policymakers. This would be so in cases where policymakers viewed the newscast and decided to act, or to change an earler city policy on the basis of the news coverage of the protest activity.

Lipsky describes the reference public activation process in the following way:

The "problem of the powerless" in protest activity is to activate "third parties" to enter the implicit or explicit bargaining arena in ways favorable to the protesters. This is one of the few ways in which they can "create" bargaining resources. It is intuitively unconvincing to suggest that fifteen people sitting uninvited in the Mayor's office have the power to move City Hall. A better formulation would be to appeal to a wider public to which the city administration is sensitive. Thus, in successful protest activity the *reference publics* of protest *targets* may be conceived as explicitly or implicitly reacting to protest in such a way that target groups or individuals respond in ways favorable to the protesters.[41]

In a study of several San Francisco Bay area cities, Rufus Browning, Dale Rogers Marshall, and David Tabb described a process in which neighborhood or minority concerns were sometimes addressed by a friendly ally in the city government acting on his or her own initiative.[42] Thus an assistant city manager in one city campaigned for policies that would aid low-income residents even though no residents had lobbied the official, nor was he a reference public activated by media coverage or protest activity. Such self-activating allies in high places are the most indirect of the indirect routes to effective access to the policy arena in local communities. Figure 1.6 is a schematic depiction of a number of typical direct and indirect routes to local policymaking bodies.

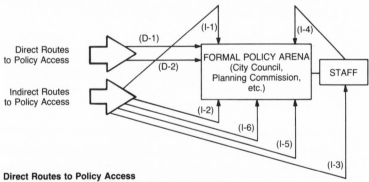

Direct Routes to Policy Access
D-1 Elections, policy mandates resulting from elections
D-2 Demands, requests presented directly to the council for specific policy action
Indirect Routes to Policy Access
I-1 Indirect lobbying via "reference publics" and third parties
I-2 Indirect lobbying by lobbyists and policy entrepreneurs
I-3 Indirect lobbying of the staff of the formal policy body
I-4 Staff-initiated policy contacts
I-5 Indirect policy input by voters via special elections (e.g., initiative, referendum, or recall elections)
I-6 "Watchdog" and agenda-setting activity by the local media

Figure 1.6 Direct and Indirect Routes to Effective Local Policy Access

Issue Networks

Hugh Heclo has coined the term "issue networks" to describe the policymaking process more accurately than the old "iron triangles" approach.[43] He cautions against looking for the two or three most powerful interest groups and assuming that these three (or four? or five?) are the whole of the policy picture. "Looking for the few who are powerful, we tend to overlook the many whose webs of influence provoke and guide the exercise of power. These webs . . . I will call "issue networks."[44] Heclo goes on to note:

> The notion of iron triangles and subgovernments presumes small circles of participants who have succeeded in becoming largely autonomous. Issue networks, on the other hand, comprise a large number of participants with quite variable degrees of mutual commitment or of dependence on others in their environment; in fact it is almost impossible to say where a network leaves off and its environment begins. Iron triangles and subgovernments suggest a stable set of participants coalesced to control fairly narrow public programs which are in the direct economic interest of each party to the alliance. Issue networks are almost the reverse image in each respect. Participants move in and out of the networks constantly. Rather than groups united in dominance over a program, no one, as far as one can tell, is in control of the policies and issues. Any direct material interest is often secondary to intellectual or emotional commitment. Network members reinforce each other's sense of issues as their interests, rather than (as standard political or economic models would have it) interests defining positions on issues.[45]

Heclo is probably correct in assuming that a picture of the policy networks and a picture of the environment or ecology of a local community would look very similar; that it might, in fact, be analytically impossible to distinguish between the two. They surely overlap. For the purposes of the present book, I will depict the local policy networks as subsumed in the policymaking life cycle and, more generally, in the overall policy ecology or environment of city government (see Figure 1.1). This ecology of city policymaking is the backdrop or stage upon which the specific local policy networks play. And like any theatre stage and building, it helps shape the way in which the play will proceed.

2

The Life Cycle of City Policymaking

> A cover of a League of Women Voter's volume fully caught
> the essence of the city's government. A Calder-like mobile
> has figures frozen in midair and interconnected in wildly
> zooming lines. A mobile is a thing of great beauty, but hardly
> functional.
>
> Frederick M. Wirt,
> *Power in the City: Decision Making in San Francisco*

Fred Wirt's characterization of San Francisco politics sums up in a
nutshell one of the leading problems in urban policy analysis—how
are we best to capture the "wildly zooming lines," "figures," and
interconnections that exist in the city policy process? The policy life
cycle theory, presented in this chapter, will explain how problems in
cities are translated into issues, and how these issues, in turn, frequently result in policy enactment, implementation, feedback, and
(occasionally) termination.

Statement of the Problem

There are several models of general policymaking that are both
widely popular and analytically rigorous. Chief among these are the
"agenda-setting" model of Roger Cobb and Charles Elder, the "policy cycle" model of Bryan Jones, and the "policy flow" model that

29

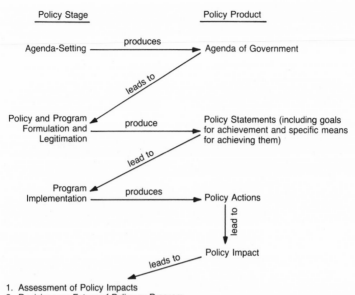

SOURCE: Randall Ripley and Grace Franklin, *Congress, the Bureaucracy, and Public Policy,* 3rd ed. (Homewood, Ill.: Dorsey Press, 1984), p. 2.

Figure 2.1 The Randall Ripley/Grace Franklin Policy Overview Model

Randall Ripley and Grace Franklin have used with great effective-ness to explain policymaking in Congress and implementation in the federal and state bureaucracies.[1] (See Figures 2.1 and 2.2.)

While each of these models is, in itself, an adequte way to view policy formation, the present chapter combines elements of all these models into a new "life cycle" model to explain policymaking. I do this not simply to add yet another model to the literature, but to cre-ate a better, more adequate way in which to understand and explain policy behavior at the municipal level. Still, it must be admitted that the new model has weaknesses as well as strengths. The life cycle model is inferior in some respects to each of the component models. The new model lacks the rich discussion and detailed analysis of the early issue-formation stage in the Cobb and Elder agenda-setting model. It also lacks the admirable economy of design found in Jones

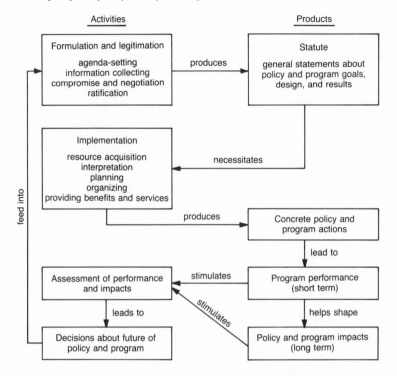

SOURCE: Randall Ripley and Grace Franklin, *Policy Implementation in the United States*, 2nd ed. (Homewood, Ill.: Dorsey Press, 1986), p. 6.

Figure 2.2 The Randall Ripley/Grace Franklin Policy Flow Model

(see Figure 2.3), as well as many of the subtleties—including the distinction between long-term and short-term policy effects—incorporated in the Ripley and Franklin policy flow model. However, and herein lies the problem for policy analysis at the local level, no current model exists that is designed primarily for the local level and which incorporates all of the major strengths of the numerous policy models currently in use.

The policy life cycle model introduced in this chapter remedies this problem. The life cycle model and the case study of a short-lived municipal gun-control policy in San Francisco should prove a useful addition to the municipal policymaking literature, and to policy-

making literature generally, for several reasons. The life cycle model
builds on earlier models and provides an integrated view of local policymaking that discusses: (1) public involvement in formulating public policy; (2) the "triggering" and "containment" mechanisms in
policy formation; (3) the time element or the temporal dimension of
local policymaking, for example how long it takes for even such a
highly emotional issue as municipal gun-control legislation to be
enacted following the assassination of San Francisco Mayor George
Moscone, and how rapidly such issues can disappear from the political arena; (4) the vulnerability of local policymaking and policymakers to outside actors and forces, particularly the impact of the
judiciary on policy formation and implementation; (5) the strengths'
and weaknesses of, in Doug Yates's terms, mayors-turned-crusaders;[2] (6) what I shall call *displacement* in the local policymaking process; and (7) the circumstances that lead not only to policy enactment
but also to policy termination.

The Jones Policy Cycle Model

In *Governing Urban America,* Bryan Jones argues that "public policy
changes come about only after traveling through a number of stages
... known as the *policy cycle.*"[3] Noting that "[n]ot all issues successfully complete the cycle; many issues never become true policy proposals and many proposals are never enacted into public policy,"
Jones presents a policy cycle[4] model to describe the policymaking
process (see Figure 2.3). This model is a valuable tool for understanding public policymaking in urban areas, and I shall use it,
slightly modified, to explain the rise and fall of gun-control legislation in San Francisco.

The Jones policy cycle (see Figure 2.3) has seven steps or stages:
problem, issue, formulation, enactment, implementation, impact,
and evaluation. As he notes, "The first transition point in the movement of a problem through the policy cycle occurs when the problem
captures the attention of a sizable segment of the public and becomes
an issue."[5] Not all problems become an identifiable public issue.
Some lack the threshold to become part of the public discourse of the
community, to be placed on what Cobb and Elder have called the

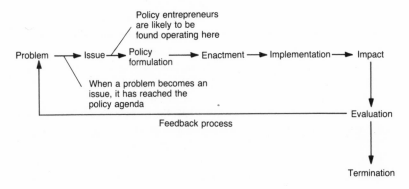

SOURCE: Bryan Jones, *Governing Urban America: A Policy Focus* (Boston: Little, Brown, 1983), p. 18.

Figure 2.3 The Bryan Jones Policy Cycle Model

"public agenda."[6] Some issues have a slightly longer life but then fade. In San Diego, for example, where environmental issues frequently dominate the public agenda, the discussion of acid rain in the northeastern United States and Canada found a curious parallel in a short-lived public discussion of acid fog—an atmospheric condition caused by the mixture of ocean fog with industrial pollutants from smokestack industries located in the Los Angeles region.[7] Thus an issue may have enough critical mass to emerge temporarily on the public agenda but later—"even if it involves a continuing problem of crucial importance to society"—may fade back into the gray zone of low priority community problems.[8]

Edward Banfield in *The Unheavenly City* and *The Unheavenly City, Revisited* has drawn a distinction between urban conditions and urban problems that is a useful corollary to the policy cycle sketched out by Bryan Jones.[9] Banfield argues that many so-called urban problems (e.g., high crime, poverty, high-density housing, gridlocked highways, and associated slow commute times) may actually be urban conditions. The distinction between problem and condition is an important one for Banfield, as well as for urban policy analysis. If an item is viewed as a condition of urban life, it is not really appropriate for it to emerge as a central issue for policymakers since it is inherently insolvable; such problems do not properly belong in the policy arena. If, on the other hand, items are seen as problems (read: solvable conditions residents are willing to tax themselves for in order to pay for attempted resolutions), then the items are appropriate for policymakers to consider and may well travel through the full seven stages of the policy cycle. But, as I noted when discussing political ethos, not all communities share similar perceptions of whether a given item is a condition or a problem, and not all residents or policy actors have the same attitude toward the proposed issue. Thus in a community that regards poor public transportation as undesirable but as a given, the matter will be treated as a condition of living in community X. In a community with mixed opinions on whether poor public transportation is a condition or an issue, the matter may require some time to incubate as a policy issue; it may even require a skilled advocate ("policy entrepreneur")[10] to articulate both the dimensions of the problem and the possible solutions available to the community. For example, F. Stevens Redburn and Terry F. Buss have demonstrated in a recent study how religious leaders in Youngstown, Ohio, served as forceful—if ultimately unsuccessful—policy entrepreneurs in viewing the closing of the Youngstown Sheet and Tube Company as a solvable problem.[11] Thus, the time invovled for the problem to ripen into a bona fide public issue (and, at a more basic level, whether the given condition is even defined as a solvable problem) depends on the type of community in which it arises, the way in which the condition/problem is viewed by that community, the presence or absence of skilled policy entrepreneurs, and—as we shall discuss later—the leadership or problem-solving style of the mayor and chief policy figures (see Figure 2.4).

Nelson Polsby has recently noted several other factors that are important in determining policy "ripeness," that is, whether and under what conditions problems will be translated into bona fide policy proposals actually scheduled for determination by public officials.[12] As Polsby notes, policy may be initiated in the formulation stage either rapidly, in response to an issue seen as immediate and threatening (Type A or "acute policies"), or more slowly (Type B or "incubatory policies"). In the case study discussed later, San Francisco represents an amalgam of both types of policy initiation. The gun-control legislation, a response to a problem of violence seen as both immediate and threatening, required four years to percolate up

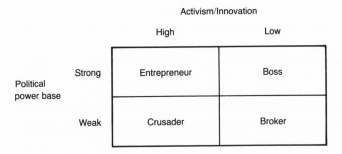

Figure 2.4 The Douglas Yates Typology of Mayoral Leadership Styles

SOURCE: Douglas Yates, *The Ungovernable City: The Politics of Urban Problems and Policy Making* (Cambridge, Mass: MIT Press, 1977), p. 164. (Arrows in the original have been deleted.)

from the public to the formal agenda of government. Furthermore, the policy style of San Francisco's Mayor Feinstein followed a pattern observed by Yates in *The Ungovernable City,* with the mayor's management style exhibiting the strengths and weaknesses of the mayor-as-crusader approach to public policy.

In *The Ungovernable City,* Yates described four types of mayoral leadership styles. (See Figure 2.4.) Mayors with high activism and innovation levels were described as "entrepreneurs" or "crusaders," while those with low levels were designated as "bosses" or "brokers." Mayors also tended to differ along two dimensions: "(1) the amount of political and financial resources that they possess in dealing with their various problems and (2) the degree of activism and innovation that they display in their daily work."[13] For Yates, the crusader style of mayor "emphasizes a symbolic politics and crisis management because he (she) does not have the resources to govern and control the city consistently through the force of political or financial clout. Instead, he must dramatize issues and develop support through the force of his principles and personality. The Lindsay administration in New York illustrated this approach to urban problem solving."[14] Lindsay's popularity was particularly weakened by the failure of several of his personal crusades to take root. Yates suggested in *The Ungovernable City* that the mayor of New Haven in the 1960s, Richard Lee, was an example of the entrepreneur style of mayor—one who uses his or her available resources to expand city services and projects and to increase their own political support. The political boss, on the other hand, is more in the mold of Chicago's Richard Daley, who possessed "strong political and/or fiscal resources but who assumes a passive attitude toward urban problem solving," adopting a motto that has been described by Milton Rakove as "don't make no waves, don't back no losers."[15] A fourth style of mayoral leadership described by Yates is that of the broker, who has few resources and is disinclined to use them, either to expand his or her political base or to push innovative programs or policies for their city. As Yates notes, "The broker accepts the limitations of his power and seems to keep peace in the city by carefully balancing and adjusting conflicts, demands, and interests. Robert Wagner and Abraham Beame of New York are illustrations of this type."[16] So, too, I might add, was the mayor of Los Angeles, Tom Bradley, *prior* to his more entrepreneurial phase associated with bringing the 1984 Summer Olympics to Los Angeles and operating the Olympics at a net profit to the city.

While many policies are stopped at various stages of the policy process, the gun-control policy in the case study I will examine was enacted, partially implemented, had impacts, and (almost immediately) was terminated. This presents the curious case of a city policy with a lengthy gestation period, followed by a rapid enactment phase, and an equally rapid termination phase.

The Policy Life Cycle Model

I have modified the Jones policy cycle in four respects (see Figure 2.5). First, the Cobb and Elder distinction between the public and formal agenda has been deliberately included into the policy life cycle model. Essentially, the public agenda is that stage when local problems become part of the public discourse of a community; when the problem shifts in the public mind from the general to the specific (e.g., pollution to acid fog) or—in Banfield's terms—from a city condition (e.g., poor public schools) to a city problem (e.g., inadequate preschool facilities).[17] The inclusion of the public agenda in the

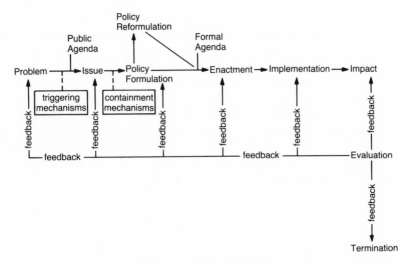

Figure 2.5 The Policy Life Cycle

model is a recognition that the problem (now viewed as an issue with pros and cons) is a part of the public debate in households of the concerned citizens of the municipality. The revised policy life cycle model also includes Cobb and Elder's formal agenda dimension. That is, when a city official places the policy on the formal agenda of government—the policy is introduced to the city council, county board, announced as policy by an elected or appointed official, or quietly or publicly implemented by city officials—the policy life cycle model takes account of this shift from the public agenda to the formal agenda of municipal government. Third, the feedback loop has been redrawn to reflect the possibility that policy feedback stages may include evaluation, termination, renewed attempts at implementation, or may recycle into the policy formation, issue, or problem stages of the policy life cycle. For example, the policy may supplant the earlier problem by creating a new problem (e.g., mayoral incompetence or high government expenditures) which dwarfs the original problem in scope and intensity. Alternatively, the policy may be implemented, judged effective or ineffective, and continued or terminated. Another possibility is that a policy deemed ineffective is reformulated, enacted, and then implemented. Thus a policy may die at any stage in the policy cycle or may take several trips and routes through the life cycle process.

A final modification is the inclusion in the policy life cycle of what Cobb and Elder have labeled containment and triggering mechanisms. Briefly stated, a triggering mechanism or device is an action or event that affects a policy problem area and serves as a catalyst for increased public attention and discussion. As Gerston notes, "a triggering mechanism is a critical development that converts a routine problem into a widely shared, negative public response."[18] A plane crash, for example, can convert vague public impressions about an airport safety problem into public issue number one for a given community. Triggering mechanisms need not always be negative. An unexpected budget surplus, for example, can serve as a triggering device promoting renewed community discussion of ways to spend the windfall income. Triggering mechanisms vary according to the degree to which they increase the scope and intensity of community dialogue, and whether the triggering event originated outside the community or within the city. Containment mechanisms are strategies or events designed to, or having the effect of, hindering the progress of a policy at the formulation, enactment, implementation, impact or evaluation, or feedback stages. Typically, containment mechanisms include studies, bipartisan panels, or blue-ribbon commissions when these are used in an effort to delay a decision, defuse an issue, or defeat a motion. Parliamentary delaying tactics and legislative counterproposals or referenda designed to moot or blunt an emerging issue are good examples of containment mechanisms commonly used in the city policy arena. Like triggering mechanisms, containment mechanisms vary according to scope and intensity, and whether they originate within or outside the city. Containment mechanisms may be viewed as "gate-keeping"[19] or "demand-screening"[20] activities undertaken by those wishing to circumvent a city policy proposal. In Jones's terms, "The ease with which an issue can reach the policy agenda, where it will be scheduled for serious consideration, is known as the penetrability of the political system."[21]

Containment mechanisms or strategies can also be used, as Cobb and Elder note, "by parties seeking to keep an issue off the agenda"[22] or, alternately, by those who wish to keep an item on the agenda but want to contain or manage the conflict level associated with the proposed policy. Generally speaking, groups employing such containment strategies divide (as suggested in Figure 2.6) into four groups:

	Group-Oriented	Issue-Oriented
Direct	Attack Group	Defusing (of issue)
Indirect	Undermine Group	Blurring (of issue)

SOURCE: Roger W. Cobb and Charles D. Elder, *Participation in American Politics: The Dynamics of Agenda-Building,* 2nd ed. (Baltimore, Md.: The Johns Hopkins University Press, 1983), p. 125.

Figure 2.6 The Cobb/Elder Conflict Containment Strategies

those who attack directly or indirectly their opponents and those who attack the policy initiative or the issue itself. This leaves several options available to those seeking to stop or contain a policy. They can attack the sponsoring group directly, or indirectly by undermining the credibility of the group purpose or leaders. More issue-oriented strategies would involve attempts to either defuse the issue or to blur it for tactical advantage.

Finally, it is important to note that, as Jones observes, "Not all policymaking takes place on the policy cycle. Off-cycle policies do not receive the necessary public attention to get them on the public agenda. They remain hidden from public view, not because anyone is trying to hide them, but because not very many people are very interested. Off-cycle policies generally affect very few people directly (although their indirect effect may be considerable)."[23] For example, city decisions concerning street sweeping, building codes, or fire department station assignments and expenditures are usually concluded off the policy cycle. Such policymaking is usually characterized, as Jones notes, by incrementalism, routinized decision making, and the use of formulas, or time-tested patterns of allocation and decision making.[24]

San Francisco, Gun Control, and the Policy Life Cycle

One of the main arguments of the present chapter is that the general policy life cycle is subject to significant influences from outside the city which may trigger, contain, delay, or cause modifications of city policy. Occasionally, a problem will emerge as an issue and succeed in traveling through the entire policy life cycle, only to be stopped by an external influence. San Francisco's gun-control legislation is a case in point; outside influences and actors exerted sufficient pressure to terminate the policy.

Politics in San Francisco, as Fred Wirt observed, can be described as "hyperpluralism" acted out inside a "restraining cage."[25] By this, Wirt means that San Francisco politics is frequently characterized by the interplay of many interest groups simultaneously demanding conflicting ends from a city policymaking structure, a structure hemmed inside the "restraining cage" of a reformist era charter approved by voters in 1932. The San Francisco charter, as Wirt notes, "succeeded admirably" in checking the then-widespread municipal corruption, "but the price for achieving this honesty was to make those who govern San Francisco impotent, to rob them of coordinated instruments for meeting emergent social problems."[26] In fact, "the charter divided the power and structure of government into so many pieces that if officials wanted to be corrupt, it would hardly be worth their while."[27] The partitioning of power is so extreme that, by the count of the executive director of San Francisco's most recent charter reform commission, there are at least nine charter-inspired, independent sources of political power with an impact on city policymaking.[28] One way for a San Francisco mayor to break out of the gridlock of hyperpluralism and the restraining cage of the city charter is to champion a major social issue that has the potential for coalescing many of the dominant interest groups into a citywide ad hoc coalition. Mayor Diane Feinstein successfully created such a policy coalition on the issue of gun control. Interestingly, she did so by creating an ad hoc citizens' commission to promote the policy. As I observed earlier, such commissions are usually used to defuse or contain a policy rather than promote it.

In 1982 the board of supervisors enacted a handgun policy that made the possession or sale of handguns a misdemeanor in San Francisco. The San Francisco handgun ban qualifies as a clear demonstration of policymaking going through the life cycle stages. The banning policy had both a policy entrepreneur (the mayor) and a tragic triggering mechanism. The 1978 assassination of Mayor George Moscone and Supervisor Harvey Milk provided the triggering event, although it took four years to evoke a policy response from city hall.

The gun ban policy is an interesting case study for four reasons. First, it shows the time it may take for vital issues to emerge onto the formal agenda—even when accompanied by the drama and tragedy of a dual assassination. Second, it shows how rapidly even highly emotional topics may fade from the public attention, and how rapidly city policy once enacted may be reversed or nullified by extramural or noncity actors or forces. Third, it shows the strengths and weaknesses of mayoral resources when, in Douglas Yates's terms, mayors become "crusaders."[29] Finally, it provides an excellent example of a policy which, once enacted, led to the emergence of a larger issue (as measured in terms of scope and intensity) that displaced the original issue on the public agenda.

San Francisco and Gun Control: From Problem to Issue

On February 25, 1982, Mayor Diane Feinstein proposed that a handgun ordinance be drafted. Triggered by the assassination of Mayor George Moscone and Supervisor Harvey Milk in 1978, and the success in court of a similar gun ban in Morton Grove, Illinois, Feinstein undertook a crusade on behalf of a handgun ban in San Francisco. The proposed ordinance made the possession or selling of handguns a misdemeanor, punishable by thirty days to six months in jail.

Nelson Polsby has suggested that policy may incubate slowly, as the result of a process of maturation, deliberation, and refinement leading to policy ripeness, or policy may emerge quickly, as a response to an issue seen as immediate and threatening.[30] The San Francisco gun-control case seems to be somewhat of an anomaly, falling in between immediate pressures to enact policy and the slower policy incubation process. The policy had as its proximate cause the assassinations of George Moscone and Harvey Milk, but required several years to ripen into a bona fide policy proposal. Such delays, while perhaps morally repugnant, are not uncommon at either the national or municipal policymaking levels. In fact, the assassination, followed by a period of public confusion and then public discussion that eventually led to legislative alternatives being placed before the appropriate policymaking body in San Francisco, is not unlike the national response to the assassination of President Garfield by Charles Giteau in 1881. Giteau, a distraught and unemployed former

Garfield campaign worker, had expected a Garfield presidency to bring him a much-desired patronage position with the federal government. When the job was not forthcoming, Giteau shot and killed the president. Despite the ensuing flood of revulsion for both the assassination and the frequently corrupt patronage system that (at least in part) prompted the assassination, it took Congress a full two years to enact the Pendleton Act, which ended the patronage system and created the U.S. Civil Service Commission.

STRATEGIES TO CONTAIN CONFLICT

Predicting "overwhelming support," Feinstein persuaded the president of the San Francisco board of supervisors to sponsor the legislation before the board.[31] Passage of an ordinance requires six of the eleven supervisor votes. The mayor created a citizens' task force to build support for the measure. The task force, supported by Police Chief Con Murphy, was headed by retired Superior Court Justice Francis McCarty and included Gina Moscone, wife of the slain mayor; George Evankovich, business manager of the Laborers International Union; Jack Crowley of the Labor Council; Arlene Sauser, chief of Adult Probation; Del Martin of the California Commission on Crime Control and Violence Prevention; Sheriff Mike Hennesey; Public Defender Jeff Brown; and representatives from the Catholic archdiocese and Jewish synagogues. The task force focused on the citywide cooperation that would be necessary to pass the gun ban ordinance, which allowed a ninety-day grace period in which to turn over one's weapons.[32] After this period the authorities would begin citing those in violation of the law. In order to help gain support for the proposal, the task force sought to heighten public awareness of the high number of gun-related crimes in San Francisco. It succeeded in gaining backing for the gun ban proposal from several prominent community groups, most notably the twenty-two-member board of the San Francisco Bar Association, which adopted unanimously a resolution stating that the "unregulated possession of handguns is not consistent with a peaceful and orderly society founded on the rule of law."[33]

POLICY FORMULATION AND REFORMULATION EFFORTS

The day after the mayor announced the proposed handgun ban, the mayor's office received 115 calls opposing and 26 favoring it.[34] In a *Chronicle* poll conducted on March 4, 1982, readers were asked: "Should handguns be banned in San Francisco?" Callers opposed the ban by a margin of 59 to 41 percent.[35] Neither of these samples were large enough or sufficiently controlled to ensure accuracy, but they do suggest that a sizable percentage of the city's population was opposed to the ban.

Although many groups, including gun dealers, the Gray Panthers, and Gays for Guns, opposed the ban, their lack of organization—particularly their inability to form one cohesive antiban umbrella group—proved a critical shortcoming. The 1,750-member San Francisco Police Officers Association, which represents all but 100 of San Francisco's police officers, opposed the ban on grounds that they believed it to be unenforceable. Nevertheless, the POA and, more surprisingly, the National Rifle Association maintained a low profile in their opposition to the proposed ordinance. The only significant public NRA protest against the ban was a full-page ad in the local newspapers on the Sunday before the supervisoral vote. This ad listed the supervisors who supported the ban and urged citizens to call and urge them to change their policy.

The opponents of the handgun ban offered many alternatives to the gun ban ordinance. The POA suggested the following: (1) toughening the existing state laws governing the use of pistols, (2) conducting a voluntary program to turn in handguns, and (3) requiring prospective pistol purchasers to attend weapon safety courses. Supervisor Ruth Silver, who opposed the ban, suggested stiffer penalties for the possession of a stolen pistol and for the possession of a firearm while under the influence of alcohol. Another supervisor, Quentin Kopp, suggested that strengthening state and federal laws should prevent the need for the San Francisco handgun ordinance.[36]

During the San Francisco debate, state ballot Proposition 15 was gaining support. This proposition, which failed by a 2 to 1 margin in the November 1982 gubernatorial election, would have prohibited the sale of unregistered pistols after April 30, 1983, and would also have required that handgun owners register their weapons with the state attorney general's office by November 1983. It is probable that many Bay area voters felt that Proposition 15 would render San Francisco's gun ban unnecessary.

Policy Enactment

Once placed on the formal agenda by the mayor, the first obstacle that the gun ban proposal had to overcome was the Public Protection

Committee, which decides whether a policy proposal in their subject will go before the full board of supervisors. This three-member committee, after hearing testimony from both sides, passed the ordinance to the board on June 11, 1982. Although the antiban groups were vocal at this stage, they still lacked cohesiveness. The ban was passed and signed into law on June 29, 1982—just four months after the proposal was first introduced.[37]

POLICY IMPLEMENTATION AND TERMINATION
From its beginning it seemed unlikely that a handgun ban would remain in effect for long. The POA protested that the ban was unenforceable and that it barred off-duty police officers from carrying guns. In March 1982, California state senator H. L. Richardson, a national spokesman for gun owners, released an opinion by the state legislative counsel which argued that San Francisco did not have the legal authority to ban guns. Following the enactment of the gun ban policy in June, Supervisor Quentin Kopp and other supervisors and citizens who opposed the ban filed one suit and the NRA filed a second suit with the state court of appeals, both groups arguing that the city ordinance violated state laws. The court of appeals ordered the city to appear at a hearing on September 22, 1982.[38] San Francisco's attorney argued that the ban was "a legally valid local supplement to state laws regulating the licensing and registration of pistols."[39] The court of appeals held otherwise, arguing that only the state legislature, through the state penal code, may regulate pistol possession in California. In a unanimous decision, the court struck down the city ordinance.

POLICY DISPLACEMENT
The Feinstein gun-control policy sparked a larger issue for San Francisco's mayor—a recall election that began as a negative response to the gun ban policy and evolved into a broader referendum on Feinstein's competence and leadership in office. I refer to this scenario—when the original policy issue is replaced by a second, more formidable, policy issue—as "policy displacement." In classic San Francisco fashion, the recall produced a hyperpluralistic aggregation of interest groups, each with a separate agenda. Controlled growth advocates and environmental groups opposed the mayor on the

grounds that she was promoting high-rise development, while other groups charged that the mayor was a tool of downtown business interests. Gays objected to Feinstein's veto of a 1982 Domestic Partner's Ordinance that would have granted unmarried couples the same employee benefit rights as married persons. The senior group Gray Panthers attacked Feinstein as soft on senior issues. The San Francisco White Panthers, a fixture of the past decade in the Haight-Ashbury neighborhood—went after Feinstein because of her sponsorship of the city pistol ban, an idea that ran head-on into their strong belief that the Constitution protects the right to bear arms. The White Panthers are a group of urban activists who are extremely vocal, well armed, and very effective at expressing deeply held populist sentiments on such grass roots issues as child care and urban homesteading. Despite the termination of the gun ban policy by the courts, the White Panthers' thirty members worked tirelessly to collect the signatures necessary to put a recall measure on the ballot.

A San Francisco *Examiner* poll taken just before the recall election showed that city dwellers, as a whole, had great confidence in Mayor Feinstein.[40] Feinstein supporters gave a number of reasons for voting to retain her. The largest group cited a good job performance and the lack of corruption in her administration as major reasons for their support of the mayor. Of the people polled, 26 percent characterized the recall as a waste of time and money, another 26 percent believed that there were insufficient grounds to recall Feinstein, while 21 percent said that she should be permitted to finish out her term. Of those who favored the recall, the largest group of recall advocates thought that she was supported by financial interests or was overly influenced by business groups. Another 13 percent disagreed with the mayor's position on housing and renter issues, while 12 percent said that they found her political views too conservative. Only 10 percent of those surveyed said they intended to vote against Feinstein because they disagreed with her support for gun control. The poll indicates how quickly the gun-control issue was submerged or displaced by other policy concerns emerging onto the public agenda. The new issues, combined with the earlier position taken by the mayor, were insufficient to unseat her. Feinstein retained her office by a margin of 81 percent to 19 percent. The mayor's wide margin of support cut across ethnic, sexual, economic, educational, partisan, and neighborhood lines.

San Francisco and the Policy Life Cycle: Conclusion

As with any research conducted in California, the author must concede the possibly idiosyncratic nature of the research environment itself. The Bay area can be a slender reed on which to base a generalization about city behavior. Still, the basic movements in the city policy formation process can be charted and analzyed. In the case of San Francisco and gun control, four important aspects can be deduced about policymaking and analysis. First, in the transition from public agenda to formal agenda, even highly emotional issues may require lengthy gestation periods to acquire policy ripeness. Second, the recall election and the lack of salience that the mayor's role in the gun-control policy had in regard to the recall effort shows how easily even a highly emotional issue such as gun control can be supplanted or *displaced* by a succeeding issue or set of issues. Third, the case study of the gun ban policy demonstrates the accuracy of Doug Yates's analysis of mayors-turned-crusaders. Such mayors may undertake bold, activist policies but "the buoyant public mood that supported political intervention, experimentation and risk taking" may raise civic expectations and force a mayor "to respond to a public mood that viewed urban crusaders with suspicion and resentment, and city life itself with increasing frustration and fear."[41] Feinstein's skill and resources were sufficient to guide the gun ban policy to enactment and, when the bubble of expectations burst and collective resentment set in, she survived the recall election. The mayor survived because of her campaign skills, because her actions on other policy fronts were viewed favorably, and because the gun ban policy was not central to the eventual voting decision of most city residents. Had Feinstein, like Lindsay of New York City, been inextricably associated with several failed city crusades, she might have fared more poorly in the recall election. And fourth, the San Francisco case study shows how closely city policy is bound to outside forces and actors. As Michael Reagan has noted, cities and their policy arenas are players in the larger system of "intergovernmental relations" (IGR)—a theme I shall return to in discussing the impact of IGR on local policymaking in chapter 5.[42] Thus city policies have recognizable life cycles, and the policies in those cycles may be initiated, accelerated, triggered, contained, delayed, reformulated, rerouted, recycled back through the cycle, or terminated by outside actors or forces.

Finally, although the policy life cycle is the basic to all U.S. cities, the ability of a city to make decisions and solve problems is not simply a consequence of activity within this policy life cycle. The life cycle is subject to influences that vary greatly from city to city, namely, the unique ecology or environment of a given city at a given point in time. Ecological factors (e.g., temporarily heightened public awareness of gun control as an issue following an assassination) play an important role in helping shape the route and timing of issues moving through the city policy life cycle. In addition to shifts in the ideology of the times for a given city, other ecological factors less ephemeral than public opinion also play key roles in the local policymaking process. The next chapter will examine how three such factors—a city's age, locale, and growth process—influence the policy life cycle in American cities.

3

Growth, Locale,
and City Policymaking

The policy life cycle discussed in the previous chapter illustrates how proposals travel from "birth" (the shift of a potential policy issue from the status of a condition to that of a municipal problem, resulting, first, in placement on the public agenda, and second, on the formal agenda of local policymakers) to "death" (policy termination). The present chapter will identify key elements in the city policymaking ecology (e.g., formal city decision-making bodies, the physical location and rate of growth of a given city) and identify how such ecological factors (as well as how *changes* in such factors) affect the overall city policymaking life cycle.

City Policymaking Bodies:
Impacts of the Growth Process and City Age

Bureaucratic and elected policy bodies pass through an identifiable aging or growth process that has been described as a "life cycle of bureaus" by Anthony Downs.[1] To avoid any confusion with the life cycle of policies discussed in chapter 2, I will refer to this as the growth or aging process of city policymaking bodies. The growth process or the age of a city council has a significant impact on municipal policymaking. An adequate understanding of the growth process is crucial to understanding how the city policy life cycle works (or, in some cases, *fails to work*) in American cities.

The Downsian Growth Process

In his now-classic study of bureaucratic decision making, Anthony Downs set forth a theory on the life cycle of bureaus. Bureaus, argued Downs, are characterized by an eight-stage developmental process: birth of the agency, early dominance by a "small band of warriors" ("advocates" or "zealots"), a struggle for autonomy followed by a similar struggle for support, rapid growth, a "decelerator effect" ending in a "crisis of continuity" ("age lump"), and, rarely, death.[2] Despite the fact that Downs was speaking of public and private agencies in democratic societies, this chapter will argue that his growth cycle theory may also be applicable to *elected* public bodies. Using case studies drawn from recently incorported cities in California (1968–74), the present chapter illustrates the growth cycle hypothesis.

Methodology and Sample

As part of a larger "Choices for Unincorporated Areas" project[3] conducted by the Institute of Governmental Affairs at the University of California at Davis, I conducted a two-round series of interviews with city officials and incorporation proponents and opponents in fifteen newly incorporated California cities from 1968 to 1974. Generally the first city manager of each newly incorporated city and at least one of the incorporation proponents elected to the first city council was interviewed. In most cases, several members of the council were interviewed in each city, as were incorporation opponents. The picture that emerged from the interviews was contrasted with newspaper accounts of both the incorporation election and the first few years of council decision making, where possible.

The sample (100 percent of the incorporation cases in the 1968–74 period) included data from metropolitan and rural as well as northern and southern areas of the state. This urban and rural mix, geographic diversity, and large sampling size have produced a reasonably solid data base from which to generalize about the behavior of new (newly incorporated) cities. However, again I must concede the possibly idiosyncratic nature of the research environment itself.

The Eight-Stage Downsian Growth Process

Downs argues that, once created or "born," bureaus are dominated in their early years by a founding "band of warriors." The early years of such bureaus are usually noted for disproportionately high numbers of strong believers in the bureau's mission ("zealots") and a large support group consisting of personnel who strongly advocate the worthwhile services provided by the bureau to "outsiders." For Downs, the combination of both zealots and advocates provides an administrative apparatus with several important survival characteristics for the new bureau. The early days of a bureau are characterized by a two-fold set of struggles. As Downs notes, "No bureau can survive unless it is continually able to demonstrate that its services are worthwhile to some group with influence over sufficient resources to keep it alive."[4] This struggle is characterized by a drive among agency personnel to portray its services as unique and to cultivate a supportive client group. A bureau which fails to do this will, as Downs observes, fall below the "initial survival threshold."[5] Even for a newly created and presumably legislatively supported agency, the possibility of failure in the first few years creates a drive by administrators to consolidate early gains and to cultivate outside support. Thus the early years are characterized by a drive for autonomy from existing (competing) governmental bureaus and a struggle for support from client groups. Once a separate identity has been established, the bureau will generally try to seek additional support and services from the very agencies from which it had earlier sought autonomy.

This early consolidation phase of a bureau is usually followed by a period of sustained and rapid growth. Once past its initial survival threshold, the new bureau seeks not to protect its flank from a killing legislative or electoral blow but to entrench old services and extend new ones. As Wildavsky notes, this is the time when bureau budget officers will wish to defend and extend the bureau "base."[6]

Downs notes a symmetrical growth pattern for bureaus. The very factors that encourage growth eventually lead to a slowing down of growth. External factors begin to impinge on the growth of the bureau. Its enlargement has altered the bureau's environment as well as its internal dynamics. The fact that the original social function of the bureau must now compete with newer programs for the allocation of attention and resources provides an internal brake on acceleration. Also, the enlarged bureau may face an increasingly hostile environment on the part of competing service deliverers. These natural brakes on bureau growth have a cumulative effect, which Downs labels the "deceleration effect." As the bureau begins to slow in growth, it tends to lose those bureau personnel who aim at achieving enhanced status or job promotion (climbers) as well as those who sought immediate societal impact (zealots).[7] If the bureau slows to a state of growth below the average of all other similarly situated bureaus, it may begin to lose agency advocates (see Table 3.1).

A bureau sustaining such an outflow of personnel experiences a crisis of advanced age—an "age lump" crisis. In such circumstances a bureau will be characterized by a different set of administrative personality types. Without zealots or climbers and with fewer advocates, the bureau will enter into a steady-state administration manned primarily by "conservers." Happily then, just as bureau growth slows, the administrative apparatus tends to be heavily populated by those predisposed to such a trimming of bureau sails. Unhappily, even a steady-state bureau requires knowledgeable personnel, and Downs believes that an exodus of such knowledgeable and upwardly mobile

TABLE 3.1   Downsian Typology of Bureaucratic Personalities

Type	Description
Climber	Purposeful overachiever—focused on promotion
Conserver	Disinclined to accept responsibility, leads by following, reluctant to initiate action or innovate—focused on standard operating procedure (SOPs) and precedent
Zealot	Loyal to a narrow set of policies—focused on a cause
Advocate	Broad loyalty to the bureau or policy body—focused on the positive aspects of the mission of the bureau/policy body
Statesman	Loyal to society as a whole—focused on the general welfare of the community

Source: Anthony Downs, *Inside Bureaucracy* (Boston: Little, Brown, 1967), abstracted from a discussion of bureaucratic personality types in chapter 9, pp. 92–111.

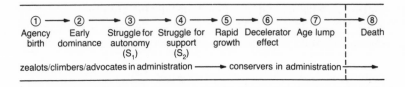

SOURCE: Robert J. Waste, "The Early Years in the Life Cycle of City Councils: A Downsian Analysis," *Urban Studies* (1983) 20:73.

Figure 3.1 The Downsian Growth Process for Public Agencies Hypothesis

people occurs in conjunction with the deceleration process. In the rare case, the age lump crisis may precipitate the final ignominy— bureau death. However, according to Downs it is a rare bureau indeed that cannot stave off its own demise. If need be, bureaus annex themselves to a former ally or even a competitor in order to survive. Twisting Mark Twain's famous quotation only a little, we may argue that—*sunset laws* notwithstanding—the reports of government bureau deaths are greatly exaggerated. (The Downsian growth process for bureaus is schematically depicted in Figure 3.1.)

The Elected "Bureau" Analogue: A Caveat

While the Downsian growth process appears to explain the policy behavior and policymaking context of new city councils, there are several significant differences between elected policy bodies and traditional bureaucratic agencies (such as a city planning department or the office of an appointed city manager).[8] Table 3.2 illustrates several of these differences. I will argue that the Downsian growth process illustrates *some* of the dynamics that occur in new city councils and policy bodies, but—and this is important to understand—the growth process illustrates only *tendencies* of behavior in such bodies rather than *inevitable* or *necessary* behavior and policy contexts in new cities.

The Elected "Bureau" Analogue: Birth and Early Dominance

Several of the interview cities passed incorporation proposals by only a slim majority (see Table 3.3). In such cities, as indeed in all

TABLE 3.2   City Bureaucratic Bodies and Elected Bodies: Some Critical Differences

Bureau (or city department)	City Council
Unit of *executive branch*	*Unit* of *legislative branch*
Employees: full-time *careerists*— selected and promoted on merit basis, many agency heads come up from ranks	*Elected Officials:* selected by the political process, emphasis on *part-time* service—most from private sector; few remain for several terms
Multiple Units: Each bureau is *one* unit of the city government that protects itself; fights for survival and seeks a bigger piece of budget pie	*Single Unit:* Only one city council per city; approves of budget and policy, some policymaking functions may be delegated to subcouncil units (e.g., planning commission, elections board, or neighborhood councils/ commissions)
Publicity Avoider: generally shuns publicity, may even defer credit to mayor–council	*Publicity Seeker:* individually and collectively seeks publicity

TABLE 3.3   Incorporation Election Percentages

City	Pro Incorporation Vote (%)	Incorporation Date
Adelanto	61	1970
Carson	66	1968
Foster City	91	1971
Hughson	90	1972
Irvine	71	1971
La Canada Flintridge	70	1976
Lafayette	55	1968
Loma Linda	90	1970
Marina	61	1975
Moraga	59	1974
Palm Desert	84	1973
Rancho Mirage	84	1973
Rancho Palos Verdes	83	1973
Simi Valley	64	1969
Waterford	51	1969

Source: Robert J. Waste, "The Early Years in the Life Cycle of City Councils: A Downsian Analysis." *Urban Studies* (1983) 20:75.

the interview cities, leaders prominent in the civic pro-incorporation
drive were elected into office as the first city council. In the hotly
contested incorporation cities, it would not stretch credulity to
describe such early council members as "a small band of warriors."[9]
In many cases this same group of incorporation proponents had
failed in at least one earlier municipal incorporation attempt. Generally, the incorporation activists were few in number, often less than
ten active individuals, of which several would subsequently become
members of the first council. Usually, the council member receiving
the most votes in the incorporation election was chosen by the council to serve as the first mayor. Even in cities where pro-incorporation
sentiments were widely shared (see Table 3.3), early council members were incorporation advocates. The first council members in all
fifteen interview cities, elected at the same time that citizens voted
to form the new city, had advocated incorporation. Interestingly, a
few individuals who had opposed incorporation also stood for council election during the vote for incorporation. These candidates, none
of whom were elected, were against incorporation but in case it succeeded wanted to be on the new council. Thus all the new cities seem
to have rejected any early council member who could not be
described as an advocate or zealot of incorporation.

In each of the cities interviewed, the overall picture produced by
the cumulative interview data was that of a first city council wherein
members saw themselves as a small band of warriors. Others not on
the council also described the members in terms that clearly paral-
leled Downs's description of advocates or zealots. City personnel, for
example, often referred to council members as treating the guidelines
of the incorporation proposal as "biblical." Staff proposals for new
services or taxes that did not correspond to those originally envisioned were often rejected by new council members. In cities that did
not provide a full complement of public services, those bureaucrats
who advocated expanding parks and recreation services, social services, or city services in general either lowered their expectations,
waited for a more propitious time (after some of the zealot/advocate
council members went back to being private citizens), or, if they
could not reconcile their view of city services with that of the council, moved on (see Table 3.4).

One southern California city staffer underlined the difference

TABLE 3.4   City Manager Turnover in New Cities

City	Incorporation Date	Hiring Date of First CM	Tenure of First CM (Months)
Adelanto	12/1970	—	—
Carson	2/1968	5/1968	122*
Foster City	4/1971	—	18
Hughson	11/1972	11/1975	13
Irvine	12/1971	3/1972	77*
La Canada Flintridge	12/1976	2/1977	18*
Lafayette	7/1968	11/1968	104*
Loma Linda	6/1970	4/1971	1
Marina	11/1975	1/1976	5
Moraga	11/1974	4/1975	40*
Palm Desert	11/1973	11/1973	2
Rancho Mirage	8/1973	8/1973	48*
Rancho Palos Verdes	10/1973	1/1974	53*
Simi Valley	11/1969	1/1970	48
Waterford	11/1969	2/1974	6

Source: Robert J. Waste, "The Early Years in the Life Cycle of City Councils: A Downsian Analysis. *Urban Studies* (1983) 20:75.

*Indicates that the first city manager is still on the job as of June 1979.

between working with an advocate-laden council and the council of an older town in which he had been previously employed. While the council in the older city had tended toward a laissez-faire administrative style, the new council was more directive. He noted, "One of the problems here is that the council is supervising and it is hard—maybe impossible—to get around this mind-set to run your own shop. It really takes until the council turns over. It's just now doing this. We still have X of our original members."

The early dominance of the council by advocates and zealots has several advantages for the new city. It means the new council administrative team will spend prodigious amounts of time in exchange for little or no monetary recompense, a quality necessary to carry it through the multiple tasks of forming and administering a new city government. Furthermore, few administrators are better suited to the task of fleshing out the new city services than the advocate/zealot team that helped draft the original incorporation report. In many ways the natural proclivity of new cities to elect an advocate/zealot council dovetails rather nicely with the sacrifices of energy and time which will be required of the newly elected body.

S_1 and S_2: The Struggles for Autonomy and Support

Having won in the incorporation election its struggle for separation, the new government must still wage a fight for autonomy from surrounding cities, special districts, regional governments, and county government. Two basic types of cities were studied: contract and full-service cities. In contract or "Lakewood Plan"[10] cities, such services as police, fire protection, parks and recreation, and public works are contracted out to county or private agencies. Full-service cities attempt to provide all or most of these services under existing or future municipal government departments.

Both contract and full-service cities exhibited a fight for autonomy. For contract cities, this was especially difficult. Newly independent from the county, these cities had to negotiate with county departments for basic public services. Respondents in the interviews often cited instances wherein they felt railroaded by the county. They felt county services were too little and too costly in the early periods. Until the city learned the negotiation process and established a base of power from which to bargain, council members generally felt "taken" in the county contract process. Autonomy from the county, however, was usually not long in arriving. Within two years, most respondents felt the city could stand on its own in its relationship with county and regional governments. Occasionally, extra leverage was achieved when an early council member won election to the county board of supervisors. In fact, as distinct from the advocates/ zealots, there are a few early council members Downs would label "climbers." Such members use council membership as a lower rung on a career ladder which frequently includes election to the county board and the state legislature. In one case, an early climber went on to Congress.

Full-service and contract cities had early struggles with special districts formed before incorporation. Often the officers of such districts were unwilling to be absorbed by the new municipal government. Respondents described such special districts as "little fiefdoms." One city mayor said, "Old-time residents of [the special district] were on the board and they were reluctant to give up their authority because the city was untried and inexperienced." Eventually, most cities were able to persuade those districts that had land, public services, and clienteles overlapping with the city's to cede their operations to the new municipal government.

In the early days the council will also need to assert its autonomy over the claims of neighboring cities and regional governments. Adjacent municipalities may attempt to annex fringe areas contiguous with the new city. "Being the new kid on the block, everyone will take a shot at you," noted one city manager. The new council will have to deal with such claims and may eventually launch annexation drives of its own. In California, these claims frequently involve regional government. Local Agency Formation Commissions (LAFCOs) in each county act as a jurisdictional referee in annexation and spheres of influence claims. The new council may seek to have one of their own members elected to LAFCO to aid in pressing their claims before the regional agency.

Even as the struggle for survival (S_1) takes place, the early council is caught up in a second struggle for support (S_2). In the early years the new council is seeking to develop the "critical mass" necessary for successfully functioning as a unilateral actor within a larger regional context. S_2 is a struggle for both internal and external support. Internal support means: (1) the council must be able to act together as an administrative team,[11] and (2) the local citizenry must support its efforts. This is crucial to the successful implementation of new city policies and programs. As mentioned earlier, all of the council members were proponents of incorporation. Most had worked together prior to incorporation, and thus working together as council members presented no immediate problems in terms of internal support. It was common, as one newly elected mayor noted, to have working meetings at his house even prior to the incorporation election. This allowed new councils to present a united image at their first public meeting. As he put it, "We lined our ducks up before that date." In the extreme case, one early council agreed to take no action on any item that could not be disposed of unanimously by the council members.

Despite the fact that most new city councils enjoy a "honeymoon period" lacking in political controversy, they still seek support from the community. A high degree of support (at least from pro-incorporation voters) is possible by carefully adhering to the guidelines of the incorporation proposal. Obtaining electoral support by simply sticking to proposal guidelines seems, perhaps, easy enough but the introduction of new issues into the political arena can create difficulties. New issues proved difficult for the recently elected councils to handle in several of the cities studied. The appearance of these issues seemed to follow a feast-or-famine pattern. Some cities appeared to have no visible new agenda for the council to address. Added to this was the fact that those who had once been the spokespersons for community grievances were now part of the system—dissenters had been transformed into council members. As one respondent commented, "Interestingly, now that we are the elected officials doing the planning, that critical element that we provided ... is missing now. We are on the council or the planning commission and there is no real watchdog monitoring us like we did the supervisors and the planning commission. There's nobody like us out there, only vested interests."

On the other hand, several issues can appear simultaneously on the city agenda. This is particulary the case in rural cities. In two of the small towns studied, it was difficult to purchase city equipment from any supplier in town without generating conflict-of-interest charges, recall elections, and voter mobilization. Four of the cities studied had trouble maintaining electoral support, as evident by grand jury investigations and recall elections.

In addition to internal support, new councils seek external support from county and regional governments. Often cities will not have city departments operating for one or two years after incorporation. For example, the council usually will have hired a police chief within a few months after incorporation, but while the new chief is getting a department together, the city must still rely on county police protection. This is especially common in California, where the county is required to continue to provide its services to the community until the close of the budget year in which the incorporation election falls.

Rapid Growth and the Decelerator Effect

Although half of the sample cities were contract cities committed to a limited scope of municipal services and a correspondingly low tax rate, all of the full-service cities and several of the contract cities expanded service beyond those originally proposed in the incorporation proposals. Council members of contract cities were able to justify such an increase by pointing to economies achieved elsewhere or by the use of state subvention funds in lieu of local taxes. Still other cities became adept at federal and state grantsmanship to provide for their extra services (see Tables 3.5 and 3.6). Of the cities which expanded their services beyond the originally proposed levels, most did not do so within the first three years. Instead, they chose to wait until nonlocal (federal or state) funds were available for expansion projects. For example, cities spent *revenue sharing (GRS)* and community development block grant *(CDBG)* funds on such projects as planning, senior citizens, and housing and rehabilitation programs.

Whether such a gradual expansion of nonbasic municipal services will continue (at least in California) is now problematic. In the late 1970s, passage of such measures as Proposition 13 in California and Proposition 2½ in Massachusetts which limited local property taxes, and the elimination of GRS and CDBG during the Reagan administration[12] has had an effect on city growth and planning. It is uncertain both how much municipal governments will be willing to expand basic services and how much nonlocal revenue for cities has been lost.

The promulgation of numerous commissions and boards is one way city councils can extend their scope without necessitating a substantial capital outlay. Several of the cities studied had increased the original number of citizens' commissions envisioned in their incorporation proposals. While all the cities had a planning commission, some councils had expanded the number of commissions to include such concerns as police review, curbs and gutters, transit, and even cable television.

Even before Proposition 13 and the demise of revenue sharing, a city council that sought to rapidly expand municipal services would be checked by a multiplicity of external factors, which may be collectively referred to as a decelerator effect. There are several external factors that tend to slow down any expansion of municipal services city council members might envision. First, the expansion of local services beyond the point anticipated by early incorporation advocates tends to be funded with nonlocal revenues. In order to qualify for more than the most basic block grants, new cities need to develop a grantsmanship capability. Even then, they are still in the risky position of competing with older, more experienced cities for scarce non-

TABLE 3.5 Federal/State Grant Matrix

City	Incorporation Date	Programme	Grant Sources	Year First Applied	Year Received
Adelanto	1970	Redevelopment	FHA	1975	1976
		Redevelopment	HUD	1975	1976
		Staff Expansion	CETA	1977	1977
		Staff Expansion	Title II, III	1977	1977
Hughson	1972	Physical Improvement	HCD	1973	1974
		Street Construction	EDA	1976	1977
		Recreation/Parks	Park Bond Act (1974)	1976	1977
		Sewer Improvements	Water Quality Control Board	1976	1977
La Canada Flintridge	1976	Planning	HCD	1977	1977
Lafayette	1968	Senior Meals	Older Americans Act	1976	1977
		Elder Housing Project	HCD	1977	1977
Marina	1975	Council Chambers	HCD	1976	1977
		Parks & Recreation		1977	1978
Moraga	1974	Planning	HCD	1974	1975
Rancho Palos Verdes	1973	Planning	HCD	1974	1975
		Staff Expansion	CETA	1975	1976
		Staff Expansion	PEP	1976	1977
		Planning	EDA	1976	1977
		Bikeway	SCAG	1976	1977
Waterford	1969	Street Improvement	HCD	1970	1971
		Parks & Recreation		1975	1976

Source: Robert J. Waste, "The Early Years in the Life Cycle of City Councils: A Downsian Analysis," Urban Studies (1983) 20:75.

FHA = Federal Housing Administration
HUD = Housing Urban Development
CETA = Comprehensive Employment & Training Act
HCD = Housing & Community Development Block Grant
SCAG = Southern California Association of Governments

EDA = Economic Development Administration
Park Bond Act, 1974 California State Legislature
EPA = Environmental Protection Agency
PEP = Public Employment Program

TABLE 3.6   Federal Grants: Illustrations of Use by Cities of Federal Grants*

Examples	Activity	Source	Amount (1977–78)
Lafayette	Senior Meals on Wheels	Older Americans Act	14,350
	Public Employees Hired	CETA	68,000
Waterford	Staff Expansion: 3 clerk-typists 1 animal control officer 1 building inspector	CETA	39,000
La Canada Flintridge	Highway Construction	FAU** (Federal Aid Urban, from fed. gas taxes)	196,000
Simi Valley	Police Service (augmented)	LEAA grant**	167,500
	Planning	HUD 701 grant	20,500
	Summer Young Program	Title III	81,000

Source: Robert J. Waste, "The Early Years in the Life Cycle of City Councils: A Downsian Analysis." *Urban Studies* (1983) 20:75.

*Grants other than revenue sharing or community development block grant funds.

**Federal Aid to Urban Areas and the Law Enforcement Assistance Administration were urban grant programs of the sixties and seventies.

local funds. Second, even when obtained, nonlocal revenues (including GRS and CDBG) cannot be relied on. Cities often cite the unpredictability of second-year funding as a major lesson learned from the demise of GRS and a major reason for using such monies to fund one-year, capital-intensive construction projects.[13] Third, a council is affected by external factors over which it may have little control but which nonetheless serve to apply the brakes to expanding municipal services (for a more extensive discussion of this, see chapter 5). Such factors include flight to the suburbs by the middle class, racial unrest, increasing crime rates, and state and federally mandated local programs. The state of the local and national economy may also adversely affect expansion. For example, inflation and/or unemployment may increase the cost of providing minimum services to such a point that expanding services becomes too expensive for the new city.

The decelerator effect has momentum even in times of financial plenty. While the funds to provide additional services might be present, factors such as increasing crime rates, racial unrest, or necessary modifications to existing programs might require a trimming of the expanding budgetary sails. Furthermore, as Aaron Wildavsky has pointed out, the traditional orientation of budget officers is to defend "base" programs over new projects, then extend the base, and then add new programs to the base, in that order.[14]

While the decelerator effect may be more pronounced and appear more rapidly to municipalities facing periods of stringent financial limitations, all municipal governments face at some time a lesser version of the decelerator effect. In the United States, due to the symbiotic relationship between cities and the federal government, even in the best of financial times federally mandated programs may force an expanding city budget into a decelerating period. Frequently, for example, cities are ordered to abide by federal standards for water and sewage treatment, thus forcing municipalities to update or construct new facilities. While the federal government provides some funds for such programs, the local share is often enough to militate against further new projects or innovations. Conversely, faced with such constraints, cities may seek additional financial assistance from their state governments. In a case in point, several California cities were temporarily able to stave off the decelerator effect by successfully applying to the state legislature for funds to bail out popular local programs.

It should be noted then—and this is true of the growth cycle process for city councils in general—that while all municipalities can expect to experience the dynamics of the Downsian growth process, the degree to which they are influenced by the different growth process stages, the speed with which they move from stage to another, and the unilinear or curvilinear pattern (see Figures 3.2 and 3.3) they may exhibit while doing so is partially affected by the cities' role and place within the larger governmental framework. While it is possible, indeed probable,that most small to medium-sized municipalities will move in a fairly regular or unilinear fashion through the first seven

Bureaus							
1 Birth of an agency	2 Early dominance	3 Struggle for autonomy (S_1)	4 Struggle for support (S_2)	5 Rapid growth	6 Decelera-tion effect	7 Age lump	8 Death

zealots/climbers/advocates ⟶ conservers ⟶

City Council							
1 Incorporation	2 Early dominance by advocates, zealots, climbers	3 Autonomy from gov. network, earlier gov. forms	4 Support from 1) electoral community 2) supportive gov. agencies	5 New goals, services added	6 Decelera-tion effect	7 Crisis of continuity, recycling original council-members	8 Death

zealots/climbers/advocates ⟶ conservers ⟶

SOURCE: Robert J. Waste, "The Early Years in the Life Cycle of City Councils: A Downsian Analysis," *Urban Studies* (1983) 20:73.

Figure 3.2 The Downsian Growth Process for Public Agencies Matched with the Growth Process of City Councils

stages of the Downsian growth process, intergovernmental actions may affect a city's progress in the process. In this sense, the Downsian growth process is a guide to what cities may expect but not a predictor. Cities may move back and forth between life process stages, or have the duration and severity of such stages as the decelerator effect shortened or exacerbated.

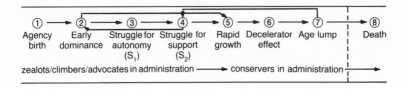

SOURCE: Robert J. Waste, "The Early Years in the Life Cycle of City Councils: A Downsian Analysis," *Urban Studies* (1983) 20:73.

Figure 3.3 Curvilinear Depiction of Growth Process for City Councils: A Hypothetical Case

Possible Impacts of Internal Deceleration and Age Lumps

In the new councils, the external catalysts for deceleration join with an internal drive for deceleration: the "wear factor." Council members of new cities are faced with heavy demands on their time, which may increase as the scope of city activity increases. The difficulty of supervising a still-new operation is compounded if the council chooses to expand the scope of city services. Often these increased demands are made at the expense of time council members could spend with their business or family. Adding to the possible discontent members may have at this stage is the fact that many may feel that they have accomplished their original goals and that any increased demands on their time have reached the point of diminishing returns. Incorporation advocates have had their original intent fulfilled; zealots may have moved on to another cause; climbers, by their very nature, are looking to move elsewhere or have already left the council.

At this stage, the council is left primarily with "conservers," to use Downs's term. All other deceleration factors aside, the mere presence of a majority of conservers on the council may spell doom for any significant expansion or innovation in city services.

The final wear factor is, of course, age itself. This occurs on the council when the original elected officials leave to go back to private life or to fill another elected position. Most of the cities studied began to lose council members as early as the second term of office, and by the fourth term were often presented with an "age-lump" crisis, a "crisis of continuity."[15] It is possible that by the fourth council term all of the original council members have left. Although senior committee chairpersons will be retiring, most councils will have new council entrants. Thus in most cases all of the upper echelons of policymaking positions will not suddenly be vacated. Nevertheless, the council "will go through a time of troubles as its remaining members struggle for control over its policies and resources."[16]

Such age-lump stages appear to present a twofold effect on young city councils. A real possibility exists that a city manager and staff that grew increasingly significant in the policy process of a conserver-dominated council would continue and extend this relationship, coming to dominate a new and inexperienced council. This trend may be checked, however, by a second trend that can develop at the same time. A new cadre of climbers and zealots, discouraged earlier by the lack of high policy positions available or the conserver domination of the council, may be attracted to service on the council at this stage. Thus while the age-lump crisis presents a problem to the city council in terms of a loss of expertise and the possible escalation of staff efforts to dominate the council policy process, it may also lead to the election of a new set of council members with relatively low levels of expertise but psychologically predisposed to resist staff domination.

New City Councils and the Growth Process: A Summary

Though the match is not perfect, scholars of local government can use Anthony Downs's theory of the growth process of public bureaus to explore policymaking dynamics in the early years of a city council. They both appear to exhibit a similar pattern or growth process.

Mature Councils: The Senior Connection

Older or mature councils (councils in cities aged ten years and older) have their own policy characteristics and sets of behavior. Extending Downs's analysis, I propose that mature councils still experience growth but this growth will be limited to the last three or four stages of the Downsian growth process. Mature councils are frequently characterized by a "go along and get along" atmosphere known as the "norm of reciprocity."[17] Also, older councils generally fall into long-term policymaking trends that reflect: (1) the city's *proximity to a core urban area* (e.g., core, suburban, and fringe cities);[18] (2) the members' *view of the proper role of the city as service provider* (e.g., economic development booster, a provider of municipal amenities, a stick-to-the-knitting caretaker government, or an arbiter of community conflict);[19] or (3) the city's *geographical locale and/or economic circumstances* (e.g., sunbelt versus frostbelt cities, fast-growth versus slow-growth cities, smokestack versus high-tech industrial base cities).[20]

Having gone through the difficult first stages of the growth process several years earlier, mature councils are likely to experience curvilinear movement back and forth between growth stages 5 (rapid growth), 6 (the decelerator effect), 7 (age lump and the crisis of continuity) and—if new members are elected to the council—stage 2 (the re-entry of zealots, climbers, and advocates, and the possible domination of the council by a small band of these actors) (see Figure 3.3). The presence or absence of policy entrepreneurs (zealots and/or advocates) will affect the formation of policy in the mature council. If, as the Downs growth process suggests, new city councils will be staffed by more advocates and zealots than will older, more mature councils, what does this imply for local policymaking? Without the entry of new zealots/advocates, city policy over time is likely to take on a decidedly more conservative hue. That is, in the absence of zealots and with fewer advocates cities are less likely to embrace new causes and new programs requiring new or larger expenditures of money, nor is the city council likely to drastically increase funding for existing programs or long-planned innovations.

Aside from the probable conservatism and fiscal restraint of mature policymaking bureaus, there are several other qualities associated with aging in local policy bodies, especially city councils. The aging process in governing institutions is usually accompanied by a relatively and consistently low voter turnout,[21] generally averaging no more than one-third of the electorate.[22] As the level of voter participation drops off from the high point associated with incorporation, or the occasional high turnout associated with controversial issues or popular or controversial candidates, councils tend to take on a characteristic that Kenneth Prewitt has called a "norm of volunteerism." Prewitt found in a study of city councils in the San Francisco Bay area that four factors combine in many cities to loosen the desirable connection between policy choices in the electorate and policy choices of incumbent council members. These are: (1) many council members are appointed rather than elected to the city council; (2) low turnouts characterize most municipal elections in the United States; (3) few incumbent council members are defeated at the polls, leading to the fact that (4) most city council members retire from office voluntarily. This results in a "norm of volunteerism," meaning officeholders "enter and leave office not at the whim of the electorate, but according to self-defined schedules."[23] Prewitt concluded that in cities where voluntarism was high, so too would be the propensity of council members to vote their own opinions (or interests) as opposed to letting public opinion guide their voting on policy options before the council. Thus mature councils may be characterized by the conservatism of conserver-advocate policymaking or by the policy detachment associated with the norm of voluntarism.

It should be noted that the antidemocratic implications of mature council voluntarism are far less disturbing in communities where "policy concurrence" exists, that is to say, in cities where the elected council members share the same policy preferences as the mass electorate. In a study of sixty-four randomly selected cities with populations of less than sixty thousand, Susan Hansen[24] found that such concurrence is higher

> where elections are conducted on a partisan basis, and where the chief executive is directly elected (rather than appointed as in council–manager cities). Concurrence is higher where either the Democratic or the Republican party is active, but declines where both are active. Finally, concurrence is higher where elections are hotly contested. (However, this relationship holds only for communities in which there is a high degree of consensus between politically active citizens and the mass of more passive citizens.)[25]

Despite the apparent problem that may arise from nonconcurrence between various members of the council and the mass electorate of a given city, it is important to note, as Heinz Eulau has oberved, that "even if particular individual councilpersons are not responsive to their constituents, the council as a corporate actor can be."[26] In fact, whatever the policy preferences of individual council members, mature councils tend to develop relatively fixed, long-term policymaking orientations or policy trends. These trends appear to reflect differences in: (1) the spatial characteristics of the city, (2) the political culture of the city, or (3) the regional or economic base of the city in question. Thus in the celebrated City Council Research Project (CCRP)—a study of over eighty cities in the San Francisco Bay area conducted by Robert Eyestone, Heinz Eulau, Kenneth Prewitt, and associates—Robert Eyestone found that cities tended to fall into one of three clusters in terms of their policy decisions on economic development. He classified the three types as core cities, suburban cities, or fringe cities (those too far out on the city's rim to serve as "bedroom communities" for commuters working in the core city but which were still affected by policies set in the core city area).

For all three groups, the density of population proved to be the best predictor of policy behavior vis-à-vis development decisions. However, aside from the decisive influence of density (presumably density decreases the further away from the core city area), "the next most important variable is different from group [type of city] to group."[27] Eyestone hypothesized that "[t]he three groups of cities represent different stages of metropolitan growth," and as such, each city "will eventually move through all the stages found in the region."[28] Hence, mature councils will generally enact policies reflective of their core, suburban, or fringe city status; however, over time it is probable that all the cities within a given region will come to adopt similar policies (e.g., downtown redevelopment strategies, approaches toward mass transit, policies toward rent control, cooperative agreements on fire protection) as each city matures in terms of age and population density.

Nevertheless, even within these three city types, subgroupings tend to arise. Oliver Williams and Charles Adrian argue that "[t]he economic climate of a city is insufficient in itself to determine the value orientation of civic policies."[29] Councils within mature cities tend to fall into one of four subgroupings: (1) boosters or promoters of economic growth; (2) providers or securers of amenities; (3) caretaker councils bent only on maintaining the city's traditional services; and (4) arbiter councils that intervene minimally in the civic affairs of the community, choosing to referee interest group conflicts but reluctant to provide leadership or to exercise governmental "muscle" on behalf of any specific policy proposals.

If differences in the policy directions of mature councils are to be expected *within* regions, it is hardly surprising to find that great differences exist in the policy preferences and actions of mature councils located in *different geographical regions*. In general, the most striking difference between mature councils and city policymakers is found between sunbelt and frostbelt cities.[30] Figure 3.4 illustrates the definition of sunbelt used for the current study. As I have noted in another work, "Sunbelt cities are those cities concentrated in the southern United States (generally but not exclusively below the 37th parallel) experiencing rapid growth, and characterized by a local industrial base in which defense and aerospace industries, military bases, high tech firms, tourism and educational institutions play a leading role."[31] Several studies have shown sunbelt cities to be more

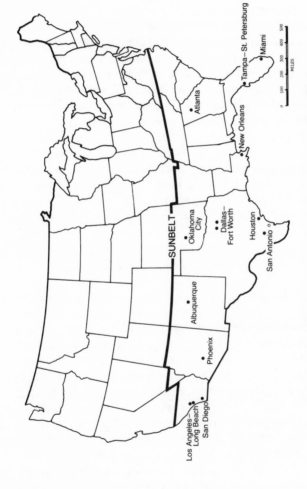

Figure 3.4 A Map of the American Sunbelt and Selected Sunbelt Cities

conservative than their northern frostbelt neighbors.[32] Carl Abbott has described the policy politics of sunbelt cities as "lifestyle liberalism" combined with "fiscal conservatism."[33] Furthermore, he has argued that another major difference between sunbelt and frostbelt cities has to do with the political role of the neighborhoods and the periphery of urban areas. In sunbelt cities, many of which have nonpartisan elections and council–manager forms of government, neighborhood politics and to a lesser extent ethnic group politics are often far less developed or pronounced than they are in eastern and older northern cities. Arguably, only recently have sunbelt city councils, particularly in the West, evolved from being more than a reflection of downtown business interests and the chamber of commerce—a policy orientation that usually emphasized spending city money to develop the downtown merchant area and to attract industries and tourists into the core city. Abbott argues that maturing sunbelt city councils have begun to extend their policy concerns and city expenditures out from the center of town to the various neighborhoods. This trend, if it continues, should produce an increase in the ethnicity and diversity of political coalitions and policy concerns in sunbelt cities.

Conclusion

I have shown that new and mature city councils exhibit various characteristics having to do with: (1) the *growth process* and *growth process stage* of the given city; (2) the *types of bureaucratic personalities* found among the membership of the council policy body; (3) the *density* of the city; (4) *spatial location* or distance of the city from the core urban area; (5) whether *mature councils* view themselves as boosters, amenity providers, caretakers, or arbiters; and (6) *regional differences* as reflected in the policy perspectives of sunbelt versus frostbelt city councils.

I have in this chapter and the preceding chapter put in place two of the key bricks in the wall of city policymaking—the life cycle of policymaking, and the influence upon that cycle of the growth process of city councils, the age of the city, and the geographic location of a municipality.

4

Policy Type, Political Conflict, and City Policymaking

There are several excellent models of policymaking that might adequately serve as a guide in analyzing city policymaking.[1] Many of these models would be helpful in explaining the emergence and escalation of political conflict—the ecological factor that is the central topic of the current chapter. None of the models, by itself, explains city policymaking conflict as well as a combination of two leading policy models advanced by Paul E. Peterson and James Q. Wilson,[2] particularly when additional elements drawn from a host of recognized policy scholars are included.[3] Thus, as in chapter 2 where the elements of several existing models were combined to enable a better understanding of the life cycle of city policy, I am once again mixing and matching explanatory models. Whether such theoretical alchemy is constructive or merely construction will ultimately be decided by others.

I believe such tinkering is justified on two grounds. First, the hybridized new model explains conflict in the municipal policy world *better* than any of the alternative models. Second, it explains *more* of the political circumstances encountered in the policy life cycle than alternative models or typologies. In fact, the entire discussion of city "policy paths" and "policy space," which is central to the present chapter, probably could not be explained adequately without resort to this model.

After a brief explanation of the policy conflict model, the current chapter will: (1) examine the Peterson and Wilson models of policymaking and illustrate some of the problems that exist with these models; (2) set forth a new typology of local policymaking; (3) discuss whether issues determine politics; (4) discuss the role of mediating influences in local politics and how these influences skew the generally valid assumption that issues determine politics; (5) discuss conflict escalation in local policymaking; (6) demonstrate the usefulness of mapping policy paths and policy space in analyzing conflict in local policymaking; and, finally, (7) set forth some general rules or guidelines regarding political conflict in the life cycle of policymaking in American cities.

The Typology of Policy Conflict: A Brief Introduction

Like the other key components of city policymaking (e.g., the growth process, the age, or the spatial location of a given city), political conflict is a component of the overall policymaking ecology or environment, and, as such, influences the operation of the municipal policy life cycle. As I have shown earlier, city policy proposals go through an identifiable life cycle. Policies that succeed in completing a full cycle—from problem identification to enactment to placement on the formal agenda and later successful implementation—are also affected by the stage of growth of the city council. The first elected council for a newly incorporated city will have a very different orientation and membership composition than an older city council. Even without the presence of zealots on a new city council, the sheer lack of experience and expertise on city matters would set the new council markedly apart from more mature ones.

Another factor compounding the policy mix in a given city is the *type* of policy that is to be considered. In many cases the type of policy proposed will determine the type of politics and conflict associated with it. The policy conflict model is premised on a division of local policymaking into five basic policy types: *autonomous, pork barrel, conventional* or *routine, distributive,* and *intrusive.* Each type has unique characteristics that, as in the case of other ecological factors (e.g., age, locale, growth process stage) discussed earlier, directly affect local policymaking. I will next examine two policy models that, when combined and modified, form the core of the policy conflict model.

The Paul Peterson Typology of City Policymaking

For Paul Peterson, city policies can be divided into three types: developmental, redistributive, and allocational. "*Developmental* policies enhance the economic position of the city. *Redistributive* policies benefit low-income residents but at the same time negatively affect the local economy. *Allocational* policies are more or less neutral in their economic effects."[4] Developmental policies are efforts to aid and strengthen the local economy (e.g., attract new industry, expand the tax base of the community, promote tourism). Because of this community-enhancing orientation, these policies are generally popular and find little opposition. Thus developmental policies, according to Peterson, "are praised by many and opposed only by those few whose partial interests stand in conflict with community interests."[5] The homeowner, for example, whose house had to be condemned and razed to lengthen the runway for the municipal airport may well object to the condemnation and relocation procedures, but most residents of the city will believe themselves to be well served by an improved and expanded airport.

A Counterexample:
The Case of the Chinatown Expressway

The proposition first advanced by Theodore Lowi[6]—that the content of the policy determines the politics associated with actually framing the policy—is a central assumption of both the Peterson policy model and that of James Q. Wilson. There are, of course, some exceptions to his theory that "policies determine politics."[7] It is not *inevitable* that all developmental policy proposals will be favorably received. They may spark a relatively high level of conflict in cases where the pro-development forces and the anti-development forces

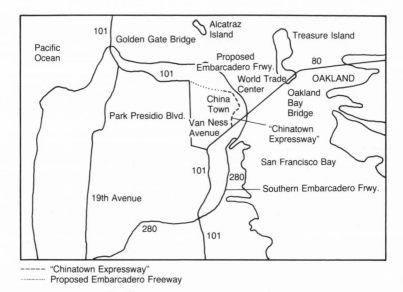

----- "Chinatown Expressway"
············ Proposed Embarcadero Freeway

Figure 4.1 A Map of San Francisco Freeways

are fairly evenly matched (e.g., a proposed freeway that makes access
to the city easier and will decrease freeway time for both city residents and suburban commuters *but* which is to be built in an environmentally sensitive area will offend environmentalists in general
and neighborhood residents in particular). Such an example, it
should be noted, is not entirely hypothetical. As the map in Figure
4.1 indicates, this is exactly what happened with the proposed
Embarcadero Freeway in San Francisco.

The Embarcadero Freeway (designated on the map by a dotted
line) was to have been a quick transportation link between the
Golden Gate Bridge and Highway 101, and the other main freeway
artery, Interstate 80 and the Oakland Bay Bridge. Since the two
opposing camps—the pro-development freeway supporters and the
environmentalists/neighborhood residents were about equal in
clout—the projected Embarcadero Freeway was never completed.
Instead, San Francisco has a curious mini-freeway (denoted in Figure
4.1 by dashed lines) that ends abruptly at the World Trade Center,
near the entrance to San Francisco's Chinatown. The partial freeway
is a monument to the conflict that can arise in developmental policymaking. The environmental forces are not sufficiently strong

enough to have the partially constructed freeway dismantled, nor are the pro-development forces sufficiently strong enough to secure completion of a freeway that, if built, would profoundly alter the landscape of Fisherman's Wharf and the waterfront views of thousands of San Franciscans. Since the partially built freeway will probably never be completed or dismantled, it is possible that in the end city supervisors will decide to make the best of a bad situation by officially naming the brief stretch of highway the "Chinatown Expressway."[8]

Peterson on Redistributive and Allocational Policymaking

Peterson notes that "[o]ne can roughly calculate whether a policy is redistributive by estimating whether those who pay for the service in local taxes are recipients of the service."[9] If the tax money is used for those who have not paid taxes, the policies are redistributive. Thus welfare programs viewed in the most general sense (e.g., general assistance, aid to the homeless, some alcohol, drug treatment, and mental health facilities) are the largest bulk of redistributive programs for a city. Interestingly, as Peterson notes, many such services (including mental health and drug rehabilitation programs, food stamps, Medicare, and Aid to Families with Dependent Children) are frequently funded by other levels of government, including the county, state, and federal governments.

Peterson sharply limits his discussion of redistributive policymaking.

> First, I speak only of redistribution from the better off to the less well off segments of the community . . . Second, I speak only of those redistributive policies that have negative effects on local economies. . . . [I]n most cases redistributive programs have negative economic effects. While they supply benefits to those least needed by the local economy, they require taxation on those who are most needed. Such a strong claim can be made on behalf of the poor and the needy that, although local governments often shy away from these painfully regressive redistributive policies, they are the one kind of regressive policy cities sometimes undertake.[10]

Peterson argues that local governments rarely engage in redistributive policies because: (1) redistribution is largely a function of the national government, (2) local redistribution efforts would do little to redress regional and/or national economic trends and conditions, and (3) redistributive policymaking is inherently conflictual. Thus, as he notes, since the Great Society programs of the 1960s, more than 55 percent of the federal budget is aimed at redistributive programs. However, the percentage of local revenues "used for redistribution was only 12.9 percent in 1962 . . . [and] even a decade after the civil rights movement and its supposed impact on local service-delivery systems, this percentage has increased by less than 1 percent."[11]

Allocational policies involve expenditures for goods and services falling in between programs to aid the poor (distributive) and programs to enhance the competitive economic position of the city (developmental). Allocational policies include "housekeeping services"[12] such as police, fire protection, and sanitation. Unlike developmental policies, which tend to produce little conflict, or redistributive policies that frequently generate sharp conflict, allocational policies (as their midpoint designation on Peterson's policy continuum would suggest) may produce some conflict but generally far less than redistributive policy proposals. Peterson classifies, for example, a city's hiring policy (political patronage versus civil service and merit hiring) as a "housekeeping" policy area that may occasionally produce some political conflicts.

A Counterexample:
Comparable Worth in San Jose and Los Angeles

Presumably, current municipal debates over "comparable worth"—the proposition that men and women working in positions of comparable responsibility ought to be paid comparable salaries—would qualify as an example of allocational policymaking. However, as the comparable worth issue illustrates, one of the troubling aspects of the Peterson typology is that the same *type of issue* (in this case, the allocational issue of comparable worth) can produce a *different type of policy politics*—that is, different levels of political conflict—in two different cities. Generally, allocational policymaking produces little or no political conflict. However, this is not always the case. In 1981 a study ordered and paid for by the city of San Jose, California, found that "salaries for 'women's jobs' were generally paid less than 'men's jobs' of comparable content. One eye-opening example is that senior librarians, typically female, earned 27% less than senior chemists, typically male, although the two jobs were rated comparably by the city."[13]

Despite the city study documenting wage inequity between men and women, and the threat of a suit against the city by the municipal employees union based on a very similar and successful comparable wage suit upheld by the U.S. Supreme Court (*County of Washington v. Gunther* 452 U.S. 161, 1981), the city of San Jose balked at a negotiated settlement. As a result, several hundred municipal employees walked off their jobs for nine days. The strike was settled on July 14, 1981, "with the city agreeing to pay $1.45 million in raises for several hundred female employees to make their pay more equitable with men."[14]

In 1981 the American Federation of State, County and Municipal Employees (AFSCME) filed a complaint with the Equal Employment Opportunity Commission (EEOC) charging the city of Los Angeles with sex and wage discrimination. After a protracted series of negotiations and collective bargaining sessions, the city eventually agreed in May 1985 to adopt a plan to address comparable worth problems. In return for a promise by AFSCME to drop its complaint before the EEOC, Los Angeles agreed to a three-year contract under which 3,900 clerks and librarians were assured of salaries equal to those of maintenance workers, gardeners, and other city workers employed in predominantly male job classifications. The agreement allowed the city to phase in various job categories and classifications over a period of several years so that all city jobs would be eventually covered, and to lessen the financial burden of salary adjustments on the city treasury.[15]

Why was the comparable worth issue handled so differently in San Jose and Los Angeles? Why did the same substantive policy generate two different political scenarios, two different levels of political conflict? This can be explained by the fact that various types of issues tend over time to correlate with various fixed or constant levels of political conflict (e.g., developmental policies and little or no conflict, allocation policies and slightly higher conflict levels, and redistributive policies and still higher levels of conflict). This is precisely Peterson's argument. But by extrapolating beyond his position, one can show that it is often the case that an issue may deviate at any given time and in a given community from the normal pattern of expected conflict. This is due to *mediating influences* within that community. There were several mediating influences in the San Jose–Los Angeles comparable worth case. For one, comparable worth was a *new issue* in San Jose, requiring the city to accept a fundamentally new idea, and indeed requiring the nation to accept a fundamentally new idea since San Jose was the first city to put comparable worth into effect. Thus by the time Los Angeles began its salary adjustment program in 1985, comparable worth was a far more known quantity to Los Angeles policymakers. Also the overall mayoral style of Mayor Bradley of Los Angeles is, using Yates's typology, that of a broker—and in this case a broker with political aspirations (Bradley ran for governor in 1982 and 1986)—which may have served as a strong incentive to avoid highly charged political conflicts (such as a strike by municipal employees). It is possible that the leadership of the municipal employees union was different in each city, with the San Jose union having a more confrontational leadership style than Los Angeles (although, as noted earlier, the newness of the issue alone could have produced the confrontation in San Jose). And finally, and more speculatively, it is possible that the conflict differed because, following the typology of cities suggested by Williams and Adrian, San Jose is primarily a promoter of economic growth, disinclined to negotiate with a union presenting a demand separate from or hostile to the city's progrowth orientation, while Los Angeles might be described as an arbiter city, more inclined to bargain with an interest group (in this case, the employees union) in a conciliatory spirit.[16]

As this example illustrates, the Peterson typology may well predict the conflict level associated with certain types of policy issues generally, but from time to time, important exceptions will arise. A second problem with Peterson's typology—and with typologies in general—is illustrated by another counterexample, the case of San Diego's Gas Lamp street sweepers.

A Counterexample:
The Case of the Gas Lamp Street Sweepers

One problem with typologies is illustrated by the fact that it is entirely possible to make the argument that at some level there are

no real differences between developmental and redistributive policies. This is the case with a pilot program in San Diego that employs
homeless transients costumed in Roaring Twenties attire to sweep
the streets of the city's "Gas Lamp Quarter"—a historic preservation
district in the downtown area. The program recipients are not taxpayers, *but* the businesses in the Gas Lamp Quarter have been economically enhanced both by the amelioration of the district's side-
walk sweeping problem(s) as well as by effectively eliminating some
of the transients whose presence discouraged patrons from frequent-
ing Gas Lamp businesses. Peterson, it should be noted, is sensitive
to the problems inherent in typologies. To avoid difficulties in this
area, Peterson explicitly eliminates cases of redistribution that are
economically beneficial to the city, choosing to include those policies
that, on balance, "have negative effects on the local economy."[17] In
using Peterson's distributive policy type in a hybrid policy conflict
model introduced later in this chapter, I will incorporate Peterson's
assumption that genuinely redistributive policies must have negative
effects on the local economy. In keeping with this distinction, the
Gas Lamp street sweeping program would be either allocational
("housekeeping," because of its connection with sanitation) *or* developmental as it enhances the overall economic position of the city
(strengthens the sales tax base, brings in both tourists and city residents to businesses in the core city area, etc.). Because of the difficulty in classifying some policies as purely allocational or purely
developmental, the policy conflict typology introduced later will rel-
egate the solely housekeeping aspects of allocational policies under
the heading of autonomous issues. The more controversial allocational issues (e.g., comparable pay for municipal employees) and all
developmental issues will be combined under the heading of conventional or routine policymaking.

The Peterson Typology: A Critique

Overall, the municipal policy typology developed by Peterson is
extremely useful. Using it, one can make meaningful distinctions
between three different types of policymaking and anticipate the
usual level of political conflict associated with each type: high conflict for redistributive issues, moderate to low conflict for allocational

issues, and little or no conflict for developmental issues. But there are four basic problems with this typology. First, the actual conflict level, as in the San Francisco freeway example, may be different than the general pattern expected for the given policy type. Second, as in the comparable worth example, the conflict level on the same issue may vary widely from one community to the next. Third, the proper classification of a proposed policy may be at issue—as in the case of the Gas Lamp street sweepers. Fourth, as I shall show later, there are several other categories (which I call pork barrel, autonomous, and intrusive) of local policymaking not explicitly included in Peterson's typology. Before presenting the hybrid model that will satisfy these objections, it is necessary to examine a second leading policymaking model, the cost-benefit policy typology of James Q. Wilson.

The Wilson Cost-Benefit Policy Typology

James Q. Wilson first introduced his cost-benefit typology in his book *Political Organizations* and further refined it in his textbook *American Government: Institutions and Policies.*[18] (See Figure 4.2.) Wilson divides policy along two dimensions—the scope of the proposed benefit(s) and the scope of those who will be asked to bear the costs for the benefit. Policies, under this schema, fall into four types: (1) those with widely distributed costs and widely distributed benefits (resulting in *majoritarian politics*), (2) those with widely distributed costs and highly concentrated benefits (resulting in *client politics*), (3) those with highly concentrated costs and widely distributed benefits (resulting in *entrepreneurial politics*), and finally (4) those with highly concentrated costs and highly concentrated benefits (resulting in *interest group politics*).[19]

As do Lowi and Peterson, Wilson argues that policies determine politics; specific types of policies will generally produce a particular type of scenario and conflict level associated with their proposal and possible adoption.[20] However, Wilson notes that focusing on different types of policies tends to blur important distinctions between costs and benefits associated with different policies, and between "the adoption of a new policy and the amendment of an old one."[21] For Wilson, new policies (e.g., the adoption of a comparable worth

If the perceived *costs* are:

	Distributed	Concentrated
Distributed	Majoritarian politics	Entrepreneurial politics
Concentrated	Client politics	Interest group politics

If the perceived benefits are: (left axis label)

SOURCE: James Q. Wilson, *American Government: Institutions and Policies*, 3rd ed. (Lexington, Mass.: D.C. Heath, 1986), p. 430, "Figure 14.1, A Way of Classifying and Explaining the Politics of Different Policy Issues."

Figure 4.2 James Q. Wilson Cost-Benefit Policy Typology

policy by the city of San Jose) require a change in public opinion in order "to place on the public agenda what had once been a private relationship and to clothe a particular program with legitimacy."[22] As noted earlier, key policy entrepreneurs or triggering events (e.g., a strike or a local political scandal) are usually required to bring such issues to the fore. Revising existing policies, on the other hand, depends on the extent to which the original policy resolved a problem and whether acceptance of the costs and benefits associated with the policy has continued.

Majoritarian Policies

For Wilson, policies with both widely distributed costs and widely distributed benefits ("majoritarian policies") tend to generate less conflict than other policy types, notably interest group politics or client politics. Because adoption of majoritarian policies "usually depends not on the pulling and hauling among interest groups, but on appealing to popular majorities . . . the politics of these issues is called 'majoritarian.'"[23] Wilson notes that majoritarian policies may involve heated ideological debates at their inception (e.g., the enactment of Social Security in 1935) but then evolve into widely popular—or perhaps more precisely widely accepted—programs and policies. Conflicts in several U.S. cities in the mid-1950s over fluoridation of public drinking water would fit into this pattern. Once hotly debated, adding fluoride to drinking water is now commonplace in the United States.

Interest Group Politics

Interest group politics, on the other hand, involves policies that will "confer benefits on one relatively small, identifiable group and impose costs on a different equally identifiable group."[24] These policies often carry with them the implication, if not the reality, of special interest politics in which public monies are being used to subsidize a specific group. They are usually more conflictual than majoritarian policies and "almost entirely dominated by interest group activity." Wilson notes:

> Each side sees the policy as hurting or helping it. Each side is small enough to make it worthwhile and relatively easy to get organized, raise money, and hire lobbyists and lawyers. Though many issues of this type involve money costs and benefits, that need not always be the case. If the American Nazi party [as in the Skokie, Illinois case] wants to march through a predominately Jewish community carrying flags with swastikas on them, the community is likely to resist strenuously out of revulsion against the disgraceful treatment of Jews by Nazi Germany. Each side organizes and hires lawyers who fight the issue out in the courts.[25]

Client Politics

Client politics covers a wide range of activities and funding scenarios. While in each case the benefits are channeled to a narrow constituency and the costs are assigned to a larger constituency, the potential for conflict varies widely depending on the legitimacy (and visibility) of the benefit being sought.

In the politics of client policymaking, "some identifiable group will benefit, but everybody—or at least a substantial portion of society—will pay whatever cost is incurred."[26] Municipal examples of client politics include subsidies to aid private developers seeking to put together large redevelopment projects. Frequently, as in the case of San Diego's multimillion-dollar downtown redevelopment project, Horton Plaza, a city will condemn land and sell it to a developer for far below the market price for such property to make the project economically affordable for the project backers. In exchange, the city will have a voice beyond the normal powers of the planning commission and the city council in determining how the project will be developed and used. Such agreements to spur downtown redevelopment are commonplace. In another example, estimates of the public costs (city, state, and federal funding) to subsidize the construction of Boston's celebrated development project, Faneuil Hall and Quincy Market, have been estimated at one hundred dollars per square foot—thus reducing the cost to the developer, the Rouse Company, to forty dollars a square foot.[27] Other costs were passed on to the tenants. In all fairness, it should be noted that building Quincy Market—with or without a subsidy—was no small task. The Rouse Company was the third firm that had tried to build the complex. Since recent estimates indicate that more people visit Quincy Market on any given day than tour Disneyland in California, the public subsidy in the case of Quincy Market has probably been an excellent investment for the city of Boston.

The benefit sought from local government is not always monetary. As Wilson notes, "certain groups may enjoy special protections from the government or have their values specially honored."[28] Examples would be a St. Patrick's Day parade or a marathon, where the cities provide activity permits and frequently low-cost or free (subsidized) police protection, traffic rerouting, and legitimacy (e.g., the mayor or council members may march in the parade or otherwise take part in the activities).

Wilson notes that "pork-barrel" policies are a prime example of client politics. In such cases narrow constituencies are given a favor (a policy that enhances their competitive position, or a physical improvement or amenity such as a park, a new dam, an improved harbor), but the costs are borne by a larger group such as state or national taxpayers in general. Frequently, pork-barrel policymaking involves heated competition between cities for a special (externally financed) favor located within or near the city limits. A good case in point was the scramble for competitive advantage set off by a U.S. Treasury department announcement in early 1986 that the department was considering twelve cities as possible sites for a new office of the U.S. Mint. Wherever it is eventually located, the Mint will bring jobs and, perhaps, increased visibility and status to the host city at the expense of national taxpayers.

Entrepreneurial Politics

In entrepreneurial politics, policies are pursued in which "society as a whole or some large part of it will benefit (or is led to believe it will benefit) from a policy that imposes a substantial cost on some small, identifiable segment of society."[29] Here, policy entrepreneurs persuade a policymaking body to enact measures that will genuinely favor the entire city, or that are actually disguised benefits targeted for a narrow client group. A one-cent increase in a local tax on liquor to fund a crackdown on drunk motorists, for example, might be an example of the former. The use of local property taxes to purchase books or recreational equipment for parochial schools might arguably be an example of the latter.

The Wilson Cost-Benefit Typology: A Critique

There are two basic problems with the cost-benefit typology of Wilson. First—and this is endemic to typologies in general, including the one presented later in this chapter—categorizing policies (e.g., majoritarian, entrepreneurial, client, or interest group politics) is oftentimes confusing. The San Francisco freeway example is a case in point. It can be considered an instance of majoritarian policymaking (distributed costs, distributed benefits) because the costs are shared by California taxpayers in general while the benefits are distributed widely to any motorists traveling throughout the Bay area. It can also be considered an example of client policymaking (costs distributed, benefits concentrated) because state taxpayers foot the bill for a benefit aimed primarily at enhancing the transportation infrastructure of San Francisco. Interest group policymaking (costs concentrated, benefits concentrated) also applies because the real costs of dislocation, visual obstruction, property devaluation, and environmental pollution will be borne by the relatively few San Franciscans actually relocated or whose view of the bay is blocked by the freeway, while the real benefits will be to the small number of motorists actually in need of a more rapid link between interstate highways. Finally, it can be considered an example of entrepreneurial policymaking (costs concentrated, benefits distributed). All Californians are benefited by better highway safety and improved roads, but the costs to achieve this desirable end are concentrated to San Franciscans, who will have to fundamentally alter their world-famous skyline.

The first problem with Wilson's typology is compounded by a second and more basic problem. Simply put, in the real world issues tend to move around, back and forth, among classifications. Such movement typically takes one of three different forms or *routes.* Thus an adequate local policymaking model must take such movement into account and explain how it occurs and why.

To some extent, Wilson's model allows for movement. Given the rational actor or rational choice orientation of the model, policy conflict is explained in each case by policy actors responding rationally to the distribution of costs and benefits of each policy type. We may assume that if the perceptions of the costs or benefits associated with a policy change, then so *necessarily* does the politics of the issue. Hence, an issue such as the Chinatown Expressway could change from entrepreneurial to interest group politics overnight if, let us say, the environmentalists were able to successfully frame the question in their terms. Indeed, shifts in the rational calculations of costs and benefits in *some* cases produce shifts in policy politics. However, movement from one policy typology to another may take place for other reasons than a rational recalculation of costs and benefits. Radically redefining an issue, escalating the amount of conflict associated with the issue, or intervening actions by a host of mediating influences may have nonrational effects on such movement. To take this into account, I have constructed an alternative view of local policymaking, the policy conflict model. The "new" model is less new than a mixture of earlier models. It incorporates the strengths of the Peterson and Wilson models, while supplementing them with a typology that tries to explain more adequately the conflict and politics associated with policymaking in American cities.

Shifting Gears: From Wilson and Peterson to a Typology of Policy Conflict

There are two clear benefits of the Wilson policy typology. First, the typology demonstrates the usefulness of the generalization that policies determine politics. Second, the Wilson typology highlights the central role played by costs and benefits (or the *perceived* costs and benefits) associated with policy proposals. This aids in understanding local conflicts, as local policy proposals with dispersed benefits and dispersed costs will generally be far less conflictual (if conflictual at all) than those policies advocating concentrated benefits financed by dispersed costs. In developing a model to better explain the politics of local policymaking, elements of Peterson's local policymaking typology have been combined with elements of Wilson's more nationally oriented cost-benefit typology. The resulting policy conflict typology (see Figure 4.3) has five major policy types—*autonomous, pork barrel, routine or conventional, redistributive,* and *intrusive*— and two major policy dimensions (*city residents only* versus *residents and nonlocals*). *Autonomous* policymaking involves the "housekeeping" dimensions of allocational issues described by Paul Peterson. These duties include such issues as staffing and logistics for police, fire protection, sanitation, and public works. Procedural matters relating to the training or conduct of municipal employees are a second type of autonomous issue. Usually these areas involve little or no conflict and will be relatively invisible to most city residents,

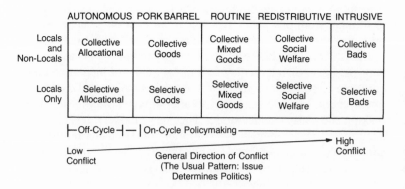

Figure 4.3 **Policy Conflict Typology**

who rarely inquire into the formula by which police or fire safety personnel are assigned to their neighborhood. Thus city policymaking—or more accurately, bureaucratic decision making—in this arena is autonomous or largely free of public scrutiny. Occasionally a policy decision made by a public official will result in a higher level of conflict and controversy, as in the decision by the Los Angeles police department to use the choke-hold on suspects resisting arrest (see chapter 1).

Like autonomous policy issues, *pork-barrel* policymaking—involving a project or policy viewed as favorable for the city and funded completely or largely by external sources (e.g., county, state, or federal government, or private institutions)—generally produces little or no conflict. This "politics of mutual gain" can escalate into a higher level of political conflict, however, if the proposed policy is viewed negatively by a small band of community members willing to defeat its implementation by elected officials.

Routine or *conventional* policymaking includes developmental issues, whereby the city stands to gain by a policy or project designed to enhance the economic position of the city, and *some* of the issues considered by Peterson to be allocational. Some procedural matters, such as the issue of comparable worth, are inherently more conflict-producing than such straightforward logistical decisions as garbage pick-up routes or fire station staffing. The conflictual matters generally involve interest group lobbying and bargaining among several community or employee groups lobbying the city for an increased amount of a limited good (e.g., services, street lights at intersections, salary or benefit increases). Both developmental and the more conflictual of the allocational policies are lumped together in the routine or conventional politics category because they can generate a higher level of conflict than autonomous or pork-barrel policymaking, frequently resulting in a scenario in which at least a few groups or individuals are willing to resist the cost or the distribution of the proposed good or policy.

Redistributive policymaking is, in the policy conflict model, the same as that described by Peterson. The issues are social welfare measures, or attempts to help the less fortunate in the community, and must, by definition, involve the city in their cost (as opposed to the city administering a welfare program both mandated and funded by the state or federal government). As Figure 4.4 illustrates, these

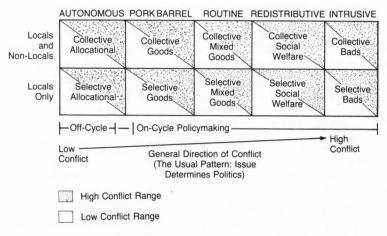

Figure 4.4 **The Policy Conflict Typology: High and Low Conflict Ranges**

issues will generally be accompanied by a higher level of conflict than autonomous, pork-barrel, or conventional policymaking. Because of this predictably high conflict level, and because redistribution usually needs to be organized by nonlocal government in order to be effective, city governments will rarely engage in redistributive policymaking.

Intrusive policymaking is the mirror image of pork-barrel policymaking. Here, the community is threatened by a project or policy (e.g., a toxic waste dump) which appears to present residents with a collective and intrusive (not easily avoided) "bad." Such issues will usually produce great discord and an acrimonious local interest group political scenario.

In his classic study, *Community Conflict*, Coleman identified seven stages (see Figure 4.5) of community conflict,[30] beginning with: (1) specific problem, which leads to (2) a disruption in the normal equilibrium of community relations, (3) escalates via the introduction of new and different issues (e.g., positions taken on downtown redevelopment projects, opposition to a health benefits package for municipal employees benefiting gay couples), (4) becomes acrimonious in character when personal antagonisms develop among the various parties to the conflict, in which the broad belief-sets and character of the opponents are called into question (e.g., the mayor

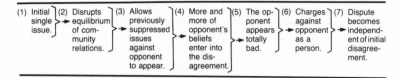

SOURCE: Reprinted with permission of The Free Press, a division of Macmillan, Inc., from *Community Conflict* by James S. Coleman. Copyright © 1957 by The Free Press, renewed 1985 by James S. Coleman.

Figure 4.5 Coleman's Conflict Escalation Pattern

is considered a secret supporter of downtown interests), thus, (5) the opponents are painted in terms that appear totally bad to the opposing camp, and as a natural consequence of this the conflict continues to escalate via (6) charges leveled against the opponent as a person, and (7) the dispute eventually becomes independent of the initial disagreement (e.g., a gun-control issue is almost buried by the numerous other charges that have surfaced, resulting in a full-scale mayoral recall election).

It is the presence of the last three conflict stages—the introduction of new and different issues, the escalation of issue antagonisms into *personal* antagonisms, and the eventual severing of the conflict from the original issue—that constitutes maximum discord and characterizes high conflict instrusive policymaking.

Issues I refer to as "collective bads"[31]—although they begin at a higher level of conflict than autonomous, pork-barrel, conventional, or redistributive policymaking—need not escalate into the maximum discord range. As Oliver Williams and Charles Adrian noted, some communities (as opposed to economic booster, amenity provider, or service provider types) have develped as arbiter communities, where the city councils are given to brokering and resolving conflicts among the various competing interest groups within the metropolitan area. Such cities are probably less likely to experience the maximum discord associated with intrusive policymaking because of the council's inherently more conciliatory role. Second, as Thomas Dye has noted, community conflict is often related to the size of cities and the homogeneity or heterogeneity of their population. Dye's basic proposition—accepted by this author—is that

> large cities have great heterogeneity of population characteristics, therefore conflict is frequent but direct citizen involvement is mini-

mized because of the apathy or alienation of the citizenry. Therefore, the intensity of conflict is reduced. Small cities, which are homogeneous in population characteristics have less conflict but when a conflict occurs it tends to be intense because of greater individual participation. The frequency and intensity of conflict will be greatest in small, heterogenous communities.[32]

As Figure 4.4 illustrates, the policy conflict model builds in the possibility of high or low conflict ranges in each policy classification. Thus, as the conflict line labeled "General Direction of Conflict" in Figures 4.3 and 4.4 indicates, this model shares with earlier ones the assumption that given policy types will *usually* have a predictable politics and level of conflict associated with it. As with the Peterson and Wilson models, policy determines politics. However, this is not *invariably* so. I have constructed the present model in an attempt to capture both the accuracy and the range of the general rule in local policymaking and the exceptions to the rule.

Use of the policy conflict typology allows us to observe and explain three troubling aspects of local policymaking. These are: (1) issues generally but do not always determine conflict levels, (2) different cities can produce different conflict levels in reaction to the same policy issue, and (3) policies frequently exhibit movement (e.g., conflict escalation or de-escalation) that defies simple categorization or permanent assignment of a given policy type. I shall divide such policy mobility into three distinct patterns of movement: policy *transfer* (movement from one policy type to another), policy *transit* (conflict escalation or de-escalation within a policy type), and policy *transposition* (vertical movement within a policy type from one range of participants to another, as conflicts involving only locals expand to conflicts involving nonlocals).

Autonomous Policymaking

Police Deployment in Los Angeles

Following a distinction raised by Bryan Jones, I have divided the housekeeping policies described by Peterson into those determined by the city council in the highly visible forum of the council chambers (on-cycle decision making, see Figures 4.3 and 4.4) and those in which policy is made by city staff out of the public view and usually guided by precedent developed over a long period of time (off-cycle decisions).

City policymakers frequently engage in off-cycle[33] or autonomous policymaking.[34] As Bryan Jones notes, "Most public decisions are made *off* the policy cycle. *Off-cycle* policies do not receive the necessary public attention to get them on the public agenda. They remain hidden from public view, not because anyone is trying to hide them, but because not very many people are very interested. Off-cycle policies generally affect very few people directly (although their indirect effect may be considerable)."[35] Eric Nordlinger has examined this dimension of policymaking at the national level and distinguished between three types of off-cycle or autonomous policymaking.[36] I shall refer to autonomous policymaking as policy enactment, meant in its broadest sense, by elected or appointed city officials that is usually not subject to public scrutiny or controversy. Such policymaking might include the staffing of city fire or police stations, the scheduling of garbage truck routes and pick-up times, enforcement practices for local housing codes, or the selection of a public hearing process to determine how to spend grant monies the city has received.

An example of autonomous policymaking is the manner in which the Los Angeles Police Department assigns police to duty areas. From 1946 to 1984, assignments were made on the basis of a formula that attempted to gauge the seriousness of crime in a particular neighborhood by calculating the numbers of crimes (with violent crimes against persons and crimes against property weighted equally) committed in an area and plugging this number into a formula which includes the value of property loss. This determined how many of the approximately 8,000 police officers would be assigned to the neighborhoods.

In 1984, the Los Angeles Police Commission voted to remove the value of property loss in a burglary from the formula because including it resulted in fewer police being assigned to poorer neighborhoods. Ironically, under the old formula fewer police were assigned to low-income neighborhoods in Los Angeles "because, although more violent crimes happen there, the overall number of crimes is lower than elsewhere."[37] Currently, the Los Angeles Police Commission is re-evaluating the formula so as to reduce the emphasis on property crimes and increase the emphasis on violent crimes.

This police assignment issue, confined to the province of *autonomous* policymaking for almost forty years, became a hotly contested issue before the police commission. This happened because, as Wilson has noted in describing pressures for enactment of new policy, the old formula was no longer seen as adequately addressing the problem of police officer deployment. Perhaps more importantly, with the decision by the city council not to hire more police officers but rather to redeploy them, the issue has undergone a radical redefinition from redeployment equity (e.g., what is the best distribution for Los Angeles) to the loss of "my police" in "my neighborhood." As a Los Angeles *Times* editorial noted, this pits "rich against poor, Valley against South-Central area."[38]

This example illustrates two characteristics—*fixity* and *mobility*—that are important in understanding the municipal policy process. First, policy can stay within one local policy arena (e.g., autonomous policymaking) for long periods of time (in this case, nearly forty years). Second, given a *radical redefinition* of the issue, policies can shift arenas rapidly to encompass the politics and conflict associated with another local policymaking arena (in this case, routine or conventional policymaking).

Autonomous policy is not constrained by high visibility, popularity, or controversy. As Jones notes, off-cycle policymaking is inherently *incremental;* it involves modest changes in past policies and programs.[39] Autonomous policymaking generally remains apolitical and noncontroversial due both to its relative lack of visibility and its inherently incremental policy logic. Policymaking in this area is guided by routines, formulas, and precedent. Fire stations, for example, are staffed each year more or less as they were in the past, using the same formula that guided the staffing decision in earlier years. Barring a triggering event in the public safety area, the same is true for police staffing.

The routines of autonomous policymaking can even be applied to new programs. For example, many urban areas faced with newly enacted federal programs for cities use formulas and citizen participation routines drawn from earlier federal–city programs (e.g., revenue sharing or Model Cities), *even when* those formulas and routines are inappropriate for the requirements of the new programs.[40]

The routinized decision making of autonomous policymaking is useful to city officials faced with the complexity and uncertainties of large, new federal or state-mandated programs.

The Case of CDBG and Citizen Participation Units

Browning, Marshall, and Tabb traced the evolution of local policymaking systems in ten northern California cities between 1966 and 1977.[41] Their policy implementation project analyzed how Bay area cities responded to and administered three federal programs designed to aid cities (Model Cities, General Revenue Sharing, and CDBG). In a small pilot study for the Bay Area Policy Implementation Project, Marshall and Waste analyzed the citizen participation units selected by city officials for use in the first year of the CDBG program.[42] For citizen participation, the Housing and Community Development Act required that cities: (1) inform local citizens of the availability of CDBG money, (2) hold at least two public hearings to obtain citizen viewpoints on possible CDBG expenditures, and (3) promote citizen participation by creating a citizen advisory board or citizen participation unit (CPU). Furthermore, the CPU must contain representatives from poor neighborhoods, and be approved by residents of low-income areas.

While all ten cities studied held more than the minimum requirement of two public meetings, public participation in the program varied widely, as did the mechanism for public participation (the CPU) used by each city. Even though citizen participation was mandated by the CDBG program, cities were free to choose the particular format for their CPU (e.g., a neighborhood-based committee, a citywide committee composed of all interested parties and/or delegates appointed by city officials or a two-tier approach combining a neighborhood-based committee with a citywide committee). (See Figure 4.6.)

In all of the ten cities studied, the city staff (typically comprised of members of the city manager's office and/or the office of planning or community development) designed a CPU based largely on their experience with past programs. Interestingly, whatever the CPU format eventually chosen, its public visibility (exemplifying the typology of conventional policymaking) remained low in eight of the ten sample cities. Richmond and San Jose were exceptions to the low

Categories	Cities
1. Citywide Committees	Berkeley, Daly City, Hayward San Francisco, Stockton, Vallejo
2. Neighborhood Committees	Oakland, Sacramento
3. Two-Tier CPU	Richmond, San Jose

SOURCE: Dale Rogers Marshall and Robert Waste, *Large City Reponses to the Community Development Act* (Davis: University of California, Davis—Institute of Governmental Affairs, 1977), p. 19, Table 2.

Figure 4.6 First-Year Citizen Participation Units: Bay Area Cities

conflict conventional policymaking rule. In these two cities, CDBG expenditure and citizen input became hotly contested and publicly visible conventional policymaking issues. In short, the policymaking politics of CDBG and CPUs was *conventional* in all the cities studied, although the *design* of the CPUs was determined via autonomous policymaking by the staff of each of the ten cities. CDBG itself is a redistributive policy issue in that it is aimed at aiding the poor in urban areas; however, in keeping with Peterson's requirement that redistributive programs must negatively affect the local economy, I will consider CDBG a conventional policy issue for this analysis. The variance in CPU formation from the low to the high range of conventional policymaking has to do with the political culture of each city, their past experience with federal–city programs, the type of policy actors present in each city, and the lack or presence of community triggering events that can spark community interest or visibility in (read: *radically redefine*) the funding and participation issues.

Thus despite newspaper advertisements and, in at least one case, public service announcements on local radio stations, CDBG/CPU policymaking remained out of public view in most of the cities studied. Because of this lack of visibility, CDBG/CPU concerns emerged as examples of the politics of both autonomous policymaking (in the design and implementation of the CPUs) and conventional policy-making (in the actual policymaking and funding recommendations of the CPUs once they were functioning).

The Bay area CDBG study also illustrates the strength of routines and precedents in autonomous policymaking. Despite the newness of the program and the unique focus of CDBG as compared to earlier federal–city ventures, several of the cities (e.g., Richmond, San Jose, Daly City, and Hayward) designed CPUs that were extensions or incremental modifications of those developed for earlier Model City or urban renewal programs. Two cities (San Jose and Stockton) considered using the earlier CPUs with no changes, while one city (Sacramento) actually did so in the first year of CDBG.

Pork-Barrel Policymaking:
The Politics of Collective and Selective Goods

Pork-barrel policies are public actions of a local government aimed at securing selective or collective goods for the city.[43] Thus city officials may lobby Congress or government agencies to select their city as a home port for a new Navy ship, or to install a military base near their city, or to award a space shuttle contract to a contractor based in their city. "Bringing home the pork," when it has beneficial economic consequences that promise to benefit the city as a whole, can be described somewhat more technically, if less appealingly, as acquiring *collective goods* for a particular electorate—in this case a city. Mayhew and others have shown that both members of Congress and voters consider pork-barrel politics important for elected officials.[44] A Congress member is expected to bring home a fair share of the loot, and if they fail to do so, voters consider their performance inadequate.

The key to pork-barrel politics in Congress is what Mayhew has labeled "universalism." As Mayhew explains, "That is, every member, regardless of party or seniority has a right to his share of benefits. There is evidence of universalism in the distribution of projects on House Public Works, projects on Senate Interior, project money on House Appropriations, project money on Senate Appropriations, tax benefits on House Ways and Means, tax benefits on Senate Finance, and . . . urban renewal projects on House Banking and Currency."[45] The influence that such expectations play in congressional budget-making, and the behavior of both Congress members and the electorate is, as Mayhew notes, a key to understanding voting behavior. Indeed, pork-barrel policymaking is a key component of what Mayhew calls "the electoral connection."[46] This study extrapolates Mayhew's discussion of pork-barrel policymaking at the congressional level to the city.

At the city level, pork-barrel policymaking is the first of four "on-cycle,"[47] or publicly visible, policy scenarios. As with conventional, redistributive, and intrusive city policymaking, discussed later in this chapter, pork-barrel policymaking takes place after an issue has evolved from the public discussion stage (the public agenda) to the formal decision making stage. Once on the formal agenda[48] of local policymakers, the issue will result in a pork-barrel policymaking scenario if the policy in question is generally perceived to be of little or no harm to the city, and of general benefit. If it promises to benefit the entire city, the policy is a *collective good;* if it benefits some parts of the city more directly than others, the policy is a *selective good.* It should be noted that, in the abstract, few policy proposals will qualify as examples of a pure collective good. Instead, it is a question of degree; some policies will benefit far more city residents than others. I will call such policies collective goods, even though it is debatable if any but a small set of public goods (e.g., clean air and political freedom) can ever be shown to benefit every citizen in the political unit. Even collective goods that appear to yield an economic benefit to an entire city (e.g., a military base or a space contract) may be viewed as selective goods by one or more residents who view militarism or space exploration in a negative light. However, for our purposes, we will categorize projects such as military bases, new Navy ships, and NASA contracts as collective goods due to the economic spin-offs of such programs for host cities.

The selective goods aspect of pork-barrel policymaking involves a program or project of general benefit to the community, but which will have as its primary beneficiary a particular area of the city or subgroup of the city population. In Peterson's terms, the policy will be *developmental*[49]—it will "enhance the economic position of the city" but those economic benefits will affect city residents differentially. For example, a state or federally financed regional transit project will benefit the city generally, but more directly suburban–to–center city commuters or north–south commuters. Such projects may later evolve into collective goods pork-barrel policymaking if the differential impacts of the project are remedied by later policy decisions (e.g., a center-city rapid transit system is added or an east–west transit link is developed). Pork-barrel policymaking emerges as the reverse coin of intrusive policymaking, which involves collective or selective bads.

Interestingly, it is possible that an issue which could be character-ized as a pork-barrel proposal in one city could be an example of a far less popular and intrusive policymaking proposal in another city. A hypothetical example might include a proposal by a state govern-ment to build a state prison near a city. Conceivably, some less afflu-ent communities would welcome the employment opportunities associated with a new prison, while much more affluent cities—as Beverly Hills, California, or Scottsdale, Arizona—would vigorously object to such proposals and would view the prison in extremely neg-ative, perhaps acrimonious, terms. This example is less hypothetical than it might seem. (See the two Los Angeles *Times* articles included in the Appendix, "Blythe Residents Look Forward to Prospect of Prison" and "Out in the Desert, They Want the Nuclear Dump." The latter article is an account of three California desert towns—Baker, Trona, and Needles—which actively lobbied the California Department of Health Services in 1987 for the unlikely prize of securing a nuclear waste dump site for their community.)

Routine or Conventional Policymaking

Peterson's threefold typology of developmental, allocational, and redistributive local policies is included in the present hybrid policy model. Given the difficulties in determining, in some cases, whether a given policy is allocational or developmental, I have collapsed these two policy types into one, labeled "conventional or routine" policymaking. This includes the more controversial of the house-keeping allocational policies and *all* developmental local policies. Conventional policymaking usually results in political scenarios characterized by little or no conflict and, when conflict arises, it is generally characterized by pluralist bargaining among competing interests groups. In this bargaining process, business groups generally and pro-development groups in particular *may,* as Lindblom and Dahl have noted, have an advantage over other groups in influencing the policy decisions of the city council.[50]

The Politics of Conventional Policymaking: The Case of the Observatory Versus the "Bug Lights"

Conventional policymaking involves the choice between *mixed goods* and/or *mixed bads.* Controversy arises because different actors and groups in the arena will calculate the mix differently, with opponents seeing the proposal as far more negative than will proponents. The San Diego streetlight controversy is a case in point.

In June 1983, the San Diego city council voted 5–4 to convert 10,000 of San Diego's street lamps from mercury-vapor lights to high-pressure sodium lamps. The council voted to do this after hearing testimony that the high pressure lamps were less expensive to maintain and more energy efficient.[51] Nine months later, on the recommendation of the city manager, the same council voted 6–3 to modify the earlier policy and to install low-pressure sodium lamps in city streetlights. The new low-pressure lamps, it was argued, were less expensive than earlier types and more energy efficient than either mercury-vapor or high-pressure sodium lamps.

Given only the above information, the reader might reasonably conclude that the street lamp decision was a straightforward example of pork-barrel or collective good policymaking. The older mercury-vapor technology was replaced with high-pressure sodium (hps) lamps, which, in turn, were replaced by the less expensive, more efficient low-pressure sodium (lps) lamps. In each case, the policy was *collective* (citywide) and a *good* (e.g., public lighting, increased savings and efficiency). However, the decision was an example of conventional policymaking because the council members did not seek to maximize a known good (e.g., economy, new technology) but instead to weigh and trade off multiple (mixed) community goods and bads.

There are several arguments that suggest that lps lights are a community good for San Diego. The new lamps are less expensive in energy use and maintenance costs, saving the city over $200,000 in annual energy costs alone.[52] Second, the "light pollution" generated by non-lps lamps is a threat to nearby Palomar Observatory. Cal Tech researchers operating the telescope at Palomar testified that lps lamps "create less interference for astronomers and that the vote by the council was particularly important to the future of Mount Palomar's 200-inch telescope, the second largest optical telescope in the world."[53] Robert Brucucato, the assistant director at Palomar, said that "if high pressure lamps were to be installed in San Diego and if the city continues to grow rapidly . . . the observatory would be virtually blinded within 15 years."[54]

On the negative side, low-pressure street lamps emit "a controversial yellow-orange glow . . . abhorred by some citizens' groups."[55] A well-organized group of Rancho Bernardo area San Diego residents strongly opposed the lps lamps—"dubbed 'bug lights' by Councilman Bill Mitchell, an opponent."[56] Other lps critics argued that the lights "made everyone look like cadavers."[57] A final set of residents argued that the lps lamps were less bright than hps or mercury-vapor lamps, and that residents were afraid of increased crime hazards attributable to the proposed lps lamps.

In the end, after a stormy and controversial meeting, council members voted 6–3 for the lps street lamps. As this example demonstrates, conventional policymaking involves choices between competing interests, community bads and community goods. This competing or *mixed good* characteristic is a central feature of on-cycle conventional policymaking in cities. Intrusive or pork-barrel policymaking is less mixed and involves the prevention of a widely perceived community harm, or the gain of a new community asset. Ironically, as the solid waste plant case discussed later illustrates, the same proposal may provoke intrusive policymaking in one city, while precipitating pork-barrel policymaking in another.

Redistributive Policymaking

For purposes of the policy conflict typology, the redistributive policymaking arena in local government is exactly the same as that described by Peterson, except for the distinction—as in the other four policy types—of policymaking which involves *locals and non-*

locals, and that which includes *locals only.* I should note that, again following Peterson, redistributive policy is not inherently developmental; in order to be purely redistributive, the policy must *cost* the city rather than benefit it.[58]

Peterson's view that redistributive policies are both conflictual and rare (because redistribution is usually a function of a larger governmental entity with the resources to make a real difference in the lives of such population groups as the poor, single parents, school dropouts, unemployed minority youth, or illegal aliens) is well-taken. Such policies, such as the example regarding the homeless in New York City, are doubly controversial when the program involves initiating rather than terminating or continuing a redistributive policy.

Rounding Up the Usual Suspects: Mayor Koch, Redistributive Policymaking, and the Homeless in Winter

In the winter of 1985, New York City's mayor, Ed Koch, was faced with three problems—temperatures dropping into the twenties, more homeless persons on New York City streets than at any time since the 1930s, and court orders dating back to 1979 requiring the city to provide safe and clean shelter to every homeless person requesting it.

On one weekend stretch that was not atypical for the 1985–86 winter, New York City housed on one Sunday evening alone 7,889 homeless men and women, and 3,959 homeless families—a total of 14,500 people.[59] For the purposes of comparison, I will note that on its busiest night in 1984, the city had housed only 7,600 homeless persons. Thus in 1985 New York City was faced with a homeless problem of almost unprecedented dimensions.

In response to this problem, Mayor Koch ordered the New York City police department to round up homeless persons and determine (by asking each person if they wished transportation to a city shelter) whether such persons were "mentally competent." The mayor announced that a negative answer was equivalent to a finding of mental incompetency since, presumably, no sane person would voluntarily sleep on the streets of New York City in the dead of winter. Under the mayor's cold weather emergency program, homeless persons who refused transport and "appeared unable to care for themselves" were found to be mentally incompetent and were taken by the police to psychiatric emergency rooms for examination, thus temporarily removing them from the streets of New York City.

The new policy, which, in effect, changed the standard of competency needed to admit homeless people into hospitals against their will, actually involved few forced assignments of the homeless to psychiatric examining rooms. Typically, from five to seven persons were rounded up on an average night (out of a homeless population at that time averaging 8,000 persons a night).[60] However, the policy did result in substantial numbers of homeless persons getting off the streets, out of the sight of metropolitan police, or voluntarily accepting transport to city shelters. In the first week of the policy, "out of 79 individuals approached [by police] in Grand Central Station and the Port Authority . . . 70 accepted shelter. In the past, only a third as many had accepted."[61]

The cold weather emergency program generated controversy among both locals and state officials. As one lawyer with the New York Civil Liberties Union argued, the program was controversial because of its coercive nature. "As long as it's not coercive, we don't mind at all," he noted. "It's not a question of the cold; it's a question of taking people to the hospital against their will."[62] In the first week of the mayor's new policy, New York governor Mario Cuomo announced that he would pay a surprise visit to several New York City shelters to determine if they could still meet state standards under the crowded conditions caused by the policy of rounding up the homeless in cold weather.

Despite mounting pressures, including "a surge in homeless people in city shelters, litigation and a controversy about the rights of the mentally ill"[63]—and even gubernatorial intervention—Mayor Koch stood his ground regarding this highly controversial policy on the homeless.

This case study illustrates five points about redistributive policymaking. First, as the general pattern of conflict in city policymaking (as indicated by the conflict arrows in Figures 4.3 and 4.4) suggests, redistributive policymaking is more likely to involve conflict than autonomous, pork-barrel, or conventional policymaking. Koch's cold weather emergency program was controversial from the beginning and was characterized by a relatively high degree of conflict, although not so high a level of conflict as to have degenerated into the acrimonious patterns associated with intrusive policymaking.

Second, in this case several of the parties to the conflict defending the homeless were, as Lipsky suggests will sometimes be the case with poor or low-resource groups in the community, third parties or "reference publics." They were perhaps activated out of genuine interest for the plight of the homeless or attracted by the media publicity which the issue produced, or both.

Third, even though the mayor issued the policy unilaterally, once announced it became subject to interest group bargaining, with groups serving as reference publics for the homeless, who had little ability to directly influence the course of policymaking themselves. The New York City American Civil Liberties Union, the governor, and a loose coalition of poverty and homeless advocacy groups (such as the Coalition for the Homeless and Project Hope) attempted to influence the mayor through lobbying, use of the media, and litigation.

Fourth, Mayor Koch—once himself a candidate for governor of New York—has a strong political power base *and* a high inclination to innovate (e.g., Koch's short-lived experiment with bicycle lanes after his return from a visit to China, or his support of nuclear freeze and sanctuary measures that were adopted by New York City). Thus, using Yates's typology of leadership styles, Koch's strong reaction to the plight of the homeless in winter was consistent with Yates's view of such mayors as entrepreneurs—a "mayor who possesses strong political and/or fiscal resources and who also takes a strongly activist posture toward urban policymaking."[64]

Fifth, perhaps one major reason that Koch was able to fend off the numerous challenges to his cold weather emergency policy was that the program was viewed as innovative but not entirely new. New programs, especially new redistributive ones, are inherently more conflictual than programs viewed as extensions or incremental modifications of existing programs.[65] In fact, the 1985 program was an extension of a windchill program that Koch had ordered put into effect in the winter of 1984. That program, patterned after a similar one initiated by Mayor Wilson Good of Philadelphia, required the police to round up homeless persons and transport them to shelters whenever the windchill factor dropped below five degrees. The windchill program was much more limited in scope than the later program. The New York City police department estimates that on ten such nights in 1984, police transported fifty people to shelters and two to hospitals.[66] Thus much of the conflict in this case centered not on the appropriateness of the policy per se but rather on the extension of the *scope* of the earlier windchill programs in the new cold weather emergency program. As a result, the normal conflict associated with a new redistributive policy was partially muted because the policy could be depicted as an extension of an earlier program in which the basic policy conflict had already been addressed.

The conflict experienced in the redistributive policymaking arena differs radically from the more personalized and acrimonious conflict found when cities engage in the politics of intrusive policymaking.

Santa Barbara and the "Tree People": Redistributive Policymaking and Local/Nonlocal Policy Conflict

Redistributive policymaking is frequently conflictual but—as with all the types of policy conflict—such conflict need not be limited to locals only. The political decisions regarding the homeless in Santa Barbara, California, is a case in point. Santa Barbara, a coastal community ninety-five miles north of Los Angeles, has a population of 77,000 homeowners and renters, and an estimated homeless population averaging between 1,000 and 1,500 persons. The homeless are referred to locally as "tree people," since many of them spend much of their day under a landmark local fig tree whose branches spread 175 feet across, making it the largest fig tree in the state of California.[67]

In 1977 Santa Barbara enacted an ordinance prohibiting sleeping in public places. The city passed the ordinance after complaints from residents and the business community about street crime and the increasing numbers of transients in Santa Barbara. The mayor of Santa Barbara, Sheila Lodge, notes that the antisleeping ordinance is not aimed at trying to rid the city of homeless but is really an attempt to protect them. She argues that the measure is for their safety: "We had five unsolved murders on our beaches before the ordinance went into effect and several more solved ones. It just isn't safe to sleep in the beaches or parks."[68] Following task force recommendations, the antisleeping ordinance was enacted and a new street crime unit was created within the police department charged specifically with enforcing the new law. The city has enforced this ordinance vigorously. In fact, more than twelve hundred people were cited for violating it between 1984 and 1986. The fine for first offenders is one hundred dollars. A local attorney that has defended several homeless clients against the antisleeping measure noted that the municipal court judge "usually sentences them to community service at $5 an hour." The attorney, Willard Hastings, argues that in his opinion such sentences are "like involuntary servitude." Enforcement has been so rigorous that, in some cases, Santa Barbara has extradited homeless persons from other California communities to face charges of violating the public sleeping ordinance in Santa Barbara.[69]

The severe Santa Barbara policy regarding the homeless has attracted the attention of various nonlocals, including national reporters assigned to cover President Reagan when he visits his ranch in the nearby Santa Ynez mountains, the Washington, D.C.-based Community for Creative Nonviolence, and the New York City-based Coalition for the Homeless. All of these groups have become players in the local policymaking process in Santa Barbara. The net result of such national attention has been to give Santa Barbara a poor image in some quarters and to broaden the scope of what was essentially a local conflict to include nonlocals. Santa Barbara probably does not care about having a negative image with one group—the homeless—but it would probably prefer not to have image problems with the others. According to one homeless man, David Conrad, Santa Barbara has "a bad rep on the road." This reputation has led some advocacy groups to bring pressure on city policymakers. Cindy Bogner, codirector of the National Coalition for the Homeless, located in New York City, notes that "Santa Barbara has been notoriously bad in its treatment of the homeless in the last few years."[70]

Mayor Lodge admitted that Santa Barbara may "be stuck with the reputation in regard to the homeless, but a lot of it has to do with being the President's town." She notes that reporters from Washington, frequently unable to gain access to Rancho Cielo, the nearby mountaintop retreat of President Reagan, "have enthusiastically covered news conferences and demonstrations by the homeless."[71]

Mitch Snyder, director of the Washington, D.C.-based Community for Creative Non-Violence, arguing that "Santa Barbara has made itself the epitome of all that is wrong in the ways that American cities are responding to the homeless,"[72] threatened to bring a large number of protesters to Santa Barbara during the first week of August 1986 when the city celebrated an annual fiesta which attracts several hundred tourists, including movie stars. This threat plus the notoriety gained by Snyder as policy entrepreneur—the "Doonesbury" comic strip creator Garry Trudeau ran a series parodying Snyder and others involved in the Santa Barbara homeless policy conflict, and a national television network broadcast a docudrama based on Snyder's work in behalf of the homeless of Washington, D.C.—eventually resulted in the summer of 1986 in the easing of Santa Barbara's hard-line policy toward the homeless.

The city's policy conflict over the influx of homeless persons had gradually broadened from what began in 1977 as an essentially local conflict to a conflict in 1986 between locals and nonlocals. Furthermore, by 1986 the situation briefly appeared as though it would escalate to the point of name-calling and intrusive policymaking. Near the end of the conflict, battle lines hardened into an "us" and "they" mentality, with both sides beginning to characterize the actions of the others in acrimonious terms. Snyder was referred to by the mayor and council members as an outside agitator threatening to descend on Santa Barbara and break up the community's main event of the year, the summer fiesta. Snyder, on the other hand, compared the Santa Barbara ordinance and policymakers to "Selma and Montgomery [Alabama] and their lunch-counter laws. . . . Sleeping ordinances may be on the books in other cities, but I know of no other place where they are used to get rid of homeless people."[73] Santa Barbara's decision on the homeless is a case of policymaking at the cusp—a highly conflictual redistributive policy scenario that escalated into the more personalized and acrimonious conflict levels associated with intrusive policymaking.

The Politics of Intrusive Policymaking

Intrusive policymaking encompasses Wilson's idea of concentrated costs and distributed benefits with their associated high level of conflict, but extends it to cover the phenomena referred to as "collective, intrusive" negatives by John Mollenkopf. For Mollenkopf, in order to generate the politics of high conflict ("maximum discord") and community mobilization, a policy proposal must threaten to fundamentally disrupt a person's life (be "intrusive") and disrupt the lives of several people simultaneously (be "collective"). Thus even relatively low-conflict intrusive policymaking will usually be more conflictual than other policy types due to the nature of the community issues usually framed in intrusive terms. Intrusive subject areas have included court-ordered busing to achieve public school integration, fluoridation of water in the mid-1950s,[74] book banning in public schools, and more recently, the presence of abortion clinics, toxic waste storage facilities, gay or lesbian bookstores/coffee houses or movie theatres, and proposals to designate cities as nuclear free zones or sanctuaries for refugees from Latin America. These issues, however, are usually—but not necessarily—intrusive. Different cities have treated the same policy issue (e.g., school integration, nuclear free zones, toxic waste disposal) so differently as to place the issue in different policy arenas.

In at least a small number of cases, then, policy type will not determine the policy politics associated with a given proposal. This is due to the role of mediating influences operating in local communities. In fact, policy movement of all types (including the movement from one type to another, differential classification of a policy depending on a city, *transit* from low to high or high to low conflict scenarios *within* one policy type) cannot be explained without resort to a satisfactory mechanism to explain local policy variations—a mechanism I shall call the local policy mediation process.

There are two basic types of intrusive policymaking scenarios: policies which, by their subject matter, begin in the intrusive policymaking arena; and policies that escalate from autonomous, pork-barrel, conventional, or redistributive scenarios to the more acrimonious conflict levels associated with intrusive policymaking. Conventional or redistributive policies which involve cultural beliefs and values (e.g., environmental issues, affirmative action, or neighborhood integration) can quickly escalate into the maximum discord that characterizes intrusive policymaking. Some cities—notably Boston and Los Angeles—treated the busing of school-age children to achieve racial integration in public schools as a collective, intrusive bad. School boards in Boston and Los Angeles were, on this issue, engaged in intrusive policymaking.

Frequently such a policy will begin as an example of conventional policymaking but will escalate if it shares three characteristics.[75] First, the issue must affect a major aspect of the lives of community members, or be intrusive.[76] Not all issues are sufficiently intrusive. Different areas of daily life are important to different people within a single community. Coleman cites religion and taxes as issues that are more likely than others to intrusively affect large numbers of city residents. Second, the policy at stake must not leave city residents feeling helpless. It must be one on which community members feel that action is possible and justified. Third, groups need forceful policy entrepreneurs (Boston and Los Angeles had Louise Day Hicks and Bobbie Fiedler, respectively, on the busing issue) who are successful in *radically redefining* the issue in intrusive terms.[77] Intrusive policymaking involves policies viewed as collective or selective bads. For example, city residents may regard an attempt by nonlocals to situate a toxic waste dump within city limits as a collective, intrusive bad that would negatively affect all city residents and which could and should be resisted as unwise public policy. The same might not be true of a proposed coal power plant, even one that planned to burn high-sulfur coal. City dwellers might judge the electricity gained from the new plant to be worth the trade-offs in air quality. Or the issue might not be sufficiently collective. It might only affect residents within a one-mile radius of the proposed plant site. In cases such as the proposed coal power plant, the policymaking scenario might still be intrusive, but selectively so. By this I mean that *some* city residents would believe the plant would have a negative impact on a significant facet of their daily lives. This segment of the city's residents—if they believe they have a chance of revising, delaying, or reversing the proposed policy—will organize around the issue and attempt to generate maximum discord in city policy circles. Thus intrusive policymaking will involve, in direct contrast to pork-barrel policymaking, collective or selective "bads." Community bads involve issues generally believed to be harmful (read: extremely concentrated costs) to all or at least part of the residents of a given city. Examples include Love Canal in New York State, Three Mile Island in Pennsylvania, the Hanaford nuclear power and weapons grade plutonium plant near Yakima, Washington, and the Union Carbide chemical plant currently operating in Institute, West Virginia. It should, however, be emphasized that, as in the case of public goods, there is no such thing as a pure public bad. Even toxic waste dumps do not qualify as pure public bads since society does gain in some respects from the uses of toxic chemicals. Thus, the continuum of selective to collective for goods and bads ranges from more good than bad to more bad than good. While the distinctions are fairly straightforward in most cases, as the example of a proposed trash-to-energy plant illustrates, the view of what constitutes a collective good or bad may shift from one community to the next and, given the involvement of significant mediating influences, may even shift within one community over time.

The Curious Case of an Intrusive and *Pork-Barrel Policy Issue: The Proposed SANDER Trash-to-Energy Power Plant*

San Diego is the seventh largest city in the United States and the third fastest growing metropolitan area. Faced with the problem of rapid growth, San Diego has recently turned to address a related problem involving the increasing difficulty of disposing of the city's muncipal waste. In an attempt to solve the increasingly severe solid waste disposal problem, San Diego County and the city of San Diego formed a joint project known as SANDER (San Diego Energy Recovery Project). Aided by funds from the state legislature, SANDER hired engineers and architects, and drew up plans for a plant to incinerate trash and use the resulting heat to generate steam and electricity. The plant would have the capacity to handle 1,200 tons of refuse daily, converting it into enough electricity to serve 30,000 homes.[78] Studies by SANDER staff indicated that, because of the estimated annual profits, the project could be privately financed, and they predicted full recovery of initial costs within the first five years of plant operation. Having solved the technical problems, the SANDER staff needed to find a suitable site for the plant.

The SANDER Authority board of directors—consisting of one state legislator, two county supervisors, and two San Diego city council members—and the SANDER staff proposed two possible plant sites, National City and Chula Vista. They met with little success in the first attempt to persuade a city to accept the proposed plant. National City community groups quickly and successfully

With landfill space dwindling, Southern California communities are turning to huge trash incinerators that generate electricity for sale to utilities. While the plants differ in design, these are the typical steps in a "mass burn" plant, the most common in the U.S. The plants usually operate 24 hours a day, all year.

1. Garbage is dumped into the pit, typically without any processing. The pit can hold 8 000 tons of trash, enough to cover the Dodger Stadium field 6 feet deep. Air from this pit is pulled into the furnace so odors do not escape.

2. Each crane load drops 2 to 3 tons of trash, including whole refrigerators and other home appliances, into the furnace hopper. A hydraulic ram pushes the trash into the furnace, which burns at 1800 degrees.

3. Burning trash is piled 3 to 4 feet deep on the furnace grate. No outside fuel is added. The special grates tumble and mix the trash for thorough burning. Air is blown through the grate from below to aid the burning, which many scientists believe helps reduce the emission of pollutants and toxic elements such as dioxin into the atmosphere.

4. Pipes in the upper furnace walls carry water, which is turned into steam by the heat of furnace. The steam is superheated before spinning the turbines to produce electricity.

5. Burned garbage falls into a quenching tank to cool. The ash and gritty residue is taken by conveyor belt and sifted to remove metals, which can be sold as scrap. Most of the residue is buried, taking up only 5% as much landfill space as the original garbage. In some states, the residue has been used in road-building or as a landfill cover.

The Gases: Exhaust from the furnace flows through a series of pollution control devices before going out a 300-foot stack. Most local plants will be required to meet more stringent emission levels than required elsewhere, although some officials are concerned about trace amounts of toxic emissions such as dioxin. From outside, there is little or no visible smoke or discernible odor.

The Ash: Small amounts of ash collected in the furnace and the pollution controls are mixed with the bulky residue taken from the furnace and trucked away for burial in landfills.

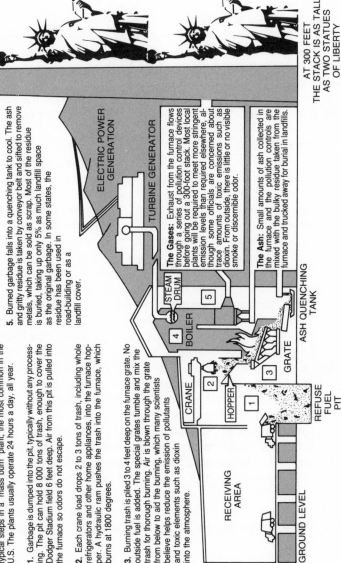

ELECTRIC POWER GENERATION

TURBINE GENERATOR

STEAM DRUM

BOILER

CRANE

HOPPER

GRATE

ASH QUENCHING TANK

REFUSE FUEL PIT

RECEIVING AREA

GROUND LEVEL

AT 300 FEET THE STACK IS AS TALL AS TWO STATUES OF LIBERTY

SOURCE: Patricia Mitchell, "Trash-to-Energy Incinerators" (March 9, 1986), p. I:3. Copyright 1986, *Los Angeles Times*. Reprinted by permission.

Figure 4.7 Trash-to-Energy Incinerators

opposed the proposed trash-burning plant as a citywide health hazard. Also, the project met stiff opposition from the Navy due to the proposed site's proximity to a nearby naval station. With the combined opposition of neighborhood groups and the Navy, the National City city council rejected the SANDER proposal unanimously.

The SANDER experience with Chula Vista was, at least initially, considerably different than with National City. Chula Vista policymakers sought out the SANDER project; they approached the proposed trash-to-energy plant as a possible collective good for their city.

In February of 1982, the Chula Vista city council expressed interest in SANDER's project. SANDER held workshops to inform Mayor Greg Cox and the city council on the objectives and costs associated with the proposed plant. In the first stage of the planning process, various city departments formed planning groups. The lead departmental group was established by the Redevelopment Agency to oversee all planning and coordination of the various city groups involved in evaluating the proposed plant. Its members consisted of the Chula Vista planning director, the city engineer, the community development director, and the director of building and housing. The public works department was responsible for project implementation. The finance department was assigned to evaluate financing options, while the chamber of commerce formed a broad-based investigative committee, which, it was hoped, would serve as an opinion and fact-gathering body that would report directly to the city council. SANDER and the city established an ecology center to help educate the public on recycling. These city and quasicity groups were central to the early planning on the proposed plant. Ad hoc citizens' groups appeared later in the process. Prior to their appearance, the major figures and groups in the planning process regarded the proposed plant as a collective good that would produce energy and jobs, and serve as a model for recycling and energy use in the future. Thus the early policy politics of the recycling plant were pork barrel in character, although this would change when ad hoc community groups appeared opposing the new plant, leading to a shift in public opinion.

After some deliberation, the city council agreed on the proposed site and indicated that they would provide the county and SANDER with a formal letter of interest after receiving a city staff report. After sending the letter of interest, the proponents of the project would be responsible for filing an environmental impact report (EIR). Mayor Cox wanted the EIR before he would decide his own position on the issue. Cox also sent city officials to similar plants in Chicago and Tampa to view operations there. The proposed ten-acre site in Chula Vista, owned by a private holding company, is near a San Diego Gas and Electric (SDG&E) power plant and adjacent to a large industrial concern, Rhor Industries. SDG&E and Rhor both favored the proposed plant and testified that the project would relieve extreme peak hour demand and reduce costly energy bills.

The issue looked as if it were ripening into a policy decision in favor of the Chula Vista site, but then a policymaking politics *transfer* took place. The city's community development director, Paul Derochers, was the first to oppose the project. Derochers preferred a light industrial and commercial complex rather than the energy plant. Hall Properties presented the Chula Vista Community Development Agency with a twenty-million-dollar plan for a commercial, light industry complex on the same site as that proposed for the trash conversion plant. Derochers argued that the energy plant would have a negative effect on the city's image and that a heavy industrial image would hurt the tourist orientation of the bayfront area. Mayor Cox strongly disagreed, countering that "SANDER would bring Chula Vista about ten times as much income annually as the commercial complex." Cox was confident of the SANDER technology and believed that building the plant in his city would be innovative and good planning for future energy needs.[79]

At this stage, the decision arena still had more SANDER proponents than opponents. However, one resident, Bud Pocklington, who lived near the proposed plant site emerged, as an anti-SANDER spokesperson. Pocklington headed CEASE (Citizens Enraged at SANDER), a group which lobbied against the SANDER project and maintained a highly visible presence at all subsequent city council meetings at which the project was discussed. In addition to the opposition of the community development director and CEASE, some council members voiced reservations about the design and aesthetics of the Chicago and Tampa plants. In response, SANDER constructed a scale model of the proposed plant, which eased city officials' fears that the plant might become a community eyesore.

SANDER assured the Community Development Agency that the facility would not resemble the "ugly boxes" now in operation in other parts of this country and in Europe. Additionally, SANDER promised landscaping to enhance the appearance of the plant site.[80]

SANDER was well-prepared for what appeared to be their final shot at gaining Chula Vista's confidence. They told the crowded council chambers that there were many pluses about the location of the facility. Agreeing, the city council voted to give SANDER's lead spokesperson—San Diego County supervisor Tom Hamilton—the formal letter of approval. After the formal letter was sent in June 1982, the Chula Vista city council gave SANDER one month to prepare the EIR. This action reserved the site for the project until January 1983. SANDER failed to complete the EIR by July 1982. The council granted SANDER an extension and decided to bring the issue to a vote by February of 1983, if the EIR was favorable. However, the council also decided that an earlier waiver of the public hearing process was inappropriate. This decision opened up the plant site proposal to a broader audience and had the eventual effect of widening the scope of conflict and controversy. The input from the public hearings, combined with the earlier resistance to the SANDER project, began to take its toll. Significantly, the council now began to shift in votes on the project. Earlier votes had favored SANDER by a 3–2 margin. The votes were now swaying in the opposite direction. The council began to see mounting opposition not only to the project itself but also on the issue of the best location for the plant. Opposition to SANDER expanded to include a changed majority on the council, the increasingly vocal dissident city staffers, and neighborhood groups. Supervisor Hamilton, a SANDER executive board member and formerly a strong SANDER advocate, began to question the future of SANDER on the bayfront and expressed a preference for relocating the proposed plant site.[81] Thus the SANDER project lost its major proponent to the council. As a result, the executive director of SANDER withdrew the application to build the plant in Chula Vista. In less than a year, the politics of SANDER had gone full circle—from collective good to collective bad. Dramatic policy transfers such as the shift in Chula Vista from pork-barrel to intrusive policymaking are relatively rare. Still, the example serves to illustrate city policymaking vis-à-vis collective goods and collective bads.

Conflict Escalation and De-escalation in Local Policymaking

While selective bads, such as the proposed installation of a coal power generating plant, will usually result in intrusive policymaking scenarios, there are natural limits that help keep the acrimony in such cases below the level experienced with collective bads. First, precisely because the policy concerns *selective bads,* the affected residents are rarely able to persuade other city residents to support their cause. While not impossible, it is unlikely that the affected population can increase the scope or the intensity of the issue. Ideally, were they able to do so, they would change the public perception of the issue, radically redefining the coal power plant as a collective rather than a selective bad. Such selective-to-collective *policymaking transfers* are relatively rare.

But it is possible that an issue which is selectively intrusive and controversial with one segment of the population may escalate into an issue considered both intrusive and collectively bad. The use of choke-holds by metropolitan police on ghetto area suspects, for example, can escalate beyond the ghetto if the issue becomes one of police brutality in general. Alternatively, the issue may begin as a selective bad in the intrusive policymaking scenario but de-escalate into the politics of conventional city policymaking. Or an issue such as a proposed zoning or environmental policy might begin as a locals-only conventional issue (or a local and nonlocal redistributive policy conflict, such as the example of policymaking on the homeless in Santa Barbara) and escalate into the highly conflictual acrimonious arena of intrusive policymaking. The next section, describing the construction policy regarding residences on canyon rims in San Diego, gives an example of exactly this sort of conflict escalation.

San Diego and Zoning for Inner-City Canyons: From Community Plan to "Outsiders" and "Elitist Social Engineering"

As Paul Peterson correctly notes, development policies—classified as conventional policies in the policy conflict typology used here—will usually involve some conflict among various community interest groups. Typically, groups that are parties to the policy conflict are seeking to: (1) expand the scope of the proposed project(s), (2) reallocate the proposed cost(s) of the projects or policy, (3) redistribute the gains associated with the proposed policy or project, or (4) to prevent the project or policy either in part or entirely. This natural conflict is the basis of interest group politics in the conventional policymaking arena at the local level. Occasionally, such conflicts heat up beyond the conflict level associated with conventional policymaking, eventually entering the intrusive policymaking arena. Such policy flare-ups need not remain permanently intrusive.

In November 1985, San Diego voters passed Proposition A, a slow-growth ballot initiative that required all new development in the city's perimeter—designated under the city general plan as the "urban reserve"—to be subject to ballot approval by San Diego voters. The initiative also retroactively rescinded approval granted by the city council for two controversial housing and industrial developments that the council had earlier approved as exceptions to the general no-growth urban reserve area. Indeed, the exceptions granted by the council—amounting to land in excess of 30 percent of the overall territory within the urban reserve—provided much of the impetus for the passage of Proposition A. The exceptions granted by the council angered many of the parties to the original growth management plan for San Diego, which had declared the 52,000-acre urban reserve off-limits to builders until 1995. The passage of Proposition A, however, served as a triggering event, affecting a second policy decision and briefly escalating it into the arena of intrusive policymaking.

Two weeks after the passage of Proposition A, the city council reviewed a plan to regulate development on canyon slopes in the downtown and near downtown areas of San Diego. The draft plan, the result of six years of community planning reviews and studies, had been amended two months earlier in October in a compromise which had removed specific density numbers from the regulation and attempted to create an air of flexibility about the regulations. The compromise between environmentalists and neighborhood groups who opposed any development, and builders who favored high density development of the hillsides, took on an acrimonious quality following the passage of Proposition A, referred to in local political and planning circles as the "Proposition A-bomb." Two weeks after Proposition A was voted into effect, pro-development forces led by council member and mayoral candidate, Bill Cleator, sought to use the lack of specific density requirements in the compromise draft of the canyon development plan to allow unlimited density (e.g., multiple multifamily units) on downtown canyon rims. Anti-development forces, led by then-mayor Roger Hedgecock, charged that the original compromise was being ignored by pro-development forces in a spirit of revenge[82] for the passage of Proposition A by a 2–1 margin. The mayor, criticizing Cleator, stated, "I believe the opponents of Proposition A made a prediction that if Proposition A passed, this council would fill up the canyons of this city with development. I think that this is the first step in fulfilling that particular prophecy. This is the revenge of Proposition A."[83]

The original plan governing canyon rims, before the October compromise, allowed no more than four units per acre. When the leader of the development forces suggested that the October compromise would allow more development than the older plan, the mayor responded that he was "horrified" at that interpretation. Hedgecock then threatened the development forces: "If it takes another initiative to protect the canyons of this city, there will be another initiative to protect the canyons of this city."[84]

Just as Proposition A, which rescinded an earlier development policy compromise, had served as a triggering event for pro-development forces to reinterpret a canyon rim development plan, so too did the threat of a second initiative—dubbed "Son of Prop A" by local political wags. At the next council meeting, one week after the original attempt by Cleator and the pro-development coalition to weaken the canyon development rules, the threat of a second and perhaps equally popular ballot initiative produced a shift in the position of Cleator and his supporters on the council. In fact, at the next council meeting Cleator led the council effort to write strict limits on canyon rim developments, announcing that he hoped "the [new] Uptown plan becomes a blueprint for citywide canyon protection."[85]

This time, the acrimonious comments came from the pro-development interests that felt deserted by Cleator and other formerly pro-development council members. "I am not pleased," said attorney Mike McDade, who represented the Uptown Property Owners Association. "I felt there was a backing off of support for property owners' rights." Acknowledging that Cleator's mayoral candicacy and the threat of a second ballot initiative timed to coincide with the election had prompted a change of position in Cleator, who "wants the broadest possible constituency" for his mayoral bid, McDade said the issue "pitted property owners against property takers," and charged that "some residents were advocating elitist social engineering of the worst sort" in supporting canyon rim preservation.[86] Cleator himself had issued some strong charges at the beginning of the meeting which resulted in a victory for anti-development forces. As one account noted, "The meeting started out with harsh words. Cleator accused 'outsiders' of trying to 'torpedo' an earlier agreement."[87] However, after a heated council session that eventually ended with Cleator leading the charge to enact a measure that would "keep everything but the barest of development off the hillsides,"[88] Cleator, in a much more amiable mood, characterized his earlier interpretation of the October compromise to reporters in the following way: "Maybe I was trying to design the perfect horse and I came out with a camel."[89]

Examining the Pattern of Community Conflicts: Escalation and De-escalation in the Canyon Rim Controversy

Figure 4.8 depicts Coleman's seven-stage community conflict escalation process and the brief escalation and de-escalation in conflict associated with the canyon rim development issue in San Diego. The canyon rim conflict began, as most redevelopment issues do, in the conventional policymaking arena but eventually progressed through each of the seven stages of conflict in Coleman's model. In stage 1, the original policy proposal met with some conflict due to the contending nature of the competing interest groups involved (builders versus environmentalists), but the original conflict over density resulted in a compromise on it. However, after this apparent end, the conflict escalated to Coleman's second stage due to a triggering event (the passage of Proposition A), which acted as a mediating influence *radically redefining* the original compromise. Supporters of Proposition A saw themselves with a new voter mandate for environmentally sensitive policies, while opponents chafed under its

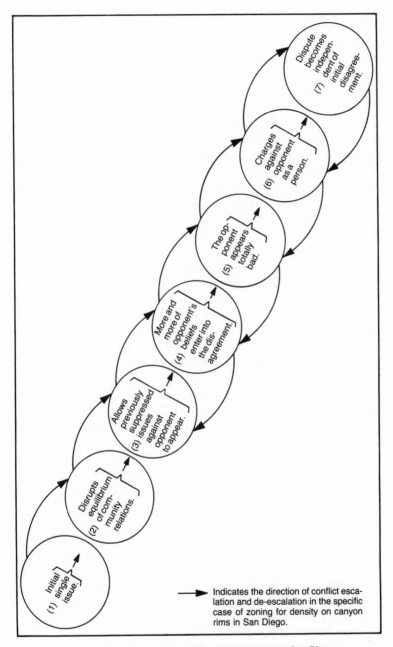

(1) Initial single issue.

(2) Disrupts equilibrium of community relations.

(3) Allows previously suppressed issues against opponent to appear.

(4) More and more of opponent's beliefs enter into the disagreement.

(5) The opponent appears totally bad.

(6) Charges against opponent as a person.

(7) Dispute becomes independent of initial disagreement.

→ Indicates the direction of conflict escalation and de-escalation in the specific case of zoning for density on canyon rims in San Diego.

Figure 4.8 Conflict Escalation/De-escalation Pattern: San Diego Canyon Rim Zoning Issue

restrictions. This served to disrupt the equilibrium that the October compromise on canyon rim development represented. This, in turn, allowed both sides to escalate to the third stage of conflict by bringing in previously suppressed issues (environmentalists alleging threats of builders to line the canyons with high-density developments versus builders' claims that the urban reserve was being held hostage for an unrealistic period). Policy entrepreneurs (the mayor and councilman Cleator) then pushed the conflict into the fourth stage by personalizing the arguments and expanding the conflict into the acrimonious realm (e.g., charges that the reinterpreted compromise was an act of revenge). In the fifth stage of conflict, opponents were painted in terms appearing to make them look totally bad (small-minded revenge seekers incapable of honorably abiding by the earlier October compromise versus "elitist social planners" willing to trample the rights of private property owners). With such emotionally charged character assessments now tossed into the policymaking arena, the conflict easily—if briefly—evolved into stage 6 (charges against the opponent as a person) and stage 7, characterized by escalation of the dispute into an issue which was independent of the initial disagreement over specific density allowances for particular canyon rims in or near the downtown area.

De-escalation (see Figure 4.8) occured due to two major mediating influences. First, a second triggering event—the possibility of a canyon rim environmental ballot initiative ("Son of Prop A")—emerged as a potent threat, quickly increasing the costs associated with pressing the conflict for pro-development forces. The proposed initiative was engineered by two policy entrepreneurs, Mayor Hedgecock and another leading member of the pro-environmental coalition, councilman and potential mayoral candidate Michael Gotch. Second, the upcoming June election in which councilman Cleator was a mayoral candidate probably encouraged Cleator to recognize the popularity of pro-environmental issues (and candidates) with San Diego voters, and to try and broaden his own base of electoral support by shifting his position on the canyon rim development issue. Thus a routine developmental issue escalated beyond the realm of conventional policymaking, only to de-escalate in conflict and return to its original routine or conventional policymaking arena.

A third aspect of the canyon rim issue that tended to reduce conflict and prevent the escalation of the issue into a full-blown collective intrusive bad is the selectivity of the canyon rim issue. While the urban reserve issue was easily visible to most San Diegans in terms of influencing the future quality of life for the city's residents, the canyon rim issue was less general in its scope, affecting only those immediately adjacent to canyons, builders, neighborhood activists, and environmentalists. While it is possible to argue that the canyons and their rims are an integral feature of the city's quality of life, it is possible that the canyon rim conflict and associated ballot measure would have produced a much smaller, less salient coalition than did the literally larger (52,000-acre) urban reserve policy controversy.

Additional Factors Determining
Conflict Escalation and De-escalation

Factors other than the selectivity of an issue may combine to defuse policymaking conflicts, to force an issue to be viewed as selectively rather than collectively bad, or to de-escalate the issue from an intrusive to a conventional policymaking scenario. The political aspects and structure of authority in a community will affect the course of an issue. If community members view the political leadership as credible and legitimate, this support may allow these leaders to facilitate the compromises necessary to defuse an issue. Furthermore, the skill of the political leadership in co-opting the various opposing factions may serve to contain the issue within the traditional authority structure. The existing local administration may also channel dissent by building in regular procedures for expressing minority viewpoints. As Coleman notes, the two-party system operating in partisan cities serves to allow expression of dissent within the system and discourages the establishment of ad hoc groups determined to escalate an issue associated with a collective or selective bad into a full-scale intrusive community controversy.[90]

Finally, forces outside a community may contribute to escalation or de-escalation of conflict. An outside event may activate the interest and participation of the city's "political stratum"[91]—those residents who actively follow and participate in political events and civic concerns. On a broader scale, a dramatic outside event may trigger large numbers of people to become interested and active in the policy

issue.[92] For example, media coverage of such dramatic and potentially dangerous events as the Love Canal toxic waste disaster in New
York State or the Three Mile Island nuclear power plant accident in
Pennsylvania may trigger broad local concern over equivalent dangers in cities across the nation. Conversely, news stories telling of
new technologies to contain the hazards of toxic and nuclear waste
may act to defuse local concerns and decrease the scope and intensity
of local policymaking conflicts. As Jane Jacobs has recently shown,
city policymaking is dramatically affected at the local level by activities in the national and international economic arena.[93]

A final force influencing local policymaking, through the sway
exerted on local beliefs and attitudes as they affect local policymaking, are shifts in the national social climate, or the mood of the country. Such shifts in the prevailing beliefs and values shared by a people—termed the "ideology of the times" by Bauer, Sola Pool, and
Dexter[94]—may act to increase or decrease the salience of an issue in
local policymaking scenarios. These shifts may even introduce
entirely new categories of collective bads to a community, which
were once viewed in the light of earlier community values and an
earlier national ideology of the times as collective goods. The emergence of nuclear weaponry on the docket of city policymaking is a
case in point. Berkeley, California, and Cambridge, Massachusetts—
which welcomed weapons research laboratories in their communities
in the 1950s—have, with a shift in both local beliefs and values and
a parallel shift in the national ideology, virtually reversed their policies regarding nuclear weapons. A measure viewed in the 1950s as
a pork-barrel victory of local policymakers—a collective good that
would simultaneously defend the country and bolster the local economy—is now debated in intrusive terms. Indeed, maximum discord
and collective bads are at the core of recent city debates on nuclear
free zones in such communities as Berkeley and Cambridge, and
sanctuary proposals in cities such as Los Angeles and New York
City.

Policy Paths and Policy Space

Borrowing a concept from Anthony Downs, I suggest that each policymaking issue has its own territory or "policy space."[95] Downs
coined this phrase to illustrate the interdependency of agencies or

bureaus in public policymaking. According to Downs, policies occupy their own territory or space; this space is not institutionally bounded but instead may involve several bureaus simultaneously. Thus Downs notes that the distinction between *policy space* and *organizational space*

> is important because a given space can be occupied by several bureaus simultaneously if they all have functions involving that space. For example, the policy space depicting U.S. nuclear bombing is occupied by SAC missile squadrons, SAC bomber squadrons, the Navy's Polaris submarines, and the Navy's carrier aircraft squadrons. Each of these has a different overall location, yet all have at least one specific location in common.[96]

Policy space, as I use it, is an extension of Downs's concept. By policy space, I refer to the fact that city issues are frequently not bounded by their original policymaking arena but instead—as in the San Diego canyon rim example—*transfer* from one policymaking arena to another (e.g., from the politics of conventional policymaking to acrimonious policymaking and back). Figure 4.9 illustrates the

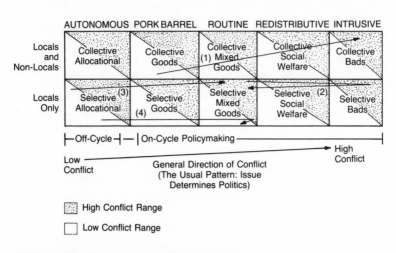

(1) Policy Space/Policy Path for SANDER Controversy
(2) Policy Space/Policy Path for San Diego Canyon Rim Policymaking
(3) Policy Space/Policy Path for Los Angeles Police Department Deployment Controversy
(4) Policy Space/Policy Path for San Diego Choke-Hold Controversy

Figure 4.9 Policy Paths and Policy Space: Unbounded Cases—Policymaking Transfers

path of the San Diego canyon rim dispute and the paths of several other policymaking scenarios used as illustrations of city policymaking in this chapter. As Figure 4.9 shows, policy paths and policy space refer to two different aspects of a single phenomena. Policy paths are the *direction* that a given policy takes, represented by the directions of the arrows in Figures 4.9 and 4.10. Policy space refers not simply to the direction (or path) of the arrow for a given case, but to the *entire length of the arrow* which, loosely speaking, may be called the policy space of an issue. Thus the space of some policy cases is unbounded (meaning that during their life cycle they cross into two or more arenas of policymaking). Figure 4.10, on the other hand, illustrates the opposite—cases in which the policy space of a given policymaking scenario is bounded by, or limited to, a single policy arena (e.g., policy which is solely autonomous, pork barrel, conventional, redistributive, or intrusive).

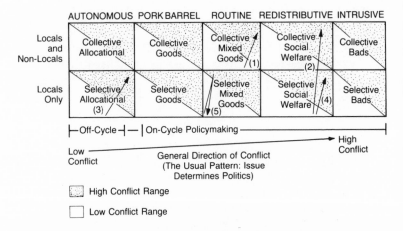

(1) Policy Space/Policy Path for San Francisco Chinatown Freeway Controversy (Policy Transit)

(2) Policy Space/Policy Path for Santa Barbara Policymaking on the Homeless (Policy Transposition)

(3) Policy Space/Policy Path for Los Angeles Choke-Hold Controversy (Policy Transit)

(4) Policy Space/Policy Path for New York City Policymaking on the Homeless (Policy Transit)

(5) Policy Space/Policy Path for San Diego Street Lamps Controversy (Policy Transit)

Figure 4.10 Policy Paths and Policy Space: Bounded Cases—Policymaking Transit and Transposition

Policymaking transfers are relatively rare. Most issues, given the general rule that issues determine politics, have a policy space that is bounded, that is, confined to one policymaking arena. It is necessary to emphasize, however, that bounded policies may still experience policy movement and thus be depicted as having policy paths. These cases include escalations or de-escalations in conflict that remain bounded within a single arena. These are referred to in the present work as examples of *policy transit* (in cases of escalation or de-escalation within a single arena) or *policy transposition* (in cases where the policy shifts in scope from a scenario involving locals only to one involving locals and nonlocals, or vice versa).

Issues and Policy Politics:
General Rules and Mediating Influences

Throughout this chapter I have insisted on three basic arguments or rules about the politics of city policymaking. First, the type of issue confronting city policymakers *usually* determines the type of politics and conflict level that will be associated with the issue. Second, even though the arena (and thus the conflict level) of a given issue is usually determined by the subject matter of the issue, such "arena-bounded" issues may still experience movement (policy transit or policy transposition or both), which may be described as a policy path. And third, such movement within policymaking arenas, as well as movement from one arena to another (policy *transfers*), and differences in assigning a classification to an issue depending on the city in which it is introduced (e.g., the SANDER project) are exceptions to the general rule that issues determine politics. These exceptions are explained by the effect of mediating influences in the policy environment of local communities.

Mediating influences, illustrated in Figure 4.11, are intervening variables that may serve to deflect policy issues from the general or expected pattern. "Issues determine politics" is a good rule of thumb *unless* the perceptions of the issue in a given community undergo a *radical redefinition.* Such redefinitions may occur because: (1) the facts surrounding an issue change (e.g., more information about a project comes to light); (2) different communities have councils and

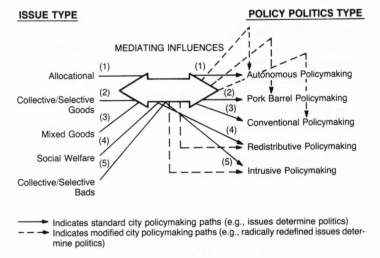

Figure 4.11 City Policymaking Paths: Typical and Atypical Patterns

policymaking bodies with different orientations (e.g., economic boosters, amenity providers, caretakers, or arbiters); (3) different communities have differences related to their unique political culture or worldview (e.g., liberal versus conservative; sunbelt versus frostbelt); (4) there are important spatial differences between cities (e.g., core, suburban, and periphery cities); (5) conflict is more probable on all issues in general in small heterogeneous cities than in larger cities or small homogeneous communities; (6) policy entrepreneurs are able to widen the scope of conflict or resist efforts to do so; (7) significant triggering events occur (e.g., Proposition A in San Diego); (8) policy entrepreneurs threaten to precipitate a significant triggering event (e.g., "Son of Prop A"); (9) policy entrepreneurs are able to escalate conflict by attacking the individual or group associated with an issue (e.g., Bobbie Fielder and the Bus Stop movement in Los Angeles that sought to block court-ordered busing) or de-escalate an issue by defusing or blurring it (e.g., the San Diego police chief, attending neighborhood meetings, defended use of the choke-hold on the grounds that it was less damaging than the use of the baton or firearms by arresting officers); (10) mayoral styles differ (e.g., the strong entrepreneurial style of Koch versus the weaker bargaining or broker style of Bradley); (11) an issue may be new or build on an existing policy (e.g., the comparable worth issue in San Jose versus the cold weather emergency program of Koch in New York City which, although innovative, was an extension of earlier programs); (12) third parties or "reference publics" may be activated, either locally or nationally; or (13) cities have differing political parties and institutions, such as strong mayor or city manager governments, consolidated city–county governments, or various reform processes including initiative, referendum, or recall elections (e.g., the recall election against Mayor Feinstein in San Francisco, the use of polling by the city manager of San Diego to lessen conflict in the street lamp case, or the use of the powers of the strong mayor system by Koch to initiate and defend the cold weather emergency program).

Conclusion

Like the life cycle of city policymaking and the growth, locale, and aging factors discussed previously, conflict is a fundamental part of the decision-making ecology of city policymaking. In large measure, the ability of a city to solve problems or make decisions rests on the interplay between the policy life cycle and the city policymaking ecology.

The hybrid policy conflict typology presented in this chapter accepts the argument advanced by Lowi, Wilson, and Peterson that, generally speaking, "issues determine politics." Thus policies are assigned to one of four arenas or policy conflict scenarios based on the type of issue under consideration. However, unlike the models of Wilson and Peterson, the policy conflict model allows for policy movement and dynamics. The hybrid model illustrates more adequately than the models of Wilson or Peterson: (1) the autonomous nature of most allocational decision making by city bureaucrats; (2) the possibility of policy shifts and movement, including policy transit, policy transposition, and policy transfer; (3) the collective goods to collective bads continuum; (4) the paradox of different cities treating the same policy issue differently (as in the case of comparable worth in San Jose and Los Angeles, or the case of choke-holds in Los

Angeles and San Diego) *and* (as in the case of SANDER) of the same city treating the same issue differently at different times.

Thus far I have considered the impact of five of the basic elements of the city policymaking ecology—age, the growth process, locale, political conflict levels, and policy type—on the life cycle of city policymaking. The final two chapters consider the impact of three additional ecological factors and the fragility of the overall municipal policymaking process in American cities.

5

Reform, Regulation, and City Policymaking

Thus far, I have examined the life cycle of city policymaking and five key components of city policymaking ecology—age, the growth process, locale, political conflict levels, and policy type. This chapter will discuss three additional major elements of the urban policymaking ecology—scandal and reform activity, regulatory activity, and other external factors (including IGR activity). I shall also examine two additional, and somewhat lesser, ecological components—the personality factor and the local political culture. After explaining the role of these additional elements in the city policy process, the last chapter presents a final set of considerations. In the closing chapter I will use the policy life cycle and the various key elements of the city policymaking ecology to illustrate fundamental and generic weaknesses in American urban policymaking—an inherent fragility in the policy process that poses problems both for those trying to understand it and for those attempting to formulate city policy on such pressing municipal concerns as poverty, homelessness, ghettos, racism, crime, and pollution.

The Reform Factor: The Ebb and Flow of Scandals and Political Reforms

Periodically, cities are gripped with the urge to reform. This urge is not a permanent feature of the municipal landscape nor is it a regular feature. Thus it is neither predictable nor particularly incremental. Instead it is episodic, like an irregular reform "tide" that ebbs and flows according to both national and local currents. While reform may, in the abstract, be desirable, the ebb and flow of reforms in American cities introduces a measure of uncertainty and added complexity to municipal deliberations. Political reform in American cities tends to follow in the wake of political scandals. For example, in the mid-1980s, both Providence, Rhode Island, and San Diego, California, reformed the absentee voter ballot process and campaign contribution laws, respectively, following the convictions of the mayor in each city on multiple felony count indictments. Without such dramatic circumstances, cities generally have little real pressure or permanent constituencies demanding—or even greatly interested in—municipal reform. Hugh Heclo has remarked on this aspect of both national and local politics whereby, unless there is a scandal, "the connection between politics and administration arouses remarkably little interest in the United States," especially when compared to "other democratic countries."[1]

One period of sustained reform in the early 1900s stands out as an exception to the ebb and flow pattern of reform efforts. The Progressive Era (*circa* 1900–20) saw the rise of good government groups (e.g., the National Municipal League and the Municipal Research Bureau movement) in many American cities. These groups eventually became powerful enough, particularly in western and midwestern cities, to defeat the immigrant-based and patronage-oriented political machines then dominant in many large metropolitan communities. The political machines were replaced with a local government system based on nonpartisan at-large elections and city manager or commission forms of administration. Banfield and Wilson have described this shift as a transfer of power from primarily immigrant groups holding a familial or *private-regarding view,* which saw "government as an instrument designed to provide jobs, protection, and housing, and to meet the particular or more selfish needs of local groups and individuals," to primarily upper and upper-middle-income white Anglo-Saxon Protestants with a *public-regarding view.* The Progressive ethic, or public-regarding view, saw city government "as a means to perform, as economically and efficiently as possible, service for the general good of the community. . . . [believing] that partisanship at the city level should be minimized and that decisions should be based on careful calculation of the community good."[2]

Bryan Jones has attacked the private-regarding versus public-regarding view of the Progressive Era reformers as an ideological camouflage, noting, "The Anglo-Saxon middle class . . . [had] a clear interest in altering municipal government forms; they were losing power to the immigrants. Public-regardingness was a justification for the changes they sought to make."[3]

The Paradox of Municipal Reform

Even reforms that seem to most observers to be absolutely crucial and desirable (e.g., ending the domination of municipal politics by corrupt political machines, replacing ward or precinct elections with at-large elections) may and frequently do have paradoxical results. As recent revisionist scholarship is making increasingly clear, this was the case with the Progressive Era municipal reforms.[4] Bryan Jones noted that the public-regarding reform rhetoric was aimed at least as much at addressing political losses by white Anglo-Saxon business groups as it was at fighting local government graft or bringing economy and efficiency to city hall. The Progressive Era reforms created, and were meant to create, an advantage for pro-business forces in local policy circles. In a study of the city manager reform movement in several cities, including Austin, Charlotte (N.C.), Dallas, Dayton, Lynchburg, Rochester, and San Diego, Harold Stone and Frederick Mosher found that "the Chamber of Commerce invariably spearheaded the movement."[5] Examining thirty-two cases of municipal reform in Oklahoma involving a shift to city manager government, Jewell C. Phillips found that "29 were initiated either by chambers of commerce or by community committees dominated by businessmen."[6] Furthermore, James Weinstein, in a more recent study, has presented what one observer described as "almost irrefutable evidence that the business community, represented largely by chambers of commerce, was the overwhelming force behind both commission and city-manager movements."[7]

This business dominance and the attendant advantage of WASP groups over predominantly white immigrant groups and (later) non-white groups—blacks, Asians, and Hispanics—created a paradox in that the so-called reforms themselves needed reform. The scenario of reforms giving rise to a set of reform-related problems is depicted in Figure 5.1.

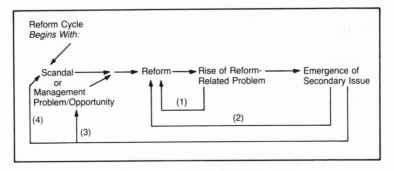

Figure 5.1 The Scandal/Reform Pattern: Four Variants

The ebb and flow pattern of municipal reform follows the basic pattern of a scandal or a management problem or opportunity (e.g., the duplication of services and lack of coordination between New York City and neighboring Brooklyn, Queens, and the Bronx in the 1890s) leading eventually to a reform to address the original issue (e.g., the consolidation of Brooklyn, Queens, and parts of the Bronx in 1898 with New York City). These reforms, in turn, can result in the rise of a new set of reform-related issues. For example, the introduction of nonpartisan at-large elections led to the dilution of immigrant and minority voting strength. In the case of consolidating the boroughs with New York City, an unnecessary layer of government was created—the New York City Board of Estimates, with automatic membership granted to the borough presidents, the city mayor, comptroller, and city council president—to oversee most land-use decisions and the noncompetitive contract bidding process, and to give the borough presidents some role in the new consolidated city government. While there are, no doubt, an almost endless number of possible permutations or routes that reforms and reform-related reactions could take in local communities, four possible scenarios seem most probable.

In the first variant, a second reform is attempted to address the new issue (e.g., the city eliminates or modifies the at-large election system, or New York City could, although it has not, eliminate the Board of Estimates or eliminate the noncompetitive bidding process). In a second variant, the rise of a set of secondary issues growing out of the reform-related problem (e.g., a growing alienation of the minority community or a disenchantment with the often scandalous conduct associated with the noncompetitive bidding process) might lead, as in the first variant, to a second reform. In a third scenario, the emergence of secondary issues leads to a management problem or opportunity to fix the problem (e.g., bilingual ballots or increased monitoring of the municipal bidding and contract process). Finally, in a fourth variant, the emergence of secondary issues could, if their discussion and tempo escalated, lead to a scandal in municipal government. Each of these variants is likely to start the reform process all over again. Thus the paradox of reforms is that they often give rise to conditions which, themselves, require reform at some future point.[8]

The Ebb and Flow of Municipal Reform

Since reform is not permanent or regular, municipal reform ebbs and flows, lurches forward and reels backwards. Recently several western and southwestern cities, including San Francisco and San Antonio, abandoned parts of their Progressive Era reforms, believing those measures now required some modifications. For example, as ethnic minorities are often disadvantaged by at-large elections in which their overall strength is diluted,[9] courts have ordered several U.S. cities to abandon the at-large "reform" structure of local elections in favor of the earlier "unreformed" ward or district election structure. In the past fifteen years, San Francisco has changed their election format twice, going from at-large to district elections, and then back again to at-large elections.

The Reform Flow: Service Delivery and Organizational Reforms

The pendulum of municipal reform swings back and forth on several dimensions—from a specific reform, to reforming the political process or the delivery of municipal services, to reforming the overall city organization. In the 1960s cities attempted to decentralize their political processes and municipal services. Among the best studies of this period is Eric Nordlinger's analysis of Boston's doomed "Little

City Hall" experiment, in which city hall was to be moved literally closer to the people by establishing several regional "little city halls."[10] The movement, featuring such elements as neighborhood or community outreach offices for municipal police departments, was extremely popular throughout the mid to late 1960s. Conversely, the 1970s saw an increased concern with consolidating and centralizing city programs, particularly the relatively autonomous federally financed neighborhood programs associated with the War on Poverty (e.g., Head Start and Model Cities). Cities faced with the fiscal stress of the 1980s are increasingly considering a number of currently popular service delivery reforms, including privatization and coproduction.

Privatization[11] is a trend toward decentralization in which functions previously managed exclusively by the city, such as trash collection and fire protection, are turned over to the private sector. As Table 5.1 indicates, several U.S. cities have shifted such traditionally city-provided services to the private sector. At the same time that cities are currently exploring the possibilities of privatization, many are also engaged in coproduction ventures with other cities. This is when two or more municipalities join forces to deliver a service (e.g., trash collection) or obtain a service (e.g., lowering the cost of liability insurance by combining the purchasing power of several cities and obtaining group rates on other significant municipal purchases).[12] Additionally, throughout the period from the 1950s through the 1980s, many cities engaged in regionally oriented political reform attempts, usually labeled "metropolitan reorganization." (See Table 5.2 and Figure 5.2.) Although metropolitan reorganization reforms span a wide spectrum or continuum (see Figure 5.2), they generally concentrate on the political, administrative, or service delivery benefits produced by consolidating several municipal units into one (or often, a two-tier) county, regional, or metropolitan government. Portland, Miami–Dade County, Jacksonville, Nashville, and Indianapolis are notable examples of communities that adopted changes designed to make the city service and management structure more regionally oriented. Several other cities, including Rochester, Tampa Bay, Sacramento, and Denver, considered but rejected adopting a metropolitan government format.[13]

The policymaking life cycle in American cities is influenced by a multitude of changing coalitions favoring or opposing various

TABLE 5.1 Privatization: Number of Cities Using Private Firms to Supply Municipal Services Under Contract*

Service	Number of Cities Contracting With Private Firms	Service	Number of Cities Contracting With Private Firms
Refuse Collection	339	Treasury Functions	14
Street Lighting	309	All Fire Services	13
Electricity Supply	258	Mosquito Control	12
Engineering Services	253	Museums	12
Legal Services	187	General Development	10
Ambulance Services	169	Alcoholic Rehabilitation	9
Solid Waste Disposal	143	Records Maintenance	9
Utility Billing	104	Election Administration	8
Animal Control	99	Police Communications	8
Planning	92	Building and Mechanical	
Water Supply	84	Inspection	7
Mapping	74	Fire Communications	7
Water Distribution		Housing	7
System	67	Recreational Facilities	7
Payroll	65	Personnel Services	6
Street Construction and		Urban Renewal	6
Maintenance	63	Crime Laboratory	5
Hospitals	57	Irrigation	5
Special Transportation		Parks	5
Services	49	Traffic Control	5
Cemeteries	47	Water Pollution	
Microfilm Services	47	Abatement	5
Nursing Services	34	All Public Health	
Assessing	31	Services	4
Public Relations	30	Juvenile Delinquency	
Bridge Construction and		Program	4
Maintenance	25	Licensing	4
Industrial Development	24	Soil Conversion	4
Tax Collection	24	Civil Defense	
Mental Health	22	Communications	2
Sewage Disposal	21	Fire Prevention	2
Management Service for		Noise Abatement	2
Publicly Owned Transit	18	Patrol Services	2
Electrical and Plumbing		Registration of Voters	2
Inspection	17	Training of Firemen	2
Libraries	17	Air Pollution Abatement	1
Zoning and Subdivision		Jails and Detention	
Control	16	Homes	1
Sewer Lines	14	Welfare	1

Source: E. S. Savas, *Privatizing the Public Sector: How to Shrink Government* (Chatham, N.J.: Chatham House, 1982), pp. 63–64.
*Based on responses of 2,375 cities to a mail survey in 1973.

TABLE 5.2   Structural Reforms in Municipal Government: Cities
Adopting Variants of Metropolitan Government, 1945–80

17 successful city–county consolidations, 1947–80, including
  Anaconda/Deer Lodge County, MT (1977)
  Anchorage/Greater Anchorage Area Borough, AK (1975)
  Lexington/Fayette County, KY (1974)
  Suffolk/Nansemond County, VA (1972)
  Columbus/Muscogee, GA (1970)
  Indianapolis/Marion County, IN (1969)
  Carson City/Ormsby County, NV (1969)
  Jacksonville/Duval County, FL (1967)
  Nashville/Davidson County, TN (1962)
  Baton Rouge/East Baton Rouge Parish, LA (1947)

Dade County, FL, metropolitan federation (1957)

Minnesota's Twin Cities Metropolitan Council (1967)
  —an appointed regional council with policy responsibilities
Portland, OR, Metropolitan Service District (1978)
  —an elected regional council with policy and operating responsibilities

671 multipurpose substate regional councils (1979) with planning and coordination responsibilities

County organization and home rule authority (1979)
  21 states with county optional forms of government set forth in law
  29 states with county home rule
  75 counties with charters
  766 counties with an elected or appointed chief executive—25% of all counties compared with less than 3% in 1960

1,039 of 3,319 cities surveyed had transferred functions to another jurisdiction
in the period 1965–75

Source: Robert Jay Dilger (ed.), *American Intergovernmental Relations Today: Perspectives
and Controversies* (Englewood Cliffs, N.J.: Prentice-Hall, 1986), p. 164. Table derived from
Advisory Commission on Intergovernmental Relations staff compilations.

reforms and by an irregular pattern of alternating strategies regarding
service delivery and metropolitan structures. The pendulum of
municipal reform swings between the extremes of partisanship or
nonpartisanship, regionalism or parochialism, patronage or civil
service professionalism, centralization or decentralization,[14] at-large
elections or ward-elected policymakers, and privatization or coproduction. As I shall argue later, despite the desirability of reform, city
policymaking is rendered considerably more difficult—and considerably more *fragile*—by the climate of uncertainty and confusion

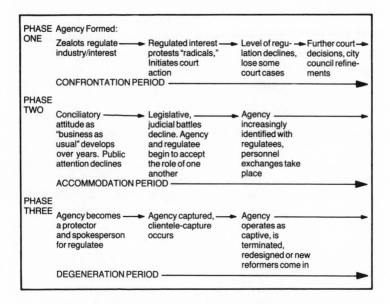

Figure 5.2 Degenerative or Weakening Process for Regulatory Agencies: The Bernstein Clientele-Capture Thesis

that accompanies the ebb and flow of municipal reform in American cities.

Clientele Capture: The Regulatory Factor

In 1986 New York City experienced one of those periodic scandals that rock American cities from time to time. In this case, "officials at three agencies—the Parking Violations Bureau, the Taxi and Limousine Commission, and the Health and Hospitals Corporation . . . [were] accused of extorting bribes from businessmen. In all, nearly a dozen people . . . [were] charged with offering or receiving bribes in return for city contracts; five have pleaded guilty." Another suspect, Queens borough president Donald R. Manes, "committed suicide in March, after prosecutors indicated that they were seeking to indict him as well."[15] It goes without saying that such examples of bribery and corruption have a negative effect on city policymaking. Such corruption is, however, episodic, and while relevant to city policymaking, hardly predictable. But there is a form of corruption—or, more precisely stated, degeneration—that is both relevant to city policymaking and predictable.

City regulatory commissions (e.g., commissions on planning, taxi license granting, or cable television) are established to oversee and regulate the behavior of certain sectors of community life. However, as with city councils and city policy bodies in general, regulatory bodies have an aging and growth process. This has been described by Marver Bernstein as the "clientele-capture thesis," in which regulatory agencies go through a three-stage weakening process—an aggressive confrontational period, a later mellowing or accommodation phase, and finally, a process of administrative degeneration, a period of outright "capture" by the very interests whose activity the commission was originally established to regulate.[16] This three-stage weakening process ending in clientele capture (depicted in Figure 5.2), although originally formulated to explain the demise of vigorous consumer advocacy by the Interstate Commerce Commission, is also applicable to municipal regulatory commissions and watchdog bodies.

The slow weakening of regulatory agencies usually begins with "youthful enthusiasm for the task of consumer protection, only to end in a senile old age in which the agency becomes, at best, a protector of the status quo and at worst the captive of the regulated agency."[17] Regulatory commissions such as a citizens' watchdog commission on police behavior are usually the result of a community incident (e.g., the choke-hold incidents in Los Angeles or San Diego, or a specific example of alleged police brutality) which typically generates a great deal of initial controversy and political pressure. Thus pressure and public attentiveness characterize the early or "gestation" period in the regulatory process, but then—importantly—such watchfulness invariably fades as the issue eventually falls off the public agenda of the community in question. As Zeigler notes, "the momentum of pressure which builds up during the 'gestation' period reaches a climax with the passage of the regulatory statute and begins to decline from that point. Support reaches a peak; the combatant interests are tired and have earned a rest. It is natural that these interests would tend to regard administration as following automatically from legislation."[18]

Hence, regulatory commissions are subject to their own version of surge and decline. Created in a period of great furor and controversy and amid media coverage and heightened public attention, the attention, furor, controversy, and coverage generally decline precipitously as soon as "the job is done"—the regulatory ordinance is enacted and the watchdog commission established. Given this decline in public and media attention, the regulatory commission is soon without any pressures except the antagonistic pressures of the interests it was supposed to regulate versus the commission's own sense of direction and purpose. In his classic text *Interest Groups in American Society,* Zeigler describes what generally happens next:

> [A]t the time of its creation, the intentions of a regulatory agency conflict with the goals of the regulated groups. The agency operates in an environment of organized, hostile interests which, having lost the legislative struggle, try to protect themselves from what they regard as the "onslaught" of administrators. In this atmosphere of animosity, the regulating agency frequently adopts an aggressive or crusading resolve to meet its opposition and not surrender its ambitions. However, although the regulated groups have lost the first round, as borne out by the passage of the enabling legislation, they can be influential both in the operation of the agency and in the securing of "sound" men as appointees.[19]

There are additional reasons why regulatory agencies tend to weaken over time, and to degenerate to a point near or including clientele capture. Regulatory degeneracy is fueled by four sets of circumstances. First, in order to be effective, agencies need accurate information on the activities of the interests they are regulating. Generally, the group(s) in the best position to provide such information are the regulated interests themselves. This necessary reliance on the regulated interests, as well as the possibility that the regulated group is likely to provide data which presents them in the best possible light, tends to blunt the early confrontational edge of the new regulatory agency. Second, it is not unreasonable to assume that an accommodation of sorts—a *modus vivendi*—develops between the regulators and the regulatees, since both must work with each other over long periods of time. Meanwhile, the original scandals and the activists who produced the clamor resulting in the creation of the regulatory agency have long since passed from the scene. This degenerative or weakening tendency has, it should be noted, been partially resisted in the few cases where crucial activists and original players are appointed to key commission or staff positions in the new regulatory body. Third, there is often a "revolving door" nature to agency–client group employment, in that former agency personnel or commission members are hired as consultants, lobbyists, or permanent employees by client groups (regulatees) seeking favorable decisions from the agency. This adds to the growing advantage that client groups have during the shift from a period of confrontation to one of accommodation. Finally, the makeup of the regulatory commission itself—the number of commissioners, their terms, and their manner of appointment—may eventually act to incline the agency in favor of the regulated interests. Typically, such bodies are comprised of members of the regulated interests, politicians with an immediate interest in the matter at hand, persons active in local political campaigns, and members of the general public. The latter may (but need not) be drawn from the circle of activists who first called for the formation of the regulatory agency. Over time, via the appointment process, it is possible for a major who is favorably inclined toward the regulated interest to change the character of the commission. This is particularly true over long periods of time and over several mayoral administrations.

Guarding Against Regulatory Weakening and Degeneration: Some Possible Safeguards

Terry Moe and Kenneth Meier have argued that chief executives have several opportunities to thwart the degeneration of regulatory zeal if they have the political resolve to do so.[20] Mayors can use the appointment process to influence the direction of regulatory bodies, although "if regulatory appointments are used as patronage rewards . . . rather than for policy reasons, then the . . . [mayor] will exercise little influence over the direction of regulatory policy."[21] Second, the mayor can use his or her leadership position, formal powers, and informal powers of persuasion and criticism to set a tone of aggressive regulation by the commission. Third, the mayor (particularly mayors in a strong-mayor form of government) may significantly influence the commission's work through the use of the city budget. Using the budget as an instrument to reward or punish the regulatory agency should not be underestimated. Fourth, the mayor can institute strict guidelines in which the goals of the regulatory agency are clearly spelled out and the manner in which their success or failure will be evaluated is clearly indicated (e.g., management by objectives or the use of zero-based budgeting techniques).[22]

Other safeguards against the degeneration of municipal regulatory bodies include, as Theodore Lowi has noted of these bodies at the national level, the drawing of explicit laws and ordinances by policymakers—in this case the city council—to make the task of the regulatory agency clear and leave little room for agency discretion.[23] The municipal, state, and federal courts may be seen as an additional safeguard against clientele-capture in that activists and/or public-interest law groups may sue the regulatory commission if it appears to be backsliding into accommodation. In the event that an agency is captured by the interests it is supposed to oversee, a new surge of activists and reformers could produce the political pressure necessary for a change of heart or of personnel in the agency. Finally, if all else fails, an activist or reform coalition could press for the elimination or abolition of the commission on the grounds that it now does more harm than good. One way to leave open this possibility from the beginning would be for cities to adopt a "sunset law" for all city boards and commissions—or at least all new regulatory commissions—in which such bodies are automatically eliminated after a specific period of time, five years for example, unless the council reaffirms the need for an additional five-year term. Such a policy could, of course, backfire if the regulated interests persuade a majority of council members to eliminate a regulatory commission that had not fallen prey to accommodation or capture.[24]

City policymaking, particularly regulatory policymaking, follows much of the same ebb and flow that characterizes municipal reform generally. Activists and interested citizens may spring forward to protest a controversial incident or situation and may even produce pressures for creation of a regulatory commission. However, this surge in activity and pressure is usually accompanied by a parallel decline. The decline, and the weakening or degenerative process of regulatory bodies in general, may produce a situation ripe for clientele-capture. If so, much of the original problem reoccurs. This back-and-forth motion in both the reform and regulatory elements of the ecology of city policymaking serves to weaken the policy process in American cities. Urban policymakers are forced to grapple repeatedly with the problems caused by the cyclical patterns of reform/response/re-reform or regulate/degenerate/re-regulate as they attempt to respond to the ebb and flow of scandals, reform constituencies, and the weakening or clientele-capture of regulatory bodies.

The Exogenous Factor

There are a host of influences originating outside the metropolitan region that nonetheless affect local policymakers, often preempting or setting the local agenda from afar. Collectively, I will refer to these external influences as the exogenous factor. Like the reform and regulatory factors, the exogenous factor (the component parts of which are depicted in Figure 5.3) does not have a predictable pattern. Instead, as with the other two factors, the exogenous factor pattern is one of ebb and flow. Sometimes more influence (and more influences) come from outside the local arena, and sometimes less affect the overall city policymaking life cycle.

Examples of exogenous factors shaping the local policy process include national policymakers, operating primarily in Washington, D.C., who can grant monies (e.g., revenue sharing or job training), set policies, offer assistance (as in the toxic waste cleanup program, Superfund), require standards to be met and enforced (e.g., affirmative action or clean air and water standards), or set the agenda of local policymakers on topics as crucial and as varied as civil rights or prayers in public schools (e.g., *Brown v. Board of Education*).[25]

A somewhat unique example of such direction—or interference—in local policymaking by a state was the passage of Proposition 4, the so-called Gann Initiative, by California voters in November 1979. The measure, written by Paul Gann, a coauthor with Howard Jarvis of California's notable Proposition 13 (1978), legally set a cap on California city spending levels by tying city budgets to a base linked to their 1978 municipal budgets. Cities may only increase their 1978

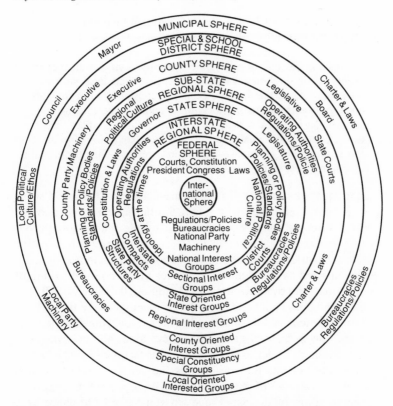

SOURCE: James L. Garnett, ''Bureaucratic and Party Politics in an Intergovernmental Context,'' in James D. Carroll and Richard W. Campbell, eds., *Intergovernmental Administration* (Syracuse, N.Y.: Department of Public Administration, Syracuse University, 1976), pg. 85. Several categories have been added to the original.

Figure 5.3 Exogenous Factors Affecting City Policymaking

spending levels by increments which match the increase in the California Consumer Price Index (CPI) since 1978.[26] Cities that raise more in tax revenues are not allowed to spend more but are required under the law to refund the difference to city residents. As the Gann Initiative demonstrates, the role of state government and state ballot initiatives can be a crucial outside or exogenous factor for local policymakers.

Fred Wirt noted that cities are affected by a number of factors from outside the city's wall,[27] including the national history and the city's own past. However, as Wirt correctly observed:

> The past is but one of many forces outside a city's wall that shape events inside it. National law increasingly affects local policies, and the conditions of the national economy constantly limit the options open to localities in their allocation of capital. The constitution and laws of the state, as well as its economic policies, affect the procedures, content, and quality of services to urban citizens. In all these forces there is a potential—and often a reality—for diluting urban autonomy, despite the rhetoric of "local control."[28]

Jane Jacobs has argued that cities are players on the world stage, and, in terms reminiscent of Adam Smith, has observed that the "wealth of cities" is greatly influenced by the international economy.[29] No American city, for example, could long resist the negative effects of a worldwide economic depression. In the same fashion, cities are affected by shifts and continuities in the political culture of their region[30] and by shifts in national opinion; these are what Bauer, Dexter, and Sola Pool have labeled the "ideology of the times."[31]

The exogenous factors affecting the urban policymaking life cycle ebb and flow in their effect on city policymaking and policymakers. This movement I refer to as the exogenous factor cycle. The lack of predictability of this flow, as well as the definitive role that such external "invasions" of the local policymaking process can play (e.g., the termination of the San Francisco gun-control ordinance by a state court), form key elements in my final argument—that the policymaking process in American cities is extremely weak or fragile.

Before I discuss this, however, it is necessary to draw together the threads of the municipal policymaking model discussed up to this point. I have argued that policymaking is both similar and different in U.S. cities. The similarity arises as a result of a general process—the policymaking life cycle—which may be used to explain policymaking in any U.S. city. Each city, however, is different from the others in possessing a unique ecological system. While the ten parts of the municipal ecology—(1) age, (2) locale, (3) the growth process of city councils, (4) policy types, (5) policy conflict levels, (6) reform activity, (7) regulatory activity, (8) exogenous factors, (9) personality factors, and (10) local political culture factors—affecting the policy life cycle are the same in each city, the composition and strength of these factors vary from city to city, producing a different set of effects, demands, cues, advantages, disadvantages, and incentives for those involved in urban politics.

The Personality and Local Political Culture Factors

Two further variables—the personality factor and the local political culture factor—need to be discussed in the ecology of municipal policymaking.

The *personality factor* refers to the Downsian-suggested pattern of movement of zealots, advocates, climbers, conservers, and statesmen in and out of city policymaking bodies and agencies. This also includes the personality types and leadership styles of the mayors, (entrepreneurs, bosses, crusaders, or brokers). As previously noted, the presence or absence of an entrepreneur or a crusader in the mayor's office has an effect on the process and substance of city policymaking.

The *local political culture factor,* while very different from the other ecological factors, still provides an important ebb and flow pattern influencing the urban policy process, as J. David Greenstone has noted at the national level.[32] The local political culture (i.e., the history, institutions, and cultural beliefs that may be said to characterize a community) often accounts for the differences in communities, which is an important consideration in analyzing and designing city policy or federal policy meant to be implemented in cities.

The ebb and flow of local political culture is patterned, as Greenstone has pointed out, in a unique way. Political culture, by definition, cannot exhibit too many shifts or variations without coming unglued as a theoretical concept. After all, the political culture of a community constitutes what is (relatively) permanent about that community over time in terms of community standards, interests, and the concept of what is public and private. Still, there can be movement within this permanence, as when two competing strains of the local political belief-set are championed by local policy activists and entrepreneurs. Many, if not most, American communities probably contain bipolar or even multipolar belief-sets, allowing for the possibility of competition (or ebbs and flows) between their opposing adherents. As Greenstone and others have noted, this occurs at the national level when two competing beliefs in the (relatively) permanent national belief-set (e.g., liberty and equality) clash on such issues as environmental protection or affirmative action.[33]

As Bauer, Dexter, and Sola Pool have observed, while Americans (and, by extension, American cities) may have a relatively fixed or permanent set of beliefs, they also have more transient beliefs and institutions (e.g., segregation, bursts of reform zeal, periods of unrestrained Levittown development, environmental sensitivity).[34] These transient beliefs are important in considering local policymaking, for they may occasionally carry the day or influence policy outcomes.

Thus cities experience ebbs and flows with the dominance or recession of one group of policy adherents who are more firmly identified with one strain of the political culture than another, or when what is transitory about the political culture comes and goes, producing changes and new permutations in the political environment.

The City Ecology Model: A Brief Overview

The *life cycle of city policymaking*—the key element in the ecology perspective on policymaking in American cities—is the process or circuit by which policy must travel to be enacted and implemented in local government. The life cycle, spanning the distance from the shift of a potential issue from condition to problem, and through enactment and implementation to evaluation and feedback or termination, is a unique way to understand the life span of city policymaking and its crucial stages. Additionally, triggering mechanisms and containment activities and strategies are central elements in explaining the success or failure of issues in traveling the policy life cycle circuit.

The *age, growth process, and locale* of a city or the age (or stage) of a city policy body produces variations in policymaking. Included in this dimension are the effects of zealots and voluntarism, the density and spatial location of the city, the differences among councils which tend toward one of four main role orientations (economic boosters, amenity providers, caretakers, or arbiters), and the impact of geographic regionalism upon local policymaking.

The *policy type and conflict level factors*—including the policy conflict typology—provide a way to understand and anticipate the general pattern of political conflict associated with policymaking in American cities, as well as a way to explain deviations from this pattern. As a rule, issues determine politics. Thus local issues can be subdivided into five issue sets—allocational, collective goods, mixed goods, social welfare issues, or collective bads—which, unless deflected by mediating influences, produce autonomous, pork-barrel, conventional, redistributive, or intrusive policy politics.

The *reform, regulatory,* and *exogenous factors* are key components in the ecology of the city policymaking process, interfering in the policymaking life cycle at irregular intervals, at times affecting the cycle greatly, and at other times, affecting it very little, if at all.

The ten ecological variables, combined with the basic city policy life cycle, constitute the ecology or environment of city policymaking. Collectively, these eleven variables make up the overall body or policymaking infrastructure of American cities. The ecological model of city policymaking is, in some respects, a mixed blessing. While it provides a better way than earlier approaches for understanding the general pattern of municipal policymaking (and for explaining its exceptions or deviations), it also provides a substantial amount of evidence for the proposition that cities are generically weak or, at best, exceedingly fragile mechanisms for making public policy.

6

The Fragility of City Policymaking

The Problems of Scale and Intractability

City policymaking—covering both policy made in behalf of cities by external actors (e.g., the federal and state governments) and that made by local actors within a city (e.g., city council, mayor, planning commission)—is an extremely problematic and fragile process. Such policymaking is problematic for three reasons. First, the sheer size and intractability of urban problems currently facing American cities present overwhelming, perhaps insurmountable, challenges to both city policymakers and those external actors attempting to aid America's ailing cities. Second, city policymaking has been made more problematic due to a series of (hopefully passing) transitory influences that have exacerbated the problems of American cities. Third, even if the problems that cities faced were of a much smaller magnitude, and even if cities were not tossed and turned like a small boat bobbing on a set of (transitory but nevertheless swelling) waves not of their own construction, cities would still be poor policymakers because the city policy process is inherently weak and fragile.

I now turn to a successive consideration of each of the following allegations: (1) city problems are, if not permanent, deeply resistant to change; (2) the ability of cities to make policy and solve problems has been eroded by several (hopefully) transitory developments since the 1960s; and (3) the basic policymaking ecology of cities is weak—cities, whether attempting to solve large or small problems, do so with a policymaking structure that is fundamentally fragile and weak.

The most serious of the problems facing city policymakers (whether attacked by the city alone, or by the combined skills and resources of federal, state, and local government) have displayed a stubborn refusal to be solved. Policymaking on behalf of cities by external actors over the last quarter century has proved to be, at best, a mixed success. While there have been innovative and successful federal–local (e.g., Head Start) and state–local programs (e.g., experimental workfare programs such as the GAIN program in California and the ET program in Massachusetts),[1] the sum total of such programs has done very little to ameliorate the worst conditions of city life (notably poverty and inner-city ghettos but also inadequate public schooling, high crime, density, urban blight, and transportation problems, to name but a few).

Michael Harrington—whose book *The Other America,* a study of poverty in America in the late 1950s, helped inspire the New Frontier and War on Poverty programs of the 1960s—has recently completed a study of poverty in the 1980s which proves beyond dispute: "The poor are still there."[2] This is so, according to Harrington, because the 1960s goal of "abolishing poverty raised issues of power and wealth."[3] Worse yet, the partial successes and "very real gains" of the War on Poverty (e.g., the food stamp program, Medicare, indexed Social Security benefits, Head Start, and short-lived Office of Economic Opportunity programs) as well as the gains of the interrelated civil rights movement (e.g., the Civil Rights Act of 1964, the Voting Rights Act of 1965, affirmative action) have "impaired the national vision; misery has become more intractable and more difficult to see."[4] Thus the few successes did not eradicate poverty but instead made it more difficult to fight.[5] The poor, as Harrington demonstrates in his study, still exist despite many of the "safety net" and opportunity programs put into place from the 1960s to the present. Indeed, poverty is so doggedly present that a good deal of productive research is currently focused on the disturbingly durable phenomenon that Ken Auletta has labeled the "underclass."[6]

Thus the problem of poverty seems, at least over the last quarter of a century, to be, if not permanent, at least stubbornly intractable.

The same may be said of urban blight and ghettos. In 1965 the predominantly black Los Angeles neighborhood of Watts exploded into a full-scale urban riot. Then-Governor Pat Brown ordered National Guard troops into the neighborhood to quell the rioting and restore order. Following the riot, a series of local, state, and national programs were initiated to improve the quality of life in Watts and other ghettos in American cities. In a moving speech following the outbreak of violence in Watts, President Lyndon Johnson clearly seemed to be giving the problems of squalid ghetto living the highest priority on the national agenda. He said, "the clock is ticking, time is moving. . . . [W]e must ask ourselves every night when we go home, are we doing all that we should do in our nation's capital, in all the other big cities of the country."[7] Yet, twenty years later, a 1985 joint report of the commissions on Human Relations of the City and County of Los Angeles found that "the overall conclusion of those testifying was that conditions are as bad or worse, in South-Central Los Angeles today as they were 19 years ago. . . . We should not have to wait for a second Los Angeles riot to erupt to bring these problems to serious public attention."[8]

Surely the scale of such problems as poverty and inner-city slums either (at the best) places *limits*[9] on city policymakers or (at the worst) makes policymaking virtually *impossible.*[10]

Paul Peterson contends that cities have limits. They can make policy on some aspects of urban life but on others—and social welfare policy is a case in point—they often need to rely overwhelmingly on the resources of the national government, for only in the federal domain are there enough resources to begin to construct policies and programs capable of making a difference.[11] And, as Harrington and the Los Angeles Human Relations Commission report suggest, even the federal government may have limitations—of political will, of resources, or of effective ideas—on solving the problems of the cities.

Edward Banfield argues in *The Unheavenly City, Revisited* that cities will always have a certain amount of poverty, crime, and violence *no matter what set of policies are adopted* to prevent or eradicate them.[12] He believes that many of the problems city policymakers attempt to address are fundamentally incurable because they are not urban problems but urban conditions. In other words, as long as there are cities, there will be poverty and crime.

The Debilitating Impact of Transitory Influences

Not everyone agrees with Banfield. Indeed, the vast majority of scholars on local policymaking probably do not.[13] Still, even if poverty and violent crime are not permanent facts of life in American cities and urban areas, they seem to have achieved a state of semipermanence.

In addition to the debilitating effects of seemingly permanent problems such as poverty, high crime, and squalid ghettos, cities have been weakened since the early 1960s by a series of largely temporary problems that collectively tend to weaken or detract from the ability of cities to make policy and find solutions. Chief among the transient problems faced by cities in this period are: (1) a series of on-again, off-again federal–local programs and policies that add to local confusion and shift the impetus for local planning to the federal government; and (2) a period of national stagflation and fiscal stress, seen most visibly in the virtual bankruptcy of New York City, but also, to varying degrees, in most other American cities.[14]

Beginning with the War on Poverty programs of the 1960s, through the general and special revenue sharing programs of the 1970s, and continuing into the current period with the elimination of most of the earlier programs such as revenue sharing and community development block grants, cities have had to adjust to several shifting federal grant strategies and federal–local programs. As William Hudson and John Mollenkopf have observed, this has led to paradox, confusion, politicization, and a weakening of the local city policy process.[15]

The paradox of such Nixon administration programs as the new federalism and general revenue sharing was that they often had the net result of strengthening the ties of the federal government to city government. Local policymakers in this period increasingly had their agenda set for them authoritatively in Washington, D.C. This "nationalization" of local politics was a two-edged sword for city governments, since it held out the promise of vast sums for needed programs (e.g., urban redevelopment, mass transit, police training) even as it took away from urban legislators some of their ability to set their own spending and program priorities.[16] Mollenkopf has convincingly pointed out that many cities were actually worse off *after* such programs because the programs succeeded in politicizing poor and minority neighborhoods and in fragmenting city governments, but did not succeed in solving the substantive problems (e.g., high crime, poverty, slums) that they were ostensibly designed to address.[17] Thus the net effect of such programs was the creation of a more politically charged and fragmented city than before—the "contested city" in Mollenkopf's terms.[18]

The result of such federal–local programs in the 1960–80s period was mixed at best. Some cities were prodded into enacting ordinances and programs that they would not have created otherwise. Also, some programs such as Head Start undeniably helped in the fight against poverty and poor public schooling.[19] Still, the net effect was to increase uncertainty in American cities, simultaneously politicizing and fragmenting subgroups within the cities and decreasing the authority and discretion of local policymakers to set their own agenda.[20] In a very real sense, after experiencing the transitory effects of recent federal–local programs, many American cities are less rather than more able to cope with local problems.

A second, presumably transitory, phenomenon affecting local governments has been the general period of fiscal stress experienced by cities from the late 1960s through the 1980s.[21] This stagflation—the curiously durable persistence of high unemployment and inflation—has increased costs for services at the same time that many of America's cities are losing large numbers of residents to the suburbs. This urban emigration has reduced many American cities to what George Sternlieb has described as "sandboxes"—places where middle to upper-class suburbanites work and play but are not compelled to pay taxes to support or maintain. Such trends render city policymaking more difficult and fragile, at least over the short term, because they reduce the financial and human resource base cities draw upon in making policy and solving problems as well as increase the complexity, expense, and dependency involved in local policymaking[22]

The City as a Weak Policymaking Unit

Cities face several difficulties that detract from their ability to make policy and solve problems. The very nature of some of the problems (e.g., homelessness, poverty, slums) limits the efforts of urban legislators to enact policies and programs to address the problems because of the sheer size of such problems, or because of their apparent intractability, or both. A second set of impediments is more transitory in nature (e.g., the stagflation experienced in the international and national economies, the mixed signals coming out of Washington, D.C., in terms of the urban programs and the priorities of federal policymakers, the increased volatility in local policy arenas because of the effects of federal–local programs). All these transitory and apparently permanent conditions combine to place limits on the ability of local policymakers to enact policy and to solve local problems.

The city policy ecology model, depicted in Figure 5.5, illustrates that the city policy process is not only weakened from externally imposed limitations (e.g., the permanent and transitory impediments discussed above) but by the very process of city policymaking, which is subjected to a multiplicity of external and internal limitations and influences. In fact one of the major benefits of the policy ecology model, aside from depicting how city policy is made, is the ability of the model to show why such policymaking is inherently weak.

Each element or factor of the policy ecology model illustrates a separate weakness or fragility of the city policymaking process. Thus the life cycle of city policymaking discussed in chapter 2 illustrates that the city governing mechanism frequently requires either a triggering event or a policy entrepreneur (or both) to bring an issue (even important or absolutely crucial issues) to the public and formal agenda. As the example of Watts depressingly demonstrates, it may well take a major riot (and perhaps, as the report of the Human Relations commissions warned, more than one such riot) before local policymakers will seriously and persistently address such issues as inner-city ghettos.

Second, as the case study of gun-control policy in San Francisco shows, city policymaking is extremely vulnerable to outside influences. The city policy agenda can be set by outside factors (see Figure 5.4) or, once enacted, policy may be terminated by outside actors or influences. The combination of both internal factors (e.g., triggering events, policy entrepreneurs, containment mechanisms) and external influences and dependencies results in an exceedingly fragile local policymaking process that is subject to both invasions from without and limitations from within.

City policymaking, as the age and growth factors discussed in chapter 3 demonstrate, is subject to the effects of age and wear. More innovative policies may be easier for new cities or new policy bodies to enact because of the overrepresentation of zealots, climbers, and advocates at the birth phase of city policy bodies. Conversely, mature policy bodies may be inherently more conservative due to the combined effects of the wear factor, voluntarism, overrepresentation of conservers in local government, the long-term crystallized policy orientation of the city council (e.g., amenity provider, economic booster, or community arbiter), the influence of regional political culture (e.g., sunbelt versus frostbelt), and the demographics of the city in question (e.g., density and spatial location—core, suburban, or periphery city types).

As chapter 4 illustrates, policies that may be easily enacted in one city can be highly conflictual in a second. While general patterns of policy politics are discernable, the role of mediating factors and the leadership style of the mayor and major policy entrepreneurs (or the lack of such actors) produces different policy scenarios and conflict levels for the same policy proposals in different cities. In some cases, a different political scenario is produced at different times for the same policy proposal in the same city. This air of general predictability (issues determine politics) combined with the frequent unpredictability helps weaken the overall city policy process by introducing into the process a combination of certainty and uncertainty. Policies will probably follow the general pattern, but they need not. Local policymakers can never be certain that the normal political expectations and rules of the game will apply to the issue at hand. Hence, while the policy conflict typology illustrates some predictability and the need for flexibility on the part of local policymakers—characteristics which strengthen the local policy process—the model also illustrates the inherent fragility of such predictability in any given case of policymaking.

The reform, regulatory, and exogenous policy ecology factors discussed in chapter 5 illustrate the temporal quality of city policymaking. Cities are caught up in an ebb and flow of reform activity which is sometimes the result of scandal and other times the result of shifting trends in management or political style (e.g., centralization versus decentralization or partisan versus nonpartisan governmental structures). Such tides ebb and flow somewhat like the hemline lengths and necktie widths of clothes fashions. Nevertheless, these alternating preferences in governmental structures and service delivery systems produce a shifting baseline for city policymakers who must sweep and police the streets no matter what the latest governmental fashion calls for.

City regulatory policy is affected by what stage the various city regulatory bodies have reached. Policymaking by the council is different when one or more regulatory bodies have degenerated to a conciliatory or clientele-capture phase. In the regulatory weakening process, cities do not make regulatory policy so much as they constantly remake it, first in response to a scandal or citizen demand, and then, as the regulatory bodies become co-opted, in response to pressures to reform the agency. Policymakers are caught between a series of alternating fashions in reform and alternating levels of regulatory decay and degeneration. This makes the overall policy process more fragile, because local policymakers are constantly formulating and reformulating local policy in response to these alternating sets of demands.

City policy processes are also, as both chapters 2 and 5 illustrate, greatly influenced by external or outside influences that may help shape local policy or even determine the outcome of local policy conflicts. The effect of the national on urban politics is a case in point. The financial restraints placed on cities by a downturn in the national or state economies, by a war, or by a change in national–local policy strategies (e.g., the elimination of revenue sharing or the community development block grant program) can greatly weaken the ability of cities to enact effective legislation. Conversely, city policymaking is strengthened in times of general economic prosperity, prolonged periods of international tranquility, or periods of more generous federal–local benefaction.

Cities and city policymakers are not and never will be free from the alternating benefits and debilitating effects of membership in this web of externalities. To steal a phrase from John Donne, cities are hardly "islands set apart from the main." When the "bell" of reform fashion, regulatory degeneration, and external factors rings, city policymakers need not wonder for whom the bell tolls; they may rest assured it tolls for them.

Conclusion

Thus the wheels of the local policymaking process turn. In studying the policymaking life cycle and different components of city policymaking ecology, we can reach a better understanding of how the city policy process works and of the limitations or fragility of that process. American cities in the modern era are faced with tremendous problems, such as insufficient financing, violent crime, homelessness, inner-city ghettos, inadequate public schools (many of which, years after *Brown versus the Board of Education,* are still bastions of *de facto* racial segregation), and ever-increasing freeway congestion and pollution. Frequently, discussions of urban life focus on these problems and proposed solutions. Such a focus is altogether appropriate. Americans, as commentators from William James to Daniel Boorstin have noted, are a pragmatic lot, given to problem identification and solution by trial and error.[23] Hence, questions such as the tractability or intractability of poverty or high crime; the desirability of various solutions such as workfare, benign neglect, or mandatory sentencing; and the benefits or lack of benefits of foot patrols by city police or the benefits of *strategic management* or other similarly innovative approaches to government spending in an era of fiscal retrenchment tend to dominate discussions of the city policy process.

This book is designed to be an addition—on two levels—to more traditional discussions of the "urban or city problem." First, the ecology of city policymaking perspective and the policy conflict typology are meant to offer a description and an explanation of how the city policy process works in American cities. Second, the policymaking life cycle model illustrates the very real fragility of that process. If city policymakers are, in the final analysis, to be the "doctors" who must—with or without hindrance or assistance from the federal government and other outside factors—eventually diagnose and treat the ills of American cities, I must insist on one point that follows from the city policymaking analysis. The point, quite simply, is this—the doctors themselves are more than a little ill.

I have examined several case studies that illustrate the fragility of city policymaking. Successful policy requires the successful interaction of ten key environmental variables. A failure in any of the environmental elements can spell doom for a city policy effort. The leadership style and personality of a major public policymaker, for example, are crucial to successful policymaking. Thus San Diego police were able to use temporarily the controversial choke-hold without raising deep mistrust in the minority community, but, because of inadequate leadership, Los Angeles police were not able to use the choke-hold without generating wide controversy in the minority community. Outside factors, such as state or federal government policies, can terminate the urban policy. This was the case with the San Francisco gun-control ordinance. City policy can also be derailed or displaced, as in the San Francisco recall election, where the issues of growth and overall mayoral leadership replaced the issue of gun control. As the trash-to-energy plant case study illustrates, city policy is fragile because what is acceptable in one community may later be unacceptable in the same community or acceptable in a second community at a still later point.

Thus city policymakers must attempt to pass policies in an atmosphere of opening and closing windows of opportunity. These windows open and close at unpredictable intervals, with severe consequences for the fate of policy proposals. Policy entrepreneurs are forced to "shop" for opportune moments when policies may be enacted. When policies such as the trash-to-energy plant proposal or the San Diego canyon rim zoning issue escalate to the acrimonious point, there is little chance for fragile city councils to contain and manage the high levels of conflict that surround such issues. At this time, either the issue is dropped (as in the case of the trash-to-energy plant in Chula Vista) or conflict de-escalation is eventually achieved (as in the case of the canyon rim zoning proposals) and policy is enacted. Sometimes city policy is fragile because the city is unwilling to act on pressing issues unless forced to do so by external factors (e.g., the homeless in Santa Barbara or the Chinatown Freeway in San Francisco). Fortunately, as in the case of Mayor Koch and the homeless in New York City, a few policymakers are capable of taking decisive action on a pressing public problem in their city. However, as this example showed, in taking action Koch came under fire from a myriad of local, state, and national policy actors.

Thus I am not saying that cities cannot make adequate and effective policy in modern times. I do claim, however, something just short of such a statement. Cities are fragile makers of public policy, and this fragility often places insurmountable barriers and costs in the way of effective policymaking. Even when cities do make policies, the very fragility that made it difficult to formulate it may make it impossible to carry it out or even more difficult to make policy again in the future.

City policymaking is, at best, a fragile and tenuous process subject to multiple influences—several of which strengthen but most of which tend to weaken or limit the ability of cities to make policy or solve problems. It is well past time that this weakness or inherent fragility in the city policy process was considered in the same light and with the same gravity that we currently discuss urban problems and proposed solutions. Indeed, in many cases the problem of local policymaking fragility may actually be more important than such other traditional urban problems as fiscal stress, poverty, and violent crime. This is so because without a solution to policymaking fragility, cities will be unable to adequately make policy on any other pressing issue of the day.

As the policy life cycle model illustrates, city policymaking can be successfully derailed at so many junctures that the miracle is not that modern cities make policies that occasionally address local problems but rather that cities make policy at all. If we are to address the problems and ills of urban life, one of the problems that we need to put at the top of the list is the exceptional fragility of the city policymaking process itself.

Appendix

Los Angeles *Times* (March 8, 1987): I:3.
"Out in the Desert, They Want the Nuclear Dump."
By Alan Goldstein, *Times Staff Writer*

NEEDLES—It is an unlikely prize, a hole in the ground where clothing, plastic gloves and medical supplies contaminated by low-level radioactivity can be buried for generations.

But a battle is brewing in the Mojave Desert over which of three dry lake basins will be selected as California's low-level nuclear waste dump. And the stakes for the communities near the chosen site are high.

As many as 40 permanent jobs would be created in the operation of the dump, no small catch for this dusty city of 5,000, just west of the Arizona border along Interstate 40, or for the other two communities in the running: Baker, 60 miles northeast of Barstow, and Trona, just west of Death Valley.

Indeed, the process has sparked competition between front-runners Needles and Baker.

Discouraging Opposition

"We want it more than Baker," said Larry DeAtley, who owns Needles Cold Storage, a food distributor, and is president of the Chamber of Commerce. "We're discouraging any kind of opposition."

Countered Lois Clark, co-editor of the Baker Valley News and owner of one of Baker's two mobile home parks: "We're elated we've

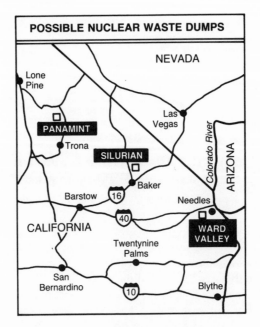

App-1

been chosen as a finalist. And I hope we get it. We certainly need it more than Needles does."

The potential sites were chosen from a list of 16 remote desert locations by U.S. Ecology, a Louisville, Ky., firm designated by the state's Department of Health Services in December, 1985, to develop, build and operate the dump.

After more studies, a site will be chosen in 1988, and U.S. Ecology will apply to the state for a license to build. The firm hopes to have the California dump taking all of the state's low-level radioactive waste, now sent to dumps in Richland, Wash., and Beatty, Nev., by 1990.

Community Support

U.S. Ecology heard plenty of organized opposition from environ-mentalists in areas it eliminated from the running, notably in Twentynine Palms. However, the company said it has significant community support from each of the remaining finalists.

"We've said from the start that public acceptance is most important," said Ronald K. Gaynor, a U.S. Ecology vice president and project manager for the California site. "We don't have to ram it down anyone's throats when other people want it."

In fact, Gaynor said, the firm has already determined that the Panamint Valley in Inyo County runs a distant third to the two San Bernardino County sites, mostly for environmental reasons. But support for the dump was so great there that it was thrown into the ring anyway.

"It would be a real asset to the people," said Robert Bremmer, an Inyo County supervisor. "It's long-term jobs, not here today, gone tomorrow."

Railroad Blues

Here in Needles, such an employer also would be welcome. For more than a century, freight trains chugging across the desert were the lifeblood of Needles. Now, the old beige depot in the center of town, a colonnaded arcade, is mostly abandoned by the Santa Fe railway.

And although Santa Fe still employs several hundred local residents, the number does not approach the 1,000 job holders the railway supported until the 1960s. Computerization and automation are responsible for the attrition. The use of refrigerated freight cars alone eliminated 300 jobs at the local ice plant.

The railroad has not been hiring for eight years. Many of the young people in town have little choice but to leave the area when they finish high school. If they are lucky, they go into the family business.

The only other choice is to work for minimum wages in any of the gas stations and fast-food restaurants that dot this place on the way to other places, serving truckers and tourists headed west toward Los Angeles or east toward Flagstaff, Ariz., and Albuquerque, N.M.

'No Future' for Youngsters

"There's no future for a lad here," said Chamber of Commerce president DeAtley, 47, a former Orange County resident who favors

T-shirts and jeans and drives a white Dodge van with the bumper sticker, "My wife, yes. My dog, maybe. My gun, never."

Of course, not everyone in town is actively lobbying for the dump. The City Council has refused to take a stand, one way or the other. "I don't know enough about it," Mayor Evelyn Connolly said.

Some confess to a little nervousness about the idea of having anything with nuclear in its name coming through town, although most of the material, refuse from the nuclear industry, hospitals and laboratories, has a relatively short half-life of about 100 years.

But reactions such as those from Gene McCall, who worked at the ice plant until it closed in 1962, are more typical. "At my age, I don't think some gloves and rags can hurt me much," said McCall, 67.

Neither does Steve Zwerner, general manager for Silver Lake Properties in Baker. Silver Lake is by far the biggest employer in Baker, keeping 80 of the community's 500 people at work at its Bun Boy restaurant, two motels, country store and three gas stations.

"Everyone plays around with radiation every day," said Zwerner, going through the company's ledgers in his office. "As far as I'm concerned, we have to build up the area. We can't just depend on tourism."

Just off Interstate 15, about 100 miles southwest of Las Vegas, Baker, like Needles, is mainly a pit stop. Around the clock, travelers flock toward the tall, brightly colored signs where they can grab burgers or buy casino show tickets as a prelude to the gambling meccas of Nevada.

The community of mostly mobile homes has a history as an oasis. Baker was developed in the 1930s as a watering hole for construction crews on their way to build Hoover Dam on the Colorado River at the Arizona–Nevada border.

Economic Hopes

Aside from the promise of better-paying jobs, Baker residents hope they can expand the economy. For example, the nearest banks and pharmacies are in Barstow, an hour's drive.

And the families of dump employees would supply an extra force of teen-agers for the local businesses, most of which run three shifts a day. The local Burger King buses in workers from Barstow; Pike's, a restaurant and gas station, has a dormitory for its employees.

Carolyn Jacobson, who with her husband owns Arne's Royal Hawaiian Motel, is resigned to the dump.

"When the subject first came up, I wasn't much in favor of it," she said. "But I've since been thinking about it, in a rational way, and I've decided, 'Why fight it? It has to be someplace.'"

> I came to this furnace because the former owners said there was going to be a prison built here and we would have lots of business.
>
> —Motel operator Carmen Vasquez

Los Angeles *Times* (July 14, 1986): I:3.
Blythe Residents Look Forward to Prospect of Prison
By Louis Sahagun, *Times Staff Writer*

BLYTHE, Calif.—Staring longingly at the swimming pool outside, Carmen Vasquez mopped the back of her neck with a handkerchief in the sweltering office of the Sea Shell Motel she bought here a year ago for $500,000.

"I came to this furnace because the former owners said there was going to be a prison built here and we would have lots of business," said Vasquez, 38, who moved here from San Diego, where she operates another motel along the Mexican border. "Right now, we're losing money."

Then she crossed her fingers and added, "We're still waiting for that prison."

Relief for Vasquez and other struggling business owners in this remote, torrid desert community of 14,000 people could come if a long-sought state prison wins final approval from the state Public Works Board next fall, California Corrections Department officials said.

Barring unforeseen difficulties, construction would begin within months on the 3,200-inmate, medium-security prison, which is

expected to bring 700 steady jobs and an estimated annual payroll of
$13 million to Blythe, said Sen. Robert Presley (D-Riverside), chair-
man of the joint legislative committee on prison construction and
operations. The first prisoners would arrive in 1988.

The proposed $125-million facility would sit 17 miles west of
Blythe at Wiley's Well, a desolate plot of desert studded with mes-
quite and greasewood that is framed in the distance by the barren
Little Chuckawalla Mountains on the south and the Mule Mountains
on the east.

"Escapees would probably die in the desert before they reached
town," said Cindy Garcia, 23, a desk clerk at Comfort Inn and strong
proponent of the prison.

Optimistic that the prison proposal will pass its final hurdles,
Blythe Mayor William Martindale said a "renaissance" is at hand for
what has existed for years as a traveler's gas and food stop straddling
the Colorado River about 200 miles east of Los Angeles.

"We are already seeing some real estate moving and new development being discussed," Martindale said. "With the prison, we'll
need more and better restaurants, shopping facilities, housing and
medical care."

That could mean a better way of life for the town, which is about
45% Latino and has an average household income of about $16,000
a year, according to Terry Matz, Blythe city manager, a little more
than half the average household income of $31,838 in Riverside
County.

The Blythe prison is one of 10 new facilities proposed by the state
Corrections Department for construction by 1991. Its approval
would have no effect on bitterly contested plans for a 1,700-bed
prison in downtown Los Angeles.

There has been near-unanimous support for the desert prison
among Blythe merchants and elected officials, some of whom
stunned legislators last February by traveling to Sacramento and
demonstrating in favor of it on the steps of the Capitol.

"One of the things we look for in siting a new prison is community
support," said Bob Gore, a spokesman for the state Corrections
Department. "It helps speed the process along."

But not everyone in the area wants the prison, and the prospect of
swift and dramatic change here has created strong friction between
businessmen and some farmers.

On one side are the mostly "mom-and-pop" business owners and realtors in town eager for the commerce associated with hundreds of prison employees and their families. On the other are farmers who believe that the town will lose its rural character in favor of a "prison subculture."

Opposition to Prison

Although much of the opposition has diminished in recent months, some farmers say their continuing opposition to the prison has caused them to lose friends in town.

"This pro-prison, anti-prison controversy has evolved into a pro-farmer, anti-farmer controversy," said Bart Fisher, spokesman for the "Stop the Prison Committee" and owner of Fisher Farms, one

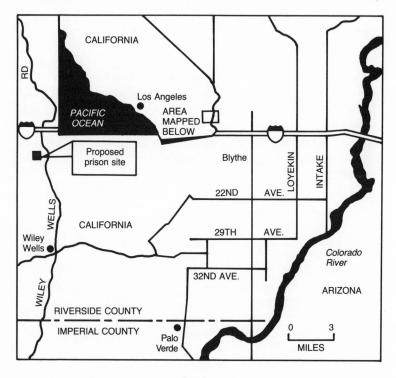

App-2

of the largest growers in the area with 9,000 acres. "The issue has driven a wedge into town and created wounds that won't heal soon."

Opponents such as Fisher believe that the prison will attract an undesirable element to Blythe, raise the crime rate, scare away winter visitors and destroy the rural, small-town atmosphere.

"What person in their right mind wants a prison in their backyard?" asked Fisher, while supervising a tomato harvest. "Besides that, it is crazy to put a prison in the middle of the desert where it is cold in the winter and hotter than hell in the summer. Can you imagine what the utility bills will be?"

Asserting that some merchants have become "starry-eyed with dollar signs," Fisher shook his head and vowed, "the fight isn't over yet."

A last-ditch effort may come in September when an Environmental Assessment Study is to be presented at a local public hearing. Opponent Ron Baker, who owns a small farm 10 miles outside of town, said prison adversaries plan to examine it closely in hopes of finding a "chink in the armor."

But even Fisher acknowledged that Blythe today "looks like ruin."

There is no skating rink, movie theater or miniature golf course here. Young people congregate instead at supermarket parking lots.

Nor are there many available jobs outside of the fast-food stands, gas stations and motels along "hamburger row"—a nickname for Lovekin Boulevard, the exit from Interstate 10—or the irrigated fields of cotton, lettuce, melons, tomatoes, corn and alfalfa surrounding the city.

"I'd Leave Tomorrow"

There are, however, lots of empty buildings, "for sale" signs and people who would like to move.

"I'd leave tomorrow if the sheriff wouldn't bring me back because of the debts I owe," said appliance store owner Bud Phipps, 65, who plans to quite business after years of "barely getting by."

But even some prison advocates are worried that stores such as Phipps' could get clobbered by potential new competition the prison would bring to town.

"Progress is sometimes painful and some of the small stores around here will adapt or die," said print shop owner and former mayor Ernest Weeks. "I wonder if some of the pro-prison people will be ready for it."

"I like competition," said Julian Hernandez, 61, sitting in the cocktail lounge of his Don Julian's Mexican Restaurant as a rock band played hard for the usual nightly crowd of locals.

"I also think the prison will double my business," he said. "The way I see it, the corrections officers will want to eat Mexican food once in a while, drink a margarita or two."

Notes

1. The Ecology of City Policymaking

1. For a recent argument that uses a biological rather than an ecological analogy (i.e., it argues that the body politic and the human body may be compared for purposes of policy analysis), see Brian H. Hogwood and B. Guy Peters, *The Pathology of Public Policy* (New York: Oxford University Press, 1985). The Hogwood and Peters work makes use of the language of medical pathology to contrast human disease processes with diseased or dysfunctional public policy scenarios.

2. Bryan Jones, *Governing Urban America: A Policy Focus* (Boston: Little, Brown, 1983), pp. 19–20.

3. Thomas R. Dye, *Understanding Public Policy,* 5th ed. (Englewood Cliffs, N.J.: Prentice-Hall, 1984), p. 42.

4. Norton Long, "The Local Community as an Ecology of Games," *American Political Science Review* 64 (November 1958): 251–61; rpt. in Harlan Hahn and Charles H. Levine, eds. *Reading in Urban Politics,* 2nd ed. (New York: Longman, 1984), pp. 120–32.

5. Ibid., p. 122.

6. Ibid., p. 121.

7. David Easton, *A Systems Analysis of Political Life* (New York: John Wiley, 1965).

8. Larry N. Gerston, *Making Public Policy: From Conflict to Resolution* (Boston: Little, Brown, 1983), p. 6.

9. "The Lebanon Strategy," *The New Republic,* December 26, 1983, pp. 5–7.

10. Jones, *Governing Urban America,* p. 17.

11. See Murray Edleman, *The Symbolic Uses of Politics* (Urbana: University of Illinois Press, 1964).

12. Michael Lipsky, "Protest as a Political Resource," *American Political Science Review* 62 (December 1968): 1155. See also his *Protest in City Politics* (Chicago: Rand McNally, 1970).

13. Lipsky, "Protest as a Political Resource," p. 1157.

14. Paul R. Schulman, *Large-Scale Policy Making* (New York: Elsevier, 1980).

15. This situation of one seller (the city) and only a few buyers (the limited number of developers able to put together the capital and planning/construction resources to build a major urban redevelopment project) is referred to as a "monopsony" by urban economists to distinguish it from the more traditional single seller, multiple-buyer scenario that characterizes a classic monopolistic situation.

16. See Charles Lindblom, *The Policymaking Process,* 2nd ed. (Englewood Cliffs, N.J.: Prentice-Hall, 1980); see also Aaron Wildavsky, *The Politics of the Budgetary Process,* 4th ed. (Boston: Little, Brown, 1984).

17. The use of the choke-hold by San Diego city police officers, while controversial, is a classic example of incremental and pluralistic policymaking of the sort that Lindblom has described as "the science of muddling through." In Lindblom's view, policy in the "real" world is not ideal or "rational-comprehensive." In the real world, the five characteristics of decision making are: (1) the policy is *incremental* (it proceeds in small steps to achieve limited objectives and frequently constitutes little more than minor changes at the margins of earlier policies); (2) the policy is *noncomprehensive* (policymakers cannot know the full range of choices actually available to them, nor can they fully predict their effects due to constraints of time, resources, and knowledge); (3) the policy involves *successive comparisons,* as policy is constantly made and remade via endless comparisons among a range of fairly limited choices; (4) the policy *suffices* rather than maximizes policy goals and social ends due to the problems mentioned previously, but if there is an up side to all this, the suffices policy helps prevent irreversible and potentially disastrous policy decisions from being made, as muddling through does not allow for irreversible decisions; and (5) the muddling through policy is based on *pluralism,* where multiple competing interest groups try to influence policy outcomes, frequently forcing policymakers and administrators to seek agreement among the competing parties. Thus the final element of incrementalism and muddling through stresses compromise and reconciliation, albeit Lindblom notes in *Politics and Markets* (New York: Basic Books, 1977) that this is not always possible in some communities or on some issues where business interests may hold a privileged position in policymaking. See Lindblom, "The Science of Muddling Through," *Public Administration Review* 19 (Spring, 1959): 79–88. See also Lindblom, *The Policy-Making Process,* 2nd ed. (Englewood Cliffs, N.J.: Prentice-Hall, 1980).

While the use of choke-holds in San Diego seems to meet Lindblom's criteria for incremental policymaking, its use by the Los Angeles police department violates several of the criteria of the admittedly dismal "science" of muddle-through policymaking. The temporary policy adopted in San Diego was controversial, and after a series of community hearings its use was extended only until the police force could be taught another tactic that would satisfy their needs as well as that of the community. William Kolender, San Diego police chief, sought out community members and explained his dilemma to them, thus facilitating a compromise. This was hardly the case in Los Angeles. There Police Chief Daryl Gates resisted community objections to the use of choke-holds and stated publicly that the choke-hold should not alarm the minority community, as in his opinion, non-Caucasians, particularly blacks, had a bulkier throat and neck structure than whites did, rendering the choke-hold less of a threat to members of the minority community.

In chapter 4, I shall show that the same policy issue (e.g., the choke-hold policy) can produce a very different form of political conflict in different communities. However, the prevailing and contrary view, set forward by Theodore Lowi, is that policies determine politics. Thus, for Lowi a given policy (A) will result in a given political scenario (X). My argument is that policy A may lead to political scenario X, or A may lead to several other scenarios, which we might label W, Y, or Z. For Lowi the policy type determines the resulting political scenario, period. My argument is less determinative and more flexible. See three articles by Lowi, "American Business, Public Policy and Political Theory," *World Politics* 16 (July 1964): 677–715; "Decision Making vs. Policy Making: Toward an Antidote for Technocracy," *Public Administration Review* 30 (May–June, 1970): 314–24; and "Four Systems of Policy, Politics, and Choice," *Public Administration Review* 32 (July–August 1972): 298–310. For an effective criticism of Lowi, see George D. Greenberg, Jeffrey A. Miller, Lawrence B. Mohr, and Bruce C. Vladeck, "Developing Public Policy Theory: Perspectives from Empirical Research," *American Political Science Review* 71 (1977): 1532–42. As I note in chapter 4, Paul Peterson and James Q. Wilson, with some modifications and qualifications, adhere to Lowi's view that, in the careful wording of Wilson, "the substance of policy influences the role of organizations in its adoption." James Q. Wilson, *Political Organizations* (New York: Basic Books, 1973), p. 330. See also Paul Peterson, *City Limits* (Chicago: University of Chicago Press, 1981).

18. Charles Lindblom, "The Science of Muddling Through," *Public Administration Review* 19 (Spring 1959): 79–88; and "Policy Analysis," *American Economic Review* (June 1958): 298–312. The first use of "satisfice" (satisfy and suffice) as the goal of actual policymakers is by Herbert Simon, *Models of Man* (New York, 1957).

19. For an argument that policy should be completely rational-comprehensive, which might actually become possible in the real world, see Yzehekyl Dror, "Optimal Models of Public Policymaking," *Public Policy-Making Re-examined* (San Francisco: Chandler, 1968), pp. 129–216.

20. Political ethos is, at best, a slippery concept which is intuitively compelling but fraught with basic problems in concept formation and possible bias. The origin of the concept and its first application to the comparative urban field is in Edward C. Banfield and James Q. Wilson, *City Politics* (Cambridge, Mass.: Harvard University and MIT Presses, 1963), and Edward C. Banfield and James Q. Wilson, "Public Regardingness as a Value Premise in Voting Behavior," *American Political Science Review* 58 (December 1964): 876–87. See also Raymond Wolfinger and John Osgood Field, "Political Ethos and the Structure of City Government," *American Political Science Review* 60 (June, 1966): 306–26.

21. For a careful discussion of some of the weaknesses in the political ethos concept, see Timothy M. Hennessy, "Problems in Concept Formation: The Ethos 'Theory' and the Comparative Study of Urban Politics," *Midwest Journal of Political Science* 15 (November 1970): 537–64. For a recent study illustrating the com-

plexity of the American national ethos and the difficulty in studying it, see the analysis by J. David Greenstone of the bipolar set of beliefs that influence American policymaking in "The Transient and the Permanent in American Politics: Standards, Interests, and the Concept of the 'Public,'" *Public Values and Private Power in American Politics,* ed. J. David Greenstone (Chicago: University of Chicago Press, 1983), pp. 3–33.

22. Raymond Wolfinger, Martin Shapiro and Fred I. Greenstein (eds.), *Dynamics of American Politics* (Englewood Cliffs, N.J.: Prentice-Hall, 1976), p. 215.

23. David Truman, *The Governmental Process* (New York: Knopf, 1951), pp. 14–17, 37–44, 506–19.

24. Robert A. Dahl, "Rethinking *Who Governs?* New Haven, Revisited," in R. Waste (ed.), *Community Power: Future Directions in Urban Research* (Beverly Hills, Calif.: Sage Publications, 1986), pp. 114–16.

25. Lipsky, "Protest as a Political Resource," p. 1148.

26. Kenneth Boulding, *Primer on Social Dynamics* (New York: Free Press, 1970).

27. Clarence N. Stone, "Power and Social Complexity," in Waste (ed.), *Community Power,* p. 66.

28. Truman, *The Governmental Process.*

29. For a vigorous statement of an alternative view, see G. William Domhoff, "The Growth Machine and the Power Elite: A Challenge to Pluralists and Marxists Alike," and Thomas R. Dye, "Community Power and Public Policy," in Waste (ed.) *Community Power,* pp. 11–43. See also Harvey Molotch, "The City as a Growth Machine," *American Journal of Sociology* 82 (September 1976): 309–30; "Capital and Neighborhood in the United States," *Urban Affairs Quarterly* 14 (March 1979): 289–312; and "Romantic Marxism: Love Is Still Not Enough," *Contemporary Sociology* 13 (March 1984): 141–43.

30. For an excellent list of community resources that may be used by community interest groups seeking to influence the formation of public policy, see Nelson Polsby, *Community Power and Political Theory,* 2nd ed. (New Haven: Yale University Press, 1980), pp. 119–20, and "How to Study Community Power: The Pluralist Alternative," *Journal of Politics* (August 1960): 474–84.

31. Robert A. Dahl, *Who Governs?* (New Haven: Yale University Press, 1961).

32. "Multiple points of access" is a key point in Truman, *The Governmental Process,* pp. 14–17, 33–44, 506–19. I am indebted to Professor William Lunch, Department of Political Science, Oregon State University, for the chart on federalism that forms the basis of Figure 1.2. For an expanded treatment of the increasing role of the federal government in setting the agenda for state and local governments, see Lunch, *The Nationalization of American Politics* (Berkeley: University of California Press, 1987).

33. For the origins of the "iron triangle" concept, see Douglas Cater, *Power in Washington* (New York: Vintage, 1964). See also J. Leiper Freeman, *The Political Process* (New York: Random House, 1965).

34. Douglas Yates, "The Mayor's Eight Ring Circus: The Shape of Urban Politics in Its Evolving Arenas," in Dale Rogers Marshall (ed.), *Urban Policymaking,* Sage Yearbooks in Politics and Public Policy, Vol. 7 (Beverly Hills, Calif.: Sage Publications, 1979): 41–70.

35. Hugh Heclo, "Issue Networks and the Executive Establishment," in Anthony King (ed.), *The New Political System* (Washington, D.C.: American Enterprise Institute, 1978), pp. 87–124, reprinted in part in Richard J. Stillman (ed.), *Public Administration: Cases and Concepts,* pp. 416–24.

36. Ibid., p. 417.

37. Ibid.

38. Robert A. Caro, *The Power Broker: Robert Moses and the Fall of New York City* (New York: Vintage, 1975).

39. See Larry Orman, "Ballot-Box Planning: The Boom in Electoral Land Use Control," (Berkeley: University of California-Institute of Governmental Studies) 25 (December 1984): 1–15.

40. Lipsky, "Protest as a Political Resource."

41. Ibid., pp. 1145–46.

42. Rufus Browning, Dale Rogers Marshall, and David Tabb, *Protest Is Not Enough: The Struggle for Black and Hispanic Equality in Cities* (Berkeley: University of California Press, 1984). See also Browning, Marshall, and Tabb, "Responsiveness to Minorities: A Theory of Political Change in Cities," a paper presented at the Annual Meeting of the American Political Science Association, August 1978; and "Implementation and Political Change: Sources of Local Variations in Federal Social Programs," a paper prepared for the Workshop on Policy Implementation, Pomona College, November 16–17, 1978.

43. Heclo, "Issue Networks and the Executive Establishment."

44. Ibid., p. 417.

45. Ibid., pp. 417–18.

2.   The Life Cycle of City Policymaking

1. Roger W. Cobb and Charles D. Elder, *Participation in American Politics: The Dynamics of Agenda-Building,* 2nd ed. (Baltimore: Johns Hopkins University Press, 1983), orig. ed., 1972; Bryan Jones, *Governing Urban America: A Policy Focus* (Boston: Little, Brown, 1982); Randall Ripley and Grace Franklin, *Congress, the Bureaucracy and Public Policy,* 3rd ed. (Homewood, Ill.: Dorsey Press, 1984), and *Policy Implementation in the United States,* 2nd ed. (Homewood, Ill.: Dorsey Press, 1986).

2. Douglas Yates, *The Ungovernable City* (Cambridge, Mass.: MIT Press, 1977), pp. 146–64.

3. Jones, *Governing Urban America,* p. 17.

4. Ibid.

5. Ibid., p. 20.

6. Cobb and Elder, *Participation in American Politics.*

7. Compared with acid rain, acid fog is a very new and still controversial concept. Early indications, however, suggest that the problem is quite serious. A recent publication of the California Air Resources Board notes that "one episode of fog measured on the Southern California coast had a pH of 1.7–8,000 times

more acidic than unpolluted precipitation. Fog in California's Central Valley near Bakersfield was measured at pH 2.6–1,000 times more acidic than unpolluted precipitation." See "Acid Fog," *Facts About* (Sacramento: California Air Resources Board, 1983), p. 3. See also Jed Waldman, J. William Munger, and Michael A. Hoffman, "Chemical Composition of Fogwater Collected Along the California Coast," *Environmental Science Technology* (August 1985): 4391–4427; B. Hileman, "Acid Fog," *Environmental Science Technology* (March 1983): 17.

8. Anthony Downs, "Up and Down with Ecology—The Issue-Attention Cycle," *Public Interest* 28 (Summer 1972): 38.

9. Edward Banfield, *The Unheavenly City* (Boston: Little, Brown, 1970), and *The Unheavenly City, Revisited* (Boston: Little, Brown, 1974).

10. The original discussion of "issue entrepreneurs" is Robert Eyestone, *From Social Issues to Public Policy* (New York: John Wiley, 1978): 88–89. See also the discussion of "policy entrepreneurs" in Jones, *Governing Urban America*, pp. 18, 25–26. See also the highly original treatment of public entrepreneurship by Eugene Lewis, *Public Entrepreneurship: Toward a Theory of Bureaucratic Political Power: The Organizational Lives of Hyman Rickover, J. Edgar Hoover, and Robert Moses* (Bloomington: Indiana University Press, 1980).

11. F. Stevens Redburn and Terry F. Buss, "Religious Leaders as Political Advocates: The Youngstown Steel Mill Closing," in Robert Eyestone (ed.) *Public Policy Formation* (Greenwich, Conn.: JAI Press, 1984), pp. 83–94.

12. Nelson W. Polsby, *Political Innovation in America: The Politics of Policy Initiation* (New Haven: Yale University Press, 1984).

13. Yates, *The Ungovernable City*, p. 146.

14. Ibid.

15. Ibid., p. 147. See also Milton Rakove, *Don't Make No Waves, Don't Back No Losers* (Bloomington: Indiana University Press, 1975).

16. Yates, *The Ungovernable City*, p. 147.

17. Banfield, *The Unheavenly City, Revisited*, pp. 279–86.

18. Larry N. Gerston, *Making Public Policy: From Conflict to Resolution* (Glenview, Ill.: Scott-Foresman, 1983), p. 24.

19. David Easton, *A Systems Analysis of Political Life* (New York: John Wiley, 1965).

20. Clarence N. Stone, *Economic Growth and Neighborhood Discontent* (University of North Carolina Press, 1976).

21. Jones, *Governing Urban America*, p. 23.

22. Cobb and Elder, *Participation in American Politics*, p. 125.

23. Jones, *Governing Urban America*, p. 39.

24. Ibid., pp. 39–41.

25. Frederick Wirt, *Power in the City: Decision Making in San Francisco* (Berkeley: University of California Press, 1974), p. 14.

26. Ibid., p. 11.

27. Ibid.

28. Glen W. Sparrow, former executive director, San Francisco Charter Reform Commission, San Diego State University, Calif., interview (February 16, 1984).

29. Yates, *The Ungovernable City*.

30. Polsby, *Political Innovation in America*.

31. E. Hsu, "Mayor Wants Pistols Banned in San Francisco," San Francisco *Chronicle* (February 25, 1982).

32. K. Butler, "S.F. Residents Taking Sides," San Francisco *Chronicle* (February 26, 1982).

33. M. Kilduff, "San Francisco Pistol Banning Measure Offered," San Francisco *Chronicle* (April 5, 1982).

34. Butler, "S.F. Residents Taking Sides."

35. M. Griego, "Deluge of Anti-Ban Calls—Mayor's Proposal Denounced," San Francisco *Chronicle* (February 25, 1982).

36. Kilduff, "S.F. Pistol Banning Measure Offered."

37. Hsu, "Mayor Signs Pistol Law Legal—Battle Seems Sure," San Francisco *Chronicle* (June 29, 1982).

38. K. Leary and W. Carlsen, "S.F. Pistol Ban Goes Into Effect," San Francisco *Chronicle* (July 29, 1982).

39. M. Kilduff, "Judges Skeptical of S.F. Gun Ban," San Francisco *Chronicle* (September 23, 1982).

40. D. Johnson and D. Cole, "Feinstein Has 75–19% Lead in Battle Against Recall," San Francisco *Chronicle* (April 17, 1982).

41. Yates, *The Ungovernable City,* p. 148.

42. Michael D. Reagan and John G. Sanzone, *The New Federalism,* 2nd ed. (New York: Oxford University Press, 1980). See also William Lunch, *The Nationalization of American Politics* (Berkeley: University of California Press, 1987.

3.   Growth, Locale, and City Policymaking

1. Anthony Downs, *Inside Bureaucracy* (Boston: Little, Brown, 1966), chapter 2, "The Life Cycle of Bureaus, " pp. 5–23. See also an earlier draft of chapter 3 of this book published as Robert J. Waste, "The Early Years in the Life Cycle of City Councils: A Downsian Analysis," *Urban Studies* 20 (1983): 73–81.

2. Downs, *Inside Bureaucracy,* pp. 5–23.

3. Alvin D. Sokolow, Priscilla Hanford, Joan Hogan, and Linda Martin, *Choices for the Unincorporated Community: A Guide to Local Government Alternatives in California* (Davis, Calif.: University of California, Davis–Institute of Governmental Affairs, 1981).

4. Downs, *Inside Bureaucracy,* p. 7.

5. Ibid., p. 9.

6. Aaron Wildavsky, *The Politics of the Budgetary Process,* 4th ed. (Boston: Little, Brown, 1984).

7. Downs, *Inside Bureaucracy,* chapter 8, "Milieu, Motives and Goals," and chapter 9, "How Specific Types of Officials Behave," pp. 88–111.

8. I am grateful to an anonymous reader for Oxford University Press for pressing this point forcefully in his/her review of an earlier draft of this chapter, and for providing the chart used as the basis for Table 3.2.

9. Downs, *Inside Bureaucracy,* p. 7.

10. The city of Lakewood, a small and relatively affluent new city near Long

Beach, California, incorporated in 1954 and contracted with the County of Los Angeles to provide the municipal services (e.g., police, fire protection, public works) normally offered by traditional full-service cities. The idea of contracting out has proved quite popular, particularly in southern California, where a large number of municipalities operate with little more full-time staff than a city manager, planning department, and a city attorney (also frequently contracted out and shared jointly with several municipalities). See Gary Miller, *Cities by Contract: The Politics of Municipal Incorporation* (Cambridge, Mass.: MIT Press, 1981). For a comparison of the Lakewood Plan communities of southern California with St. Louis and Detroit, see David R. Reynolds, "Progress Toward Achieving Efficient and Responsive Spatial-Political Systems in Urban America," in John S. Adams (ed.), *Urban Policymaking and Metropolitan Dynamics* (Cambridge, Mass.: Ballinger, 1976), pp. 463–538.

11. I use the phrase "administrative team" to refer to the elected city council as opposed to an administrative team composed of a city manager and selected department heads.

12. Several states have enacted measures similar to California's 1978 Jarvis-Gann property tax limitation initiative (Proposition 13) or the 1979 Gann spending cap measure (Proposition 4), which supporters called the "Spirit of 13" initiative. Californians—both detractors and supporters alike—frequently refer to the two measures as "Jaws I" and "Jaws II." These new tax limitations have, in many cases, greatly reduced the funds available to local governments. See David O. Sears and Jack Citrin, *Tax Revolt: Something for Nothing in California* (Berkeley: University of California Press, 1982). For ways in which cities are coping with the prolonged period of fiscal stress that has characterized the late 1970s and the 1980s, see Terry N. Clark and Lorna C. Ferguson, *City Money: Political Processes, Fiscal Strain and Retrenchment* (New York: Columbia University Press, 1983); and Irene S. Rubin, *Running in the Red: The Political Dynamics of Urban Fiscal Stress* (Albany: SUNY Press, 1982), especially chapter 5, "Political Process and Fiscal Stress: Council Behavior," pp. 51–74.

Despite the economic stress that the national, state, and local governments are currently facing, it should be emphasized that public agencies have, as David Cameron noted, multiple "internal pressures for self-aggrandizement and expansion." David Cameron, "The Expansion of the Public Economy: A Comparative Analysis," *American Political Science Review* 72 (1978): 1243–61. See also Downs, *Inside Bureaucracy;* William A. Niskanen, *Bureaucracy and Representative Government* (Chicago: Aldine Publishing, 1971); Wildavsky, *The Politics of the Budgetary Process;* and Daniel Tarschys, "The Growth of Public Expenditures: Nine Models of Explanation," *Scandinavian Political Studies* 10 (1975): 9–31.

13. E. J. Dionne, Jr., "Mayors, at Conference, Are Looking to the End of the Reagan Era," New York *Times,* (June 21, 1987): Y-14. See also Dale Rogers Marshall and Robert J. Waste, *Large City Responses to the Community Development Act* (Davis: University of California, Davis—Institute of Governmental Affairs, 1977).

14. Wildavsky, *Politics of the Budgetary Process.*

15. Downs, *Inside Bureaucracy,* p. 21.

16. Ibid.

17. Kenneth Prewitt, "Political Ambitions, Volunteerism, and Electoral Accountability," *American Political Science Review* 64 (March 1970): 5–17.

18. Robert Eyestone, *The Threads of Public Policy: A Study in Policy Leadership* (Indianapolis: Bobbs-Merrill, 1971), chapter 6, "The Roots of Policy Development," pp. 132–52.

19. Oliver P. Williams and Charles R. Adrian, "Community Types and Policy Differences," in James Q. Wilson (ed.), *City Politics and Public Policy* (New York: John Wiley, 1968), pp. 17–37.

20. The literature on this point is voluminous. A representative sample includes: Carl Abbott, *The New Urban America: Growth and Politics in Sunbelt Cities* (Chapel Hill: University of North Carolina Press, 1981); Richard M. Bernard and Bradley R. Rice (eds.), *Sunbelt Cities: Politics and Growth Since World War II* (Austin: University of Texas Press, 1983); David Caputo, "Research and Practice Note—Reaganomics and Midwestern Cities: An Initial Assessment," *Journal of Urban Affairs* 4 (Summer 1982): 79–87, and "American Cities and their Future," *Society* (January/February, 1985): 59–64; Caputo and Steven Johnson, "New Federalism and Midwestern Cities, 1981–1985," *Publius* (February 1986), a special issue dealing wih the "New Federalism"; R. L. Cole and D. A. Taebel, *Attitudes of Local Officials to President Reagan's New Federalism and the Interactive Effects of Metropolitan Type, Partisan Orientations and Sunbelt-Frostbelt Distinctions* (Arlington: Institute of Urban Studies, University of Texas at Arlington), and "Initial Attitudes of Local Officials to President Reagan's New Federalism," *Journal of Urban Affairs* 5 (Winter 1983): 57–78; and Robert J. Waste and Roger W. Caves, "New Federalism, Reaganomics and Western Cities: The View of Municipal Officials," a paper presented at the Annual Meeting of the Western Political Science Association, Eugene, Oregon, March 21–23, 1986.

21. Howard Hamilton, "The Municipal Voter: Voting and Nonvoting in City Elections," *American Political Science Review* 65 (December 1971): 1135.

22. Robert Alford and Eugene Lee, "Voting Turnout in American Cities," *American Political Science Review* 62 (September 1968): 796–813.

23. Prewitt, "Political Ambitions, Volunteerism, and Electoral Accountability," p. 10.

24. Susan B. Hansen, "Participation, Political Structures, and Concurrence," *American Political Science Review* 69 (December 1975): 1181–99.

25. This summary of Hansen's findings is contained in Bryan Jones, *Governing Urban America: A Policy Focus* (Boston: Little, Brown, 1983), p. 110.

26. Heinz Eulau, "From Labyrinths to Networks: Political Representation in Urban Settings," in Robert J. Waste (ed.), *Community Power: Future Directions in Urban Research* (Beverly Hills, Calif.: Sage Publications, 1986), p. 89.

27. Eyestone, *The Threads of Public Policy: A Study in Policy Leadership*, p. 144.

28. Ibid., pp. 151–52.

29. Williams and Adrian, "Community Types and Policy Differences," p. 36.

30. The term "sunbelt" was coined by Kevin Phillips in *The Emerging Republican Majority* (New Rochelle, N.Y.: Arlington House, 1969). The sunbelt concept is theoretically slippery at best. For a trenchant criticism, see Clyde E. Browning

and Wil Gesler, "Sun Belt–Snow Belt: A Case of Sloppy Regionalizing," *Professional Geographer* 31 (February 1979): 66–74. Several versions of what constitutes the sunbelt exist in the literature. Among these are a sunbelt map by Thomas R. Dye that includes Colorado, Utah, and Nevada but fails to include Oklahoma; a volume by Perry and Watkins that includes Memphis as a sunbelt city in one chapter but places it in the frostbelt in another chapter; and the curious definition of sunbelt in Carl Abbott's *The New Urban America: Growth and Politics in Sunbelt Cities,* which places Portland in the sunbelt region of the country. See Thomas R. Dye, *Politics in States and Communities,* 4th ed. (Englewood Cliffs, N.J.: Prentice-Hall, 1981), p. 13; David C. Perry and Alfred J. Watkins (eds.), *The Rise of Sunbelt CititEs,* Vol. 14, Urban Affairs Annual Reviews (Beverly Hills, Calif.: Sage Publications, 1977); and Bernard and Rice, *Sunbelt Cities: Politics and Growth Since World War II,* pp. 3–10.

31. Waste and Caves, "New Federalism, Reaganomics and Western Cities: The View of Municipal Officials," p. 16.

32. Identifiable policy differences exist among local officials (both *elected* officials such as mayors and council members, and *appointed* officials such as city managers, budget officers, and finance directors) from different regions. All other factors being held constant, officials in the Frostbelt tend to be more liberal, while local officials in the Sunbelt are more conservative. Differences among officials on support or opposition to the new federalism policies of the Reagan administration for example, are best explained, as in the earlier findings of the CCRP comparative study of Bay area cities, by city *size* and (unlike the CCRP study) by *locale,* measuring, in this case, sunbelt-frostbelt residency. Locale proved to be one of the best variables accounting for differences in policy positions (frequently exceeding such other presumably important policy explanations as partisan indentification, size of city, or rate of growth). See Caputo, "Research and Practice Note—Reaganomics and Midwestern Cities: An Initial Assessment"; Caputo and Johnson, "New Federalism and Midwestern Cities: 1981–1985; "Cole and Taebel, *Attitudes of Local Officials to President Reagan's New Federalism and the Interactive Effects of Metropolitan Type, Partisan Orientations and Sunbelt-Frostbelt Distinctions,* and "Initial Atitudes of Local Officials to President Reagan's New Federalism"; and Waste and Caves, "New Federalism, Reaganomics and Western Cities: The View of Municipal Officials."

33. Abbott, *The New Urban America: Growth and Politics in Sunbelt Cities.*

4. Policy Type, Political Conflict, and City Policymaking

1. There are several models specifically designed to analyze local policymaking. An illustrative, but not exhaustive, list of such models would included the following: the life cycle model in Bryan Jones, *Governing Urban America: A Policy Focus* (Boston: Little, Brown, 1983); the allocative-developmental-redistributive model in Paul E. Peterson, *City Limits* (Chicago: University of Chicago Press, 1981); the non-decisionmaking models in Matthew Crenson, *The Unpolitics of Air Pollution* (Baltimore: Johns Hopkins University Press, 1971), and John Gaventa,

Power and Powerlessness (Urbana: University of Illinois Press, 1980); the political system model in Robert L. Lineberry and Ira Sharkansky, *Urban Politics and Public Policy,* 3rd ed. (New York: Harper & Row, 1978); the stages of decision and the hyperpluralist models in Douglas Yates, *The Ungovernable City* (Cambridge, Mass.: MIT Press, 1977); the pluralist model in Robert A. Dahl, *Who Governs?* (New Haven: Yale University Press, 1961); the elite models in G. William Domhoff, *Who Really Rules?* (Santa Monica, Calif.: Goodyear, 1978), Harvey Molotch, "The City as a Growth Machine," *American Journal of Sociology* 82 (September 1976): 309–30, and Clarence N. Stone, "Systemic Power in Community Decision Making," *American Political Science Review* (December 1980): 978–90; the policy–networks model of Heinz Eulau, "From Labyrinths to Networks: Political Representation in Urban Settings," in Robert Waste (ed.), *Community Power: Future Directions in Urban Research* (Beverly Hills, Calif.: Sage Publications, 1986), pp. 85–116; and finally, the density and diversity model set forth by Robert Eyestone in *The Threads of Public Policy: A Study in Policy Leadership* (Indianapolis: Bobbs-Merrill, 1971).

See also anthologies containing local policymaking models: James Q. Wilson, *City Politics and Public Policy* (New York: John Wiley, 1968); Willis D. Hawley, Michael Lipsky, Stanley Greenberg, J. David Greenstone, Ira Katznelson, Karen Orren, Paul E. Peterson, Martin Shefter, and Douglas Yates (eds.), *Theoretical Perspectives on Urban Politics* (Englewood Cliffs, N.J.: Prentice-Hall, 1976); and Dale Rogers Marshall (ed.), *Urban Policymaking,* Sage Yearbooks in Politics and Public Policy, Vol. 7 (Beverly Hills, Calif.: Sage Publications, 1979).

Other, more general, policy models could, in most cases with only slight modification, be usefully applied to urban or local policymaking. Among these are the following: the seven models used in Thomas R. Dye, *Understanding Public Policy* (Englewood Cliffs, N.J.: Prentice-Hall, 1984); the agenda-building model in Roger W. Cobb and Charles Elder, *Participation in American Politics: The Dynamics of Agenda-Building,* 2nd ed. (Baltimore: Johns Hopkins University Press, 1983); and the policy process models in Randall Ripley and Grace Franklin, *Policy Implementation in the United States,* 2nd ed., (Homewood, Ill.: Dorsey Press, 1986), David Easton, *A Systems Analysis of Political Life* (New York: John Wiley, 1965), James E. Anderson, *Public Policy and Politics in America* (North Scituate, Mass.: Duxbury Press, 1978), Charles O. Jones, *An Introduction to the Study of Public Policy,* 2nd ed. (North Scituate, Mass.: Duxbury Press, 1977), and Grover Starling, *The Politics and Economics of Public Policy* (Homewood, Ill.: Dorsey Press, 1979).

2. Paul Peterson, *City Limits;* James Q. Wilson, *Political Organizations* (New York: Basic Books, 1973), chapter 16, "Organizations and Public Policy," pp. 327–46; Wilson (ed.), *The Politics of Regulation* (New York: Basic Books, 1980), chapter 10, "The Politics of Regulation," pp. 357–94; and Wilson, *American Government: Institutions and Policies* (Lexington, Mass.: D. C. Heath, 1980), Part IV, "The Politics of Public Policy," pp. 409–41.

3. Cobb and Elder, *Participation in American Politics;* James S. Coleman, *Community Conflict* (New York: Free Press, 1957); Dahl, *Who Governs?;* Lewis Anthony Dexter, *Representative Versus Direct Democracy in Fighting about Taxes: Conflicting Notions of Sovereignty, Legitimacy, and Civility in Relation to*

a Tax Fight, Watertown, Massachusetts, 1953–59 (Cambridge, Mass.: Schenkman, 1983); Jones, *Governing Urban America;* John Kingdom, *Agendas, Alternatives, and Public Policies* (Boston: Little, Brown, 1984); Charles E. Lindblom, "The Science of Muddling Through," *Public Administration Review* 19 (1959): 79–88, and "Still Muddling, Not Yet Through," *Public Administration Review* (November/December 1977): 511–16, and *Politics and Markets* (New York: Basic Books, 1977); Theodore Lowi, "American Business, Public Policy, Case Studies and Political Theory," *World Politics* 16 (July 1964): 677–725, ""Four Systems of Policy, Politics, and Choice," *Public Administration Review* 32 (July/August 1972): 298–310; David Mayhew, *Congress: The Electoral Connection* (New Haven: Yale University Press, 1974); John Mollenkopf, "On the Causes and Consequences of Neighborhood Political Mobilization," a paper presented at the 1973 Annual Meeting of the American Political Science Association, New Orleans, September 4–8; Eric Nordlinger, *On the Autonomy of the Democratic State* (Cambridge, Mass.: Harvard University Press, 1981); and Aaron Wildavsky, *The Politics of the Budgetary Process,* 4th ed. (Boston: Little, Brown, 1984).

4. Peterson, *City Limits,* p. 41.

5. Ibid, p. 41.

6. Lowi, "American Business, Public Policy, Case Studies, and Political Theory," and "Four Systems of Policy, Politics, and Choice."

7. For a criticism of this position, see George D. Greenberg, Jeffrey A. Miller, Lawrence B. Mohr, and Bruce C. Vladeck, "Developing Public Policy Theory: Perspectives from Empirical Research," *American Political Science Review* (December 1977): 1532–42.

8. For an excellent account of the hyperpluralistic politics of San Francisco, in which collectively the multiple contending interest groups frequently appear stronger than the government, see Frederick Wirt, *Power in the City: Decision Making in San Francisco* (Berkeley: University of California Press, 1974).

9. Peterson, *City Limits,* p. 44.

10. Ibid., p. 43.

11. Ibid., p. 78.

12. Ibid., p. 44.

13. Michael F. Carter, "Comparable Worth: An Idea Whose Time Has Come?" *Personnel Journal* (October 1981): 792–93.

14. Ibid., p. 793.

15. "Pay Equity Plan Backed for City Workers in L.A.," San Diego *Union* (May 9, 1985), p. A-1.

16. Oliver P. Williams and Charles R. Adrian, "Community Types and Policy Differences," in James Q. Wilson (ed.), *City Politics and Public Policy* (New York: John Wiley, 1968), pp. 17–36.

17. Peterson, *City Limits,* p. 43.

18. James Q. Wilson, *Political Organizations,* and *American Government: Institutions and Policies.* See also Wilson, (ed.), *The Politics of Regulation,* chapter 16.

19. James Q. Wilson, *American Government: Institutions and Policies,* p. 419.

20. James Q. Wilson, *Political Organizations,* p. 330.

21. Ibid.

22. Ibid.

23. James Q. Wilson, *American Government: Institutions and Policies,* p. 419.

24. Ibid., p. 420.

25. Ibid.

26. Ibid.

27. The one hundred dollars per square foot figure is drawn from an interview the author conducted with urban planner and architect Kenneth Ornstein, executive director of the Providence (Rhode Island) Foundation.

28. James Q. Wilson, *American Government: Institutions and Policies,* p. 420.

29. Ibid., p. 423.

30. Coleman, *Community Conflict,* pp. 10–11.

31. It should be noted that collective bads is a term I have employed to denote the mirror image of the much more developed concept of collective goods. For a more complete discussion of collective goods, see Vincent and Elinor Ostrom, "Public Goods and Public Choices," in E. S. Savas (ed.), *Alternatives for Delivering Public Services: Toward Improved Performance* (Boulder, Colo.: Westview Press, 1978), pp. 7–49.

32. Edward B. Laverty, "Assessing and Affecting Community Power: A Blueprint for Action," *Municipal Management* 7 (Fall 1984): 55.

33. Jones, *Governing Urban America,* pp. 39–41.

34. Nordlinger, *On the Autonomy of the Democratic State.*

35. Jones, *Governing Urban America,* p. 39.

36. Nordlinger, *On the Autonomy of the Democratic State.*

37. "Rationing a Police Force," op-ed commentary article, Los Angeles *Times* (October 11, 1984), p. II-10.

38. Ibid.

39. Jones, *Governing Urban America,* pp. 39–41, 304. For more detailed explanations of incremental policymaking, see Lindblom, "The Science of Muddling Through," and "Still Muddling, Not Yet Through"; and Aaron Wildavsky, "Toward a Radical Incrementalism," in Alfred DeGrazia, *Congress: The First Branch of Government* (Washington, D.C.: American Enterprise Institute, 1966), and Wildavsky, *The Politics of the Budgetary Process.*

40. Dale Rogers Marshall and Robert Waste, *Large City Responses to the Community Development Act* (Davis: University of California, Davis–Institute of Governmental Affairs, 1977).

41. Rufus Browning, Dale Rogers Marshall, and David Tabb, *Protest Is Not Enough: The Struggle for Black and Hispanic Equality* (Berkeley: University of California Press, 1984), and "Responsiveness to Minorities: A Theory of Political Change in Cities," a paper presented at the Annual Meeting of the American Political Science Association, 1978.

42. Dale Rogers Marshall and Robert Waste, *Large City Responses to the Community Development Act.*

43. On pork barrel policymaking, see David Mayhew, *Congress: The Electoral Connection* (New Haven: Yale University Press, 1974); Donald R. Matthews, *U.S. Senators and Their World* (New York: Vintage, 1960); and D. Marvick, *A Quantitative Technique for Analyzing Congressional Alignments,* Ph.D. dissertation, Columbia University, 1960. For greater detail on the nature of collective goods, see also Norman Folich and J. A. Oppenheimer, *Modern Political Econ-*

omy (Englewood Cliffs, N.J.: Prentice-Hall, 1978); and Mancur Olson, *The Logic of Collective Action* (Cambridge, Mass.: Harvard University Press, 1965).

44. Mayhew, *Congress: The Electoral Connection;* M. Fiorina, *Congress: Keystone of the Washington Establishment* (New Haven: Yale University Press, 1977); and R. S. Erickson, "The Electoral Impact of Congressional Roll Call Voting," *American Political Science Review* 65 (December 1971): 1032.

45. David Mayhew, *Congress: The Electoral Connection,* pp. 88–89.

46. Ibid.

47. Jones, *Governing Urban America,* pp. 39–41.

48. Cobb and Elder, *Participation in American Politics.*

49. Peterson, *City Limits,* p. 41. This illustrates another problem with Peterson's otherwise strong policy typology. The politics of a developmental issue are likely to differ depending on *who pays* for the proposed development. As Wilson acknowledges, the question of who pays is as important as whether or not the city as a whole will benefit from a policy or project. A "free" project is inherently less conflict-producing and more popular than one that must be paid for with hard-earned local tax revenues.

50. For an analysis of the special advantage that business interests often have in national and local policymaking, see Lindblom, *Politics and Markets* and *The Policy-Making Process,* 2nd ed. (Englewood Cliffs, N.J.: Prentice-Hall, 1980). See also Robert A. Dahl, "Rethinking *Who Governs?:* New Haven, Revisited," in R. Waste (ed.), *Community Power: Future Directions in Urban Research,* pp. 113–15, 120–22; and, Matthew A. Crenson, "Urban Bureaucracy in Urban Politics: Notes Towards a Developmental Theory," in J. David Greenstone (ed.), *Public Values and Private Power in American Politics* (Chicago: University of Chicago Press, 1982).

Perhaps the classic work stating that small constituencies such as local governments are far easier for dominant local groups, whether business or not, to "privatize" and control is Grant McConnell, *Private Power and American Democracy* (New York: Knopf, 1966). As Peterson notes in *City Limits* (p. 90):

> McConnell has argued that the central government, with a larger constituency, can be expected to serve broader and more diffuse interests. In local government, which has a smaller constituency, it is easier for dominant economic interests to control policy to the exclusion of weaker, less well organized interests. In government with a larger constituency, the mutal checking of powerful interests and the need to build coalitions of diverse interests permit consideration of weaker, broader, more diffuse concerns, perhaps including even those of the poor.

See also J. David Greenstone, "The Public, the Private and American Democracy: Reflections on Grant McConnell's Political Science," in Greenstone (ed.), *Public Values and Private Power in American Politics,* pp. ix–xiv.

51. K. MacDonald, "Cal Tech Astronomers Win Battle Over Street Lamp Issue," *Chronicle of Higher Education* 27 (1984), p.7.

52. Michael Smolens, "City to Use Low-Pressure Streetlights," San Diego *Union* (February 7, 1984), p. A-3.

53. K. MacDonald, "Cal Tech Astronomers Win Battle Over Street Lamp Issue," p. 9.

54. "San Diego to Dim Lights for Astronomy's Sake," New York *Times* (February 8, 1984), p. 14.

55. Michael Smolens, "City to Use Low-Pressure Streetlights," San Diego *Union* (February 7, 1984) p. 1.

56. Ibid.

57. "San Diego to Dim Lights for Astronomy's Sake," New York *Times* (February 8, 1984), p. 14.

58. While it is usually possible in the short run to make such distinctions (e.g., whether or not a given policy proposal will cost the city instead of benefit it, and is redistributive in nature), I have serious doubts whether such distinctions can be drawn with any definitive clarity in the long run. For that reason, I have labeled these policy cells collective or selective *social welfare*. This labeling avoids the problem, but does not solve it. One can imagine many social welfare programs that initially cost the city, but in the long run made the city a better place to live in, benefited the city materially, or both. A workfare program that trained a welfare recipient at city expense but which later hires a now-experienced park grounds worker at an entry-level or trainee salary would be a hypothetical case in point—a traditionally classified social welfare program may simultaneously cost and benefit the city. Most income transfer programs fall into this heading.

59. "Cold Forces Homeless into Shelters; Police Take Few from Streets," New York *Times* (December 3, 1985), p. II-3.

60. Josh Barbanel, "8,084 Jam City Shelters; 157 Taken off Streets," New York *Times* (December 4, 1985), p. 1.

61. "Cold Forces Homeless into Shelters," New York *Times*, (December 3, 1985), p. II-3.

62. Ibid.

63. Josh Barbanel, "Saving Homeless from Themselves: A New Policy Creates New Disputes," New York *Times* (December 7, 1985), p. 29.

64. Yates, *The Ungovernable City*, p. 147.

65. Another reason that Koch was able to fend off challenges to his innovative approach to housing the homeless is that he was on fairly firm legal ground. In fact, recently (May 1986) the Appellate Division of the State Supreme Court in Manhattan "ruled unanimously that all homeless families are legally entitled to shelter—and that the city must adhere to state regulations requiring clean linen, window guards and other sanitary and safety measures. . . [but] the Court did say that state and local oficials have broad discretion in determining how shelter is to be provided." [emphasis added] "The Homeless Have Another Day in Court," New York Times (May 18, 1986), p. E-6.

66. Josh Barbanel, "8,084 Jam City Shelters; 157 Taken off Streets," p. 1.

67. Murray Dubin, "Homeless? Snooze and You'll Lose in Santa Barbara," San Diego *Union* (May 12, 1986), p. B-8.

68. Ibid.

69. Ibid.

70. Ibid.

71. Ibid.

72. Ibid.

73. Ibid.

74. It should be emphasized that most but not all municipal fluoridation controversies were limited to the 1950s. San Diego, for example, which twice (1954 and 1969) rejected efforts to fluoridate the public drinking water, will attempt to persuade voters to opt for fluoridation in 1988. San Antonio also rejected fluoridation in a 1985 election in which the pro-fluoridation position was defeated by 52 percent of the vote. Interestingly, region (e.g., sunbelt vs. frostbelt) seems to play a role in fluoridation disputes. Forty-one of the fifty largest U.S. cities now add fluoride to their public drinking water. Seven of the nine fluoride holdouts are in the sunbelt—San Diego, San Antonio, Los Angeles, San Jose, Phoenix, Tucson, and Honolulu. One of the remaining cities, Portland, is in the sunbelt according to one leading sunbelt analyst (Abbott), and only one, Newark, N.J., is not. While such an inquiry is outside the bounds of the current study, an analysis of municipal fluoridation decision making might well illustrate strong differences between sunbelt and frostbelt cities. See Carl Abbott, *The New Urban America: Growth and Politics in Sunbelt Cities* (Chapel Hill: University of North Carolina Press, 1981); and Cheryl Clark, "Fluoride Try Still on Tap but on Hold," San Diego *Union* (May 18, 1986), p. B-5.

75. Coleman, *Community Conflict.*

76. John H. Mollenkopf, "On the Causes and Consequences of Neighborhood Political Mobilization," and "Neighborhood Political Development and the Politics of Urban Growth: Boston and San Francisco 1958–78," *International Journal of Urban and Regional Research* 5 (1981): 17–38.

77. Paul Peterson, *School Politics: Chicago Style* (Chicago: University of Chicago Press, 1981); and J. Anthony Lukas, *Common Ground: A Turbulent Decade in the Lives of Three American Families* (New York: Knopf, 1985) for detailed and careful studies of polarization and conflict over the issue of public school integration.

78. M. Haas, "Council to Look at Sander," Chula Vista *Star News* (January 1, 1982), p. 1.

79. M. Miller, "Chula Vista Report Favors Bayfront Commercial Site," San Diego *Union* (June 17, 1982), pp. 2, 6.

80. H. Fuentes, "Council Ok's Trash Energy Plant," San Diego *Union* (June 18, 1982), p. 6.

81. L. Heywood, "SANDER's Days Numbered?" Chula Vista *Star News* (October 3, 1982), p. 1.

82. Ralph Frammolino, "City Canyon Dispute May Lead to New Growth Vote," Los Angeles *Times* (November 19, 1985), p. B-1.

83. Michael Smolens, "Mayor Sees Canyons a Development Battleground," San Diego *Union* (November 19, 1985), p. B-1.

84. Ibid.

85. Michael Smolens, "City Puts Brakes on Canyon Development," San Diego *Union* (November 27, 1985), p. B-1.

86. Ibid.

87. Ibid.

88. Ralph Frammolino, "City Council Places Cap on Building in Inner-City Canyons," Los Angeles *Times* (November 27, 1985), p. II-1.

89. Ibid.

90. Coleman, *Community Conflict.*

91. Dahl, *Who Governs?*

92. Cobb and Elder, *Participation in American Politics.*

93. Jane Jacobs, "Cities and the Wealth of Nations," *The Atlantic* 253 (March 1984): 41–66. The argument that cities are caught up in an environmental web that extends to the national and international political and socioeconomic spheres was made earlier and somewhat more eloquently by Fred Wirt in his Preface to *Power in the City.*

94. R. A. Bauer, I. de Sola Pool, and L. A. Dexter, *American Business and Public Policy* (Chicago: Aldine-Atherton, 1963.)

95. Anthony Downs, *Inside Bureaucracy* (Boston: Little, Brown, 1959), p. 212.

96. Ibid.

5.   Reform, Regulation, and City Policymaking

1. Hugh Heclo, "Issue Networks and the Executive Establishment," in Anthony King (ed.), *The New American Political System* (Washington, D.C.: American Enterprise Institute, 1978), p. 87.

2. Edward Banfield and James Q. Wilson, as quoted in James MacGregor Burns, J. W. Peltason, and Thomas E. Cronin, *State and Local Politics: Government by the People* (Englewood Cliffs, N.J.: Prentice-Hall, 1984), pp. 160–61.

3. Bryan Jones, *Governing Urban America: A Policy Focus* (Boston: Little, Brown, 1983), p. 243. See also Richard Hofstadter, *The Age of Reform: From Bryan to FDR* (New York: Knopf, 1935); and Samuel P. Hayes, "The Politics of Reform in Municipal Governments in the Reform Era," *American Journal of Sociology* (September 1968): 158–71, reprinted with the same title in Harlan H. Hahn and Charles H. Levine (eds.), *Readings in Urban Politics: Past, Present and Future* (New York: Longman, 1984), pp. 54–73.

4. See also Raymond Wolfinger, "Why Political Machines Have Not Withered Away and Other Revisionist Thoughts," *Journal of Politics* 34 (May 1972): 365–98; Kenneth Mladenka, "The Urban Bureaucracy and the Chicago Political Machine: Who Gets What and the Limits to Political Reform," *American Political Science Review* 74 (December 1980): 991–98; Elmer E. Cornwell, "Bosses, Machines and Ethnic Groups," *The Annals of the American Academy of Political and Social Science* (May 1964): 27–39; and Martin Shefter, "The Emergence of the Political Machine: An Alternative View," in Willis D. Hawley et al. (eds.), *Theoretical Perspectives on Urban Politics* (Englewood Cliffs, N.J.: Prentice-Hall, 1976), pp. 14–44.

5. See Hayes, "The Politics of Reform in Municipal Governments in the Reform Era," p. 57.

6. Ibid.

7. Ibid.

8. See Charles Brecher, "Curbing the Role of Party Regulars," New York *Times* (May 18, 1986), p. 4:6.

9. See Richard L. Engstrom and Michael D. McDonald, "The Election of Blacks to City Council: the Impact of Electoral Arrangements on the Seats/Population Relationship," *American Political Science Review* 75 (June 1981): 344–54; Thomas R. Dye and Theodore P. Robinson, "Reformism and Black Representation on City Councils," *Social Science Quarterly* (June 1978): 133–41; Albert R. Karnig, "Black Representation on City Councils," *Urban Affairs Quarterly* 12 (December 1976): 223–43; and Timothy Bledsoe and Susan Welch, "The Effect of Political Structures on the Socioeconomic Characteristics of City Council Members," *American Politics Quarterly* 13 (October 1985): 467–84.

10. Eric Nordlinger, *Decentralizing the City: A Study of Boston's Little City Halls* (Cambridge, Mass.: MIT Press, 1972).

11. See E. S. Savas, *Privatizing the Public Sector: How to Shrink Government* (Chatham, N.J.: Chatham House, 1982). See also a recent symposium on "Market Based Public Policy" in *Policy Studies Review* 5 (February 1986): 583–672, especially Michael R. Fitzgerald, "The Promise and Performance of Privatization: The Knoxville Experience," pp. 606–13.

12. See Robert Warren, Mark S. Rosentraub, and Karen S. Harlow, "Coproduction, Equity, and the Distribution of Safety," *Urban Affairs Quarterly* 19:447–64.

13. For an excellent account of metropolitan reorganization with several carefully drawn case studies, see John J. Harrigan, *Political Change in the Metropolis,* 3rd ed. (Boston: Little, Brown, 1985), especially chapter 11, "The Politics of Metropolitan Reform," pp. 308–40.

14. For an excellent summary of municipal experiments in decentralization, see Douglas Yates, "Political Innovation and Institution Building: The Experience of Decentralization Experiments," in Hawley et al. (eds.), *Theoretical Perspectives on Urban Politics,* pp. 146–75. For an analysis of budgetary decentralization in New York City, where each of the city's fifty-nine community districts is represented by a community board, see Robert F. Percorella, "Community Input and the City Budget: Geographically Based Budgeting in New York City," *Journal of Urban Affairs* 8 (Winter 1986): 57–70. See also the discussion of the decentralization option by David Caputo in *Urban America: The Policy Alternatives* (San Francisco: W. H. Freeman, 1976), pp. 215–22.

15. "Preventive Medicine for Municipal Scandals," New York *Times* (May 28, 1986), p. 4:6.

16. Marver Bernstein, *Regulating Business by Independent Commission* (Princeton: Princeton University Press, 1955), pp. 74–102. See also an earlier expression of the same basic theme in Samuel Huntington, "The Marasmus of the ICC," *Yale Law Journal* 61 (April 1952): 467–509.

17. James Q. Wilson (ed.), *The Politics of Regulation* (New York: Basic Books, 1980), p. 360. It should be emphasized that Wilson is a vigorous critic of the Bernstein clientele-capture thesis. See especially pp. 360–61. See also a second and equally telling criticism of Bernstein by Theodore Lowi, *The End of Liberalism,* 2nd ed. (New York: Norton, 1979), pp. 112–13.

18. Harmon Zeigler, *Interest Groups in American Society* (Englewood Cliffs, N.J.: Prentice-Hall, 1964), pp. 119–20.

19. Ibid, p. 119.

20. Terry M. Moe, "Regulatory Performance and Presidential Administration," *American Journal of Political Science* 26 (May 1982): 197–225. See also Kenneth J. Meier, *Regulation: Politics, Bureaucracy, and Economics* (New York: St. Martin's Press, 1985); and Frank J. Thompson and L. R. Jones, *Regulatory Policy and Practices* (New York: Praeger, 1982).

21. Meier, *Regulation: Politics, Bureaucracy and Economics,* p. 26.

22. Ibid.

23. Theodore Lowi, *The End of Liberalism.*

24. This, however, is far from the only problem with the sunset concept. As Meier points out, sunset laws, although popular, have tended to work very poorly—generally eliminating only the most marginal of agencies or agencies with no supportive clientele group. Unfortunately, as Meier notes, "even the least effective agencies have some supporters." In addition, "the sunset process is expensive. . . . Funds must be spent to analyze agency missions and performance. In Colorado, the first sunset review abolished 3 of the 13 agencies reviewed (agencies that regulated boxing, sanitarians, and shorthand reporters); this saved $11,000, but the process itself cost $212,000." Meier, *Regulation: Politics, Bureaucracy, and Economics,* p. 296. See also Alan Stone, *Regulation and Its Alternatives* (Washington, D.C.: Congressional Quarterly Press, 1982).

25. See *Brown v. Board of Education of Topeka* 347 U.S. 483 (1954); *Engel v. Vitale* 370 U.S. 421 (1962); and *Abington School District v. Schempp* 374 U.S. 203 (1963).

26. For an analysis of both Proposition 13 and Proposition 4, see David O. Sears and Jack Critin, *Tax Revolt: Something for Nothing in California* (Cambridge, Mass.: Harvard University Press, 1982).

27. See Fred Wirt, *Power in the City: Decision Making in San Francisco* (Berkeley: University of California Press, 1974). Most local government scholars have argued that cities are not isolated "islands," to paraphrase John Donne, but are strongly affected by external, particularly national and international, events. Forceful examples of this argument may be found in Paul Peterson, *City Limits* (Chicago: University of Chicago Press, 1981); and Jane Jacobs, "Cities and the Wealth of Nations," *Atlantic* 253 (March 1984): 41–66.

28. Wirt, *Power in the City,* pp. 3–4.

29. Jacobs, "Cities and the Wealth of Nations," 41–66.

30. Thomas R. Dye, *Politics in States and Communities,* 5th ed. (Englewood Cliffs, N.J.: Prentice-Hall, 1985), pp. 12–20. See also Daniel Elazar, *American Federalism: A View from the States* (New York: Thomas Y. Crowell, 1966), chapter 4; Ira Sharkansky, "The Utility of Elazar's Political Culture," *Polity* 2 (Fall 1969): 6–83; Leonard G. Ritt, "Political Cultures and Political Reform," *Publius* 4 (Winter 1974): 131–34; Raymond E. Wolfinger and John Osgood, "Political Ethos and the Structure of City Government," *American Political Science Review* 60 (June 1966): 306–26; and Roger Durand, "Ethnicity, 'Public Regardingness' and Referenda Voting," *Midwest Journal of Political Science* 16 (May 1972): 259–68.

31. R. A. Bauer, I. de Sola Pool, and L. A. Dexter, *American Business and Public Policy* (Chicago: Aldine-Atherton, 1963). See also J. David Greenstone (ed.), *Public Values and Private Power in American Politics* (Chicago: University of Chi-

cago Press, 1982), chapter 1, for the interplay between the permanent and the transient in national political culture and ideals.

32. Greenstone, *Public Values and Private Power in American Politics.*

33. Ibid. See also an illuminating analysis by Ira Katznelson of the bipolar political culture of the American working class, which is plagued, according to Katznelson, by an inherent split between workplace politics and community politics. Katznelson, *City Trenches: Urban Politics and the Patterning of Class in the United States* (New York: Pantheon, 1981).

34. Bauer et al., *American Business and Public Policy.*

6. The Fragility of City Policymaking

1. See Barbara Goldman, Daniel Friedlander, Judith Gueron, and David Long, with Gayle Hamilton and Gregory Hoerz, *California: The Demonstration of State Work/Welfare Initiatives* (New York: Manpower Demonstration Research Corporation, March 1985); and Michael Wiseman, "Workfare," *California Journal* 16 (July 1985): 289–92. See also David L. Krip, "Poverty, Welfare and Workfare: The California Work/Welfare Scheme," *The Public Interest* 83 (Spring 1986): 34–48. For a less sanguine view of workfare, see Leonard Goodwin, "Can Workfare Work?" *Public Welfare* (Fall 1981): 19–25, and *The Causes and Cures of Welfare* (Lexington, Mass.: Lexington Books, 1983), especially pp. 138–45 on the "workfare hoax."

2. Michael Harrington, *The New American Poverty* (New York: Penguin Books, 1984), p. 1. See also Benjamin I. Page, *Who Gets What from Government* (Berkeley: University of California Press, 1983).

3. Harrington, *The New American Poverty,* p. 2.

4. Ibid, p. 3.

5. There is considerable controversy as to what constitutes a successful antipoverty program. See, for example, the differing assessments of the War on Poverty in John E. Schwartz, *America's Hidden Success: A Reassessment of Twenty Years of Public Policy* (New York: Norton, 1983); and Charles Murray, *Losing Ground: American Social Policy, 1950–1980* (New York: Basic Books, 1984).

6. See also William Julius Wilson, "The Urban Underclass in Advanced Industrial Society," in Paul E. Peterson (ed.), *The New Urban Reality* (Washington, D.C.: The Brookings Institution, 1985); Ken Auletta is cited in Richard Nathan, "The Underclass—Will It Always Be with Us?", an unpublished paper delivered at the New School for Social Research, November 14, 1986. Despite President Reagan's protestations to the contrary in May 1986 that the only hungry people in America were those who didn't know where to go to find soup kitchens or government meal programs, the poor are still with us. At a gathering of high school students, the President said, "I don't believe that there is anyone that is going hungry in America simply by reason of denial or lack of ability to feed them." He noted that the real problem is "people not knowing where or how to get this help." President Reagan was both correct and incorrect in his assessment.

There are, as a staff member for the House Select Committee on Hunger concurred, "large numbers of poor people [that] are not taking advantage of federal programs designed to assist them. For example, 13.9 million, or 41% of the 33.7 million Americans eligible for food stamps are not receiving them. And more than 70% of the 20.4 million who are eligible for the Women, Infants and Children Supplemental Feeding Program are not being served." Many of these people, as President Reagan noted, don't know about or don't understand that they have a right to such assistance. This does not mean, however, that everyone who needs food receives it upon request. As a January 1986 report by the U.S. Conference of Mayors, which surveyed twenty-five cities, indicated, "the demand for emergency food in the nation's urban centers exceeds donations by an average of 17%. And in some cases, like Boston and San Francisco, that figure hits 50% and 55%, respectively." Eleanor Clift, "Reagan Blames Hunger on 'Lack of Knowledge,'" *Los Angeles Times* (March 22, 1986), p. 1.

7. Address by President Lyndon Johnson following the Watts riot, August 1965, cited in Edward Banfield, *The Unheavenly City, Revisited* (Boston: Little, Brown, 1974), p. 1. See also "Statement by the President upon Sending a Federal Team to Work with Local Officials," August 26, 1965, in *Weekly Compilation of Presidential Documents* (August–December, 1965), p. 153.

8. Joint Report of the Human Relations Commissions, City and County of Los Angeles, January 1985.

9. Paul E. Peterson, *City Limits* (Chicago: University of Chicago Press, 1981).

10. Banfield, *The Unheavenly City, Revisited*.

11. Peterson, *City Limits*.

12. Banfield, *The Unheavenly City, Revisited*.

13. Banfield's argument that urban problems such as crime and poverty may be incurable, and incurable because of the "psychologically lower class" orientation of some city residents is, to say the least, highly controversial. See, for example, Robert E. Agger, "Class, Race and Reaction: A Trivial but Dangerous Analysis," *Social Science Quarterly* 51 (March 1971); Duane Lockard, "Patent Racism," *TRANS-Action* 8 (March/April, 1971): 69–78; Irving Kristol, "The Cities: A Tale of Two Classes," *Fortune* (June 1970); Richard Sennett, "Survival of the Fattest," *New York Review of Books* (August 13, 1970). For two accounts of the Banfield controversy, see Theodore Marmor, "Banfield's 'Heresy,'" *Commentary* (July 1972): 86–88; and Patricia McLaughlin, "Is Banfield Really Diabolical?" *The Pennsylvania Gazette* 72 (November 1973): 25–30.

14. See Terry N. Clark and Lorna Crowley Ferguson, *City Money: Political Processes, Fiscal Strain, and Retrenchment* (New York: Columbia University Press, 1983); and Irene Rubin, *Running in the Red: The Political Dynamics of Urban Fiscal Stress* (Albany: State University of New York Press, 1982).

15. See John Mollenkopf, *The Contested City* (Princeton: Princeton University Press, 1983). See also William Hudson, "The New Federalism Paradox," *Policy Studies Journal* (Summer 1980): 900–05.

16. William Lunch, *The Nationalization of American Politics* (Berkeley: University of California Press, 1987).

17. Mollenkopf, *The Contested City*.

18. Ibid.

19. Schwartz, *American's Hidden Success.*

20. Mollenkopf, *The Contested City.*

21. Clark and Ferguson, *City Money;* and Rubin, *Running in the Red.* See also J. H. Carr (ed.), *Crisis and Constraint in Municipal Finance: Local Fiscal Prospects in a Period of Uncertainty* (New Brunswick, N.J.: Center for Urban Policy Research, Rutgers University, 1984).

22. George Sternlieb, "The City as Sandbox," *The Public Interest* 25 (1971): 14–21. For a more recent analysis of the price that the inflow and outflow of urban migration extracts upon American cities and their residents, see the "two cities" hypothesis presented by Sternlieb and James W. Hughes, "Back to the Central City: Myths and Realities," in Sternlieb and Hughes (eds.), *America's Housing: Prospects and Problems* (New Brunswick, N.J.: Center for Urban Policy and Research, Rutgers University, 1980).

23. William James, *Pragmatism: A New Name for Some Old Ways of Thinking* (New York: Longmans, Green, 1902). See also F.C.S. Schiller, "William James and the Making of Pragmatism," *Personalist* 8 (1927): 81–93; and Daniel Boorstin, *The Genius of American Politics* (Chicago: University of Chicago Press, 1953).

Glossary

This glossary defines several of the terms used in this book. The chapter number in which the term or concept is discussed is bracketed at the end of each definition. In many cases the name of the scholar primarily associated with the term or concept appears within parentheses following the chapter citation.

acute versus incubatory policy: Nelson Polsby has distinguished between Type A (acute) policies, which are treated as emergencies and require rapid action from policymakers, and Type B (incubatory) policies, which require a lengthy gestation period prior to enactment. [2] (Polsby)

allocational, developmental, and redistributive policy: Paul Peterson has distinguished three basic types of city policy: (1) allocational—those policies that are housekeeping in nature and involve little controversy, (2) developmental—those aimed at strengthening the local economy and which may from time to time generate controversy, and (3) redistributive—those policies involving the spending of funds to help a specific subset of the city's population, such as the poor or homeless, and generate more controversey. [4] (Peterson)

autonomous, pork-barrel, conventional, redistributive, and intrustive policy issues: In this book, five types of policy issues are discussed: (1) autonomous policymaking, which, like the allocational policy type of Peterson, involves housekeeping concerns such as staffing and the logistics for the police department, fire stations, or sanitation; (2) pork-barrel issues, which involve policies or programs that benefit all or most members of the community; (3) conventional issues, involving policies and programs that have advantages and disadvantages for the community; (4) redistributive issues, the same category developed by Peterson, involving social welfare programs to help the less fortunate in the community; and (5) intrusive issues, involving policies or programs viewed as harmful or mostly harmful, creating discord and acrimonious politics. [4]

ballot-box planning: Increasingly, in local governments that use initiative and referendum, planning policies are being determined by voters at elections rather than by city councils, planning commissions, or professional staff in planning departments. [1] (Orman)

client politics, majoritarian politics, entrepreneurial politics, and interest group politics: James Q. Wilson divides public policies into four camps: (1) client politics, in which the proposed costs are widely distributed and benefits will be highly concentrated; (2) majoritarian politics, in which both the proposed costs and benefits are widely distributed; (3) entrepreneurial politics, with highly concentrated costs and widely distributed benefits; and (4) interest group politics, with highly concentrated costs and highly concentrated benefits. [4] (Wilson, 1973; 1977)

coercive power, exchange power, and symbolic power: Kenneth Boulding believes groups and individuals exercise three kinds of power—the ability to force a change due to having overwhelming resources, the ability to trade favors in exchange for a desired policy outcome, and the ability to bestow legitimacy or credibility on public policymakers, individuals, groups, or policies. [1] (Boulding)

conflict escalation: James S. Coleman has described a seven-step pattern of community discord. According to Coleman, conflict: (1) begins with a specific problem, (2) which can lead to a disruption of the normal equilibrium in community relations, (3) which in turn escalates when new issues are introduced, and may (4) cause political debate to become acrimonious in character if personal antagonisms emerge between parties to the conflict, leading to (5) each side painting opponents in terms that appear totally bad to the opposing camp, leading in turn to (6) charges leveled against the opponent as a bad person, and possibly resulting in (7) a situation in which the new dispute becomes independent of the initial disagreement. [3, 4] (Coleman)

collective goods/bads: Collective goods are policies, projects, or programs—such as a new non-polluting industry for a city or a new military base located near a city—viewed as benefiting all the members of a community. Collective bads are the reverse—the policy, project, or program is viewed as harmful and intrusive. [4] (Mollenkopf)

commission government: This is a form of city government in which council members and the mayor each have direct day-to-day responsibility for running one or more city departments. [1]

containment mechanism: This is an event, action, or strategy that has the effect of delaying or defeating a given policy proposal. Containment mechanisms such as blue-ribbon commissions may also be used by policymakers to build support for or contain opposition to a controversial policy proposal. [2] (Cobb and Elder)

coproduction: This is a policy whereby one or more municipalities join together to deliver city services, such as road maintenance or garbage collection. [5] (Warren, Rosentraub, and Harlow)

ecological power: This refers to the ability of a group or individual to secure a new or changed policy not desired by other individuals or groups in a community. [1] (Stone)

ecology of city policymaking: Policymaking in all American cities is influenced by ten key variables which, collectively, comprise a policy system, or policymaking ecology. These ten elements of cities are: (1) age, (2) locale, (3) the growth process and the rate of growth, (4) the local political culture, (5) the personality of key policy actors, (6) the presence of scandals and political reform movements, (7) the type of policy conflict surrounding a given issue, (8) the type of policy being proposed, (9) the ebb and flow of regulatory activity in the city in question, and (10) the affect of exogenous factors and intergovernmental relations. [1]

effective access: Individuals or groups have differing degrees of access to the political arena. Generally those with more social status, higher incomes, and better organization will have greater access than those with less of these key variables. [1] (Truman)

federalism: This refers to the division of government authority into national and subnational units, with each unit having a genuine measure of power and political authority. [1]

fiscal conservative: This describes the views of a person with an inclination to view additional government spending skeptically and to seek ways to reduce the scope and scale of spending in the public sector. [2]

frostbelt cities: Frostbelt cities are those located north of a line drawn, roughly, from Richmond, Virginia, to San Francisco, California. They are frequently characterized by: (1) weak local economies, often due to a once-strong but now troubled heavy industrial base, (2) population emigration, resulting in a decreasing tax base, and (3) increasingly serious infrastructure costs and problems, often associated with the age of the city itself and the severity of winter conditions. [3]

full-service city: Full-service cities, as opposed to Lakewood Plan cities, provide a wide range of services to residents by establishing and funding city departments and city mechanisms to perform these services. [3]

go/no go policy: This refers to a project that must be done entirely or not done at all; it is not subject to the normal pluralistic forces of bargaining and compromise. [1] (Schulman)

hyperpluralism: Pluralism is the belief that public policy is the result of the pull and tug of multiple interest groups and individuals in society. Hyperpluralism is a special case of pluralism in which the interest groups and individuals making demands on government are stronger than the government policymaking body, creating a chaotic and frequently paralyzed policy scenario. [2] (Lineberry; Waste, 1986; Wirt; Yates)

ideology of the times: This is the prevailing national mood that characterizes a given period. Thus historians speak of the Depression mentality of the 1930s, the war mentality of the 1940s, the quiet 1950s, the activism of the 1960s, the 1970s "me-generation," and so forth. Bauer, Sola Pool, and Dexter have used this term to describe the prevailing set of beliefs among national policymakers that characterizes a given issue, for example, in the 1950s Congress viewed tariffs as a means of protecting domestic producers but in the 1960s tariffs were viewed in Congress as an instrument of foreign policy. [1] (Bauer, Sola Pool, and Dexter)

incremental policy: This is an approach to public policymaking which argues that policymaking occurs incrementally and is noncomprehensive, involving successive comparisons to or an extensive reliance on past behavior as a guide to current behavior. It is characterized by pluralist politics designed to suffice or satisfice, rather than maximize, services or goals. [1] (Lindblom, 1959, 1979; Wildavsky, 1984, 1988)

initiative, referendum and recall elections: Introduced in South Dakota in 1898, initiative elections force a vote on public issues if a specified number of voters—usually 5–10%—sign a petition to place the measure on the ballot. Twenty-one states and the District of Columbia permit initiative elections at the state or local level. All but two of these states (Maine and Mississippi) are west of the Mississippi River.

In a referendum election, a state or local legislative body may put a question of public policy on the ballot to determine the will of the electorate. Thirty-seven states, including Connecticut and New York, have provisions allowing referendum elections.

Several states and local governments also provide for recall elections in which a specified number of voters—typically 20–30%—can, by signing a petition, force an election to determine whether an elected official should be removed from office.

Initiative and referendum elections are becoming increasingly important in land use and growth policy decisions in the West. As Iver Peterson noted in a recent New York *Times* article, "In California, where the practice is most advanced, there have been 69 no-growth or slow-growth issues on state or local ballots since 1971, 28 of them in 1986 alone, according to a survey by the Urban Land Institute." (Iver Peterson, 1988; see also Orman, 1984).

interest groups: These are temporary or permanent coalitions seeking a common objective from government policymakers. [1]

iron triangle: This refers to a three-sided policy subgovernment, composed of client groups, a policymaking body with budgetary and review authority, and a government agency. [1] (Cater)

issue network: This expands the concept of an iron triangle and is meant to convey the complex patterns of interaction among policymakers, agencies, and clients, which often includes far more than three sides or sets of actors. [1] (Heclo)

Lakewood Plan city: Named after one of the first cities to pioneer this approach, the Lakwood Plan refers to a policy in which a city offers few services directly to its citizens, preferring to contract out such essential public services as police and fire protection, sanitation, and street repair to other public and private entities. [3]

life cycle of new city council: New city councils go through an identifiable pattern of growth, or a life cycle, that includes the following stages: (1) birth, (2) early dominance by zealots and advocates, (3) a struggle for autonomy, (4) a struggle for support, (5) rapid expansion, (6) a period of expanding city services, (7) a decline as the early enthusiastic members leave and are replaced by conservers, and—improbably—(8) death. [3] (Downs; Waste; 1983)

local federalism: This refers to the division of local government authority into several units (e.g., cities, counties, special districts, regional governments), each with a genuine measure of power and political authority. [1]

mandated city programs: Cities are often ordered to undertake certain programs—water or sewage treatment, equal employment hiring, or mental health programs—by the county, state, or federal governments. Because they are ordered to do so, these programs are referred to as "mandated" programs, a reference to the Latin verb *mandare,* meaning "to order."

mature city council: City councils in cities that have been incorporated for ten or more years tend to exhibit several characteristics, including: (1) a well-developed policy orientation, such as amenity provider, caretaker, booster, or arbiter councils; (2) low voter enthusiasm combined with long tenures for incumbents, and (3) the troubling possibility, as Susan B. Hansen has noted, of policy nonconcurrence between elected policymakers and the general citizenry. [3] (Hansen; Prewitt; Williams and Adrian)

mayor–council government: In *strong mayor–council governments,* the mayor is elected in a citywide election while the council members are elected from districts. The mayor has the advantage of hiring and firing department heads, vetoing legislation, and appointing council members as members or chairs of key council committees. In *weak mayor–council governments,* the mayor is a council member selected by his or her peers to serve a brief term as mayor. Weak mayors share appointment and hiring powers with the full council and do not possess veto powers. [1]

mayor–council–manager government: In this governmental form, the mayor and council are both weaker than in either the strong or weak mayor–council form of government, because the authority to hire and fire department heads and the day-to-day management of the city is assigned to a city manager hired by the council. In theory, the mayor and the council set policy, while professional administrators manage the day-to-day affairs of the city. In reality, this distinction between politics and administration is less clear-cut. [1]

monopsony: A situation in which there is one seller (the city) and only a limited number of buyers. A common example of an urban monopsony would be the limited numbers of developers able to put together the capital and planning/construction resources to build a major urban redevelopment project. Because the city wishes to build the project and there are only a few developers willing or able to build it, the political economy of the situation is unique. Monopsonies are notably different from classical monopolies, in which there is only one seller and several qualified buyers.

nationalization: This is used to refer to the increasing tendency of the federal government to set the agenda of state and local governments. [1] (Lunch)

New England town meeting government: This is a form of city government in which citizens have a legal right to meet in assembly at least once a year to approve or disapprove the town budget. Many towns have several town meetings a year, depending on the number of issues considered serious enough to warrant calling a town meeting. One small

Rhode Island town studied by the author in the early 1980s had four meetings in one year to consider, in turn, the town budget, a government loan to renovate the town hall, a state highway project widening roads in the town, and an infestation of gypsy moths threatening local agriculture. [1] (Waste, 1987)

off-cycle policymaking: Most of the decision making for a city takes place out of the public view, or off-cycle. This exercise of power by city bureaucrats or by elected officials usually covers logistical decisions to be made in a city, such as staffing of police departments. [2] (Jones)

policy concurrence: City policymakers may agree, or concur, with voters and the general citizenry, or they may not. Susan Hansen has argued that cities with strong political parties where officeholders face active challenges tend to have a higher level of policy concurrence than cities without these characteristics. [3] (Hansen)

policy displacement: This refers to the instance when an event or policy overshadows an earlier policy and—at least temporarily—replaces the earlier policy as a topic on the public agenda. [2]

policy entrepreneur: This refers to an individual who is instrumental in "selling" a program or policy to a policymaking body. Such individuals may be inside government, such as New York city planner Robert Moses, the city bureaucrats discussed by Browning, Marshall and Tabb, or they be outside actors such as Howard Jarvis, Ralph Nader, or the Reverend Jerry Falwell. Policy entrepreneurs are skilled at quickly taking advantage of triggering events or of planning and causing desired triggering events. [2] (Caro; Lewis)

policy life cycle: Public policy goes through an identifiable growth pattern or life cycle, which includes the following stages: (1) a shift from condition to issue, (2) placement on the public agenda, (3) policy formulation and reformulation, (4) placement on the formal agenda of government, (5) enactment, (6) implementation, (7) an impact phase, (8) evaluation, and (9) termination or feedback into one of the earlier stages. [2]

political culture: This is a set of beliefs and attitudes that characterize a given place or group of people. [1]

political ethos: This is the tendency of citizens in a given locale to view the world in either "public-regarding" or "private-regarding" terms. Public-regarding beliefs, associated primarily with governments west of the Mississippi, hold that government should be reformist in character, abiding by abstract principles of neutrality and nonpartisanship. Citizens in such cities tend to believe in the efficacy of a mayor–council–manager form of government, the value of nonpartisan elections, the need for at-large elections, large council districts, and a civil service-based city employment system. Private-regarding beliefs, associated primarily with cities in the eastern and midwestern United States, hold that government should be regarded as an institution whose primary emphasis should be on supporting, often through the use of patronage jobs, as many citizens as economically feasible. Citizens in such cities frequently believe in a strong mayor form of government, partisan elections, ward instead of at-large council districts, and a small or no civil service employment system for municipal employees. [1] (Banfield and Wilson; Hennessy; Wolfinger and Field)

privatization: This is the process of contracting out to the private sector the performance of services such as road repair or garbage collection, which are normally carried out by city departments. [5] (Savas)

psychological outlooks of bureaucratic personnel: Anthony Downs has presented five types of people that compose public agencies: (1) climbers, who are oriented to personal gain and professional and political opportunity; (2) conservers, who seek primarily to maintain the status quo; (3) zealots, who have a narrow loyalty to a special cause or policy; (4) statesmen, who have a broad loyalty to society as a whole; and (5) advocates, who have a genuine belief in the worth of the agency and the mission which the agency is assigned to accomplish. [3] (Downs)

public policy: This covers the actions, commitments, or expenditures of elected or appointed public officials. [1] (Gerston)

rational-comprehensive policy: This is an approach to public policymaking that seeks to be rigorously scientific and neutral, and which contends that all policy proposals should be evaluated professionally and neutrally in every respect each time that such policies are under consideration. [1] (Dror)

reference publics: These are third parties who may be drawn into a policy dispute to aid groups unable to successfully articulate their needs to policymakers. [1] (Lipsky)

reform city government: Progressive Era reforms in many cities, notably in those west of the Mississippi River, resulted in reformed cities, featuring: (1) weak mayor–council or mayor–council–manager forms of government, (2) nonpartisan elections and weak political parties, (3) civil service hiring procedures for city employees, and (4) the potential for more grass-roots influence on city policymakers through the use of ballot initiatives, referenda, and recall elections. [1]

salience: This is the intensity citizens may or may not feel for a given policy area or proposal. [2]

satisfice: The term is a combination of "satisfy" and "suffice," used to denote the fact that public policymakers must often make do with less than perfect options and results. [1] (Simon)

slack resources: This refers to the phenomenon when low-resource groups may sometimes have a greater impact than their numbers or lack of funds might suggest due to their willingness to "pull up the slack," to use all of their available resources in one tightly directed effort to influence policymakers. [1] (Dahl)

substantive policy: This covers policy concerned with such bread-and-butter issues as the economy and war and peace at the national level, and at the local level large expenditures of money, schools, crime, and highways. [1]

sunbelt city: Kevin Phillips coined the term "sunbelt" to describe a region of the United States south of a line drawn, roughly, from Richmond, Virginia, to San Francisco, California. The area south of this line is generally considered more politically conservative than the area north of the line. The northern area has also been referred to as the frostbelt or rustbelt. Sunbelt cities are characterized by political conservativism; strong local economies, often based on defense industries and military bases; university and research centers located in or near them; strong population growth pressures; and a growing political unrest between residents of newer suburbs and supporters of downtown or core city commercial and residential revitalization. [3] (Abbott; Bernard and Rice; Phillips)

sunset law: Believed by many to be a safeguard against the apparently inherent degeneration of regulatory agencies, sunset laws provide a specific timetable—generally from five to ten years after the creation of a public agency—for the death of an agency if it cannot be shown to have produced a definite public benefit. Without a convincing showing of benefit, the "sun will set" on the agency in question. [3]

symbolic policy: This is policy concerned primarily with the manipulation of emotions and beliefs, usually those deeply held. Rarely involving the expenditure of large amounts of money, such policy is meant to give the impression that something significant is being done, when, in fact, the action is primarily window dressing rather than substantive. [1] (Edleman)

triggering device: This is an event that converts a widely held routine perception of a public "condition" into a newly perceived public "issue." Triggering mechanisms differ in scope, intensity, and whether their origins are internal or external to the city. [2] (Cobb and Elder)

types of city councils: Williams and Adrian have distinguished among cities with four different policy orientations of cities: (1) amenity providers are those cities with councils that concentrate on providing key services such as police, fire protection, and recreation, occasionally adding a new service when, in their opinion, it is needed; (2) caretaker cities focus on adding few, if any, new services and on making minor adjustments to existing service levels; (3) booster cities have councils that champion cultural and economic development for the city; and (4) broker or arbiter cities have councils that serve as referees for important community disputes and play a role as facilitators and conciliators. [3] (Williams and Adrian)

unanticipated consequences: Murphy's Law states that if anything can go wrong, it will. Unanticipated consequences are the many things, both positive and negative, not envisioned by policymakers, that will crop up once implementation of a project has begun. [1]

urban conditions versus urban problems: Edward Banfield has drawn a useful distinction between city facts of life—conditions—and city concerns with sufficient influence on daily life—problems—that citizens are willing to tax themselves for to pay for their solution. [2] (Banfield, 1970, 1974)

voluntarism: Kenneth Prewitt has correctly observed that mature city councils are often characterized by a "norm of volunteerism." This means city election turnouts are generally low, averaging 30 percent of the registered voters or less, and council incumbents rarely lose reelection efforts. This lack of interest in local elections, combined with apparent long-term job stability for incumbents, allows the incumbents to choose when they leave the council; they volunteer to leave as opposed to voters forcing them off after an unpopular decision. This serves to insulate council members from their constituencies and makes them largely independent of election threats and voter challenges. [3] (Prewitt)

zero-sum policy: This refers to a policy whereby policymakers must accept all of a proposal or reject it entirely. [1]

Bibliography

The following are key books, articles or sources used in the current study of city policymaking.

Abbott, Carl. 1981. *The New Urban America: Growth and Politics in Sunbelt Cities.* Chapel Hill: University of North Carolina Press.

Banfield, Edward. 1970. *The Unheavenly City.* Boston: Little, Brown.

———. 1974. *The Unheavenly City, Revisited.* Boston: Little, Brown.

———, and James Q. Wilson. 1963. *City Politics.* Cambridge: Harvard and MIT Press.

———. 1964. "Public Regardingness as a Value Premise in Voting Behavior." *American Political Science Review* 58 (December): 876–87.

Bauer, R. A., I. de Sola Pool, and Lewis A. Dexter. 1963. *American Business and Public Policy.* Chicago: Aldine-Atherton.

Bernard, Richard M., and Bradley R. Rice (eds). 1983. *Sunbelt Cities: Politics and Growth Since World War II.* Austin: University of Texas Press.

Bernstin, Marver. 1955. *Regulating Business by Independent Commission.* Princeton: Princeton University Press.

Blesdoe, Timothy, and Susan Welch. 1985. "The Effect of Political Structures on the Socioeconomic Characteristics of City Council Members." *American Politics Quarterly* 13 (October): 467–84.

Boorstin, Daniel. 1953. *The Genuis of American Politics.* Chicago: University of Chicago Press.

Boulding, Kenneth. 1970. *Primer on Social Dynamics.* New York: Free Press.

Browning, Rufus, Dale Marshall, and David Tabb. 1984. *Protest is Not*

Enough: The Struggle for Black and Hispanic Equality in Cities. Berkeley: University of California Press.

Caputo, David. 1976. *Urban America: The Policy Alternatives.* San Francisco: W. H. Freeman.

Caro, Robert. 1975. *The Power Broker: Robert Moses and the Fall of New York City.* New York: Vintage.

Carter, Michael F. 1981. "Comparable Worth: An Idea Whose Time Has Come." *Personnel Journal* 60 (October): 792–93.

Cater, Douglas. 1964. *Power in Washington.* New York: Vintage.

Clark, Terry N., and Lorna C. Ferguson. 1983. *City Money: Political Processes, Fiscal Strain and Retrenchment.* New York: Columbia University Press.

Cobb, Roger W., and Charles D. Elder. 1983. *Participation in American Politics: The Dynamics of Agenda-Building.* 2nd ed. Baltimore: Johns Hopkins University Press.

Cole, Richard L., and David A. Taebel. 1981. *Attitudes of Local Officials to President Reagan's New Federalism and the Interactive Effects of Metropolitan Type, Partisan Orientations, and Sunbelt-Frostbelt Distinctions.* Arlington: University of Texas at Arlington, Institute of Urban Studies.

———. 1983. "Initial Attitudes of Local Officials to President Reagan's New Federalism." *Journal of Urban Affairs* 5 (Winter): 57–78.

Coleman, James S. 1957. *Community Conflict.* New York: Free Press.

Cornwell, Elmer, E. 1964. "Bosses, Machines and Ethnic Groups." *The Annals of the American Academy of Political and Social Science* (May): 27–39.

Crenson, Matthew. 1971. *The Unpolitics of Air Pollution.* Baltimore: Johns Hopkins University Press.

Dahl, Robert. 1961. *Who Governs?* New Haven: Yale University Press.

DeGrazia, Alfred. 1966. *Congress: The First Branch of Government.* Washington, D.C.: American Enterprise Institute.

Dexter, Lewis Anthony. 1983. *Representative versus Direct Democracy in Fighting about Taxes: Conflicting Notions of Sovereignty, Legitimacy, and Civility in Relation to a Tax Fight: Watertown, Massachusetts, 1953–59.* Cambridge, Mass.: Schenkman.

Domhoff, G. William. 1978. *Who Really Rules?* Santa Monica, Calif.: Goodyear.

Downs, Anthony. 1959. *Inside Bureaucracy.* Boston: Little, Brown.

Dror, Yzehekyl. 1968. *Public Policy-Making Re-examined.* San Francisco: Chandler.

Durand, Roger. 1972. "Ethnicity, 'Public Regardingness,' and Referenda Voting." *Midwest Journal of Political Science* 16 (May): 259–68.

Dye, Thomas R. 1985. *Politics in States and Communities,* 5th ed. Englewood Cliffs, N.J.: Prentice-Hall.

———. 1987. *Understanding Public Policy.* 6th ed. Englewood Cliffs, N.J.: Prentice-Hall.

———, and Theodore P. Robinson. 1978. "Reformism and Black Representation on City Councils." *Social Science Quarterly* 59 (June): 133–41.

Easton, David. 1965. *A System Analysis of Political Life.* New York: John Wiley.

Edleman, Murray. 1964. *The Symbolic Uses of Politics.* Urbana: University of Illinois Press.

Elazar, Daniel. 1966. *American Federalism: A View from the States.* New York: Thomas Y. Crowell.

Engstrom, Richard L., and Michael D. McDonald. 1981. "The Election of Blacks to City Council: The Impact of Electoral Arrangements on the Seats/Population Relationship." *American Political Science Review* 75 (June): 344–54.

Eyestone, Robert. 1971. *The Threads of Public Policy: A Study in Policy Leadership.* Indianapolis, Ind.: Bobbs-Merrill.

———. 1978. *From Social Issues to Public Policy.* New York: John Wiley.

———. (ed). 1984. *Public Policy Formation.* Greenwich, Conn.: JAI Press.

Erickson, Robert, S. 1971. "The Electoral Impact of Congressional Roll Call Voting." *American Political Science Review* 65 (December): 1018–32.

Fiorina, Morris. 1977. *Congress: Keystone of the Washington Establishment.* New Haven: Yale University Press.

Freeman, J. Leiper. 1965. *The Political Process.* New York: Random House.

Frolich, Norman, and J. A. Oppenheimer. 1978. *Modern Political Economy.* Englewood Cliffs, N.J.: Prentice-Hall.

Gaventa, John. 1980. *Power and Powerlessness.* Urbana: University of Illinois Press.

Gerston, Larry N. 1983. *Making Public Policy: From Conflict to Resolution.* Glenview, Ill.: Scott, Foresman.

Goldman, Barbara, Daniel Friedlandler, Judith Gueron, and David Long, with Gayle Hamilton and Gregory Hoerz. 1985. *California: The Demonstration of State Work/Welfare Initiatives.* New York: Manpower Demonstration Research Corporation. (March).

Goodwin, Leonard. 1981. "Can Workfare Work?" *Public Welfare* 39 (Fall): 19–25.

————. 1985. *The Causes and Cures of Welfare.* Lexington, Mass.: Lexington Books.

Greenberg, George D., Jeffrey A. Miller, Lawrence B. Mohr, and Bruce C. Vladeck. 1977. "Developing Public Policy Theory: Perspectives from Empirical Research." *American Political Science Review* 72 (December): 1532–42.

Greenstone, J. David. (ed). 1983. *Public Values and Private Power in American Politics.* Chicago: University of Chicago Press.

Hansen, Susan. 1975. "Participation, Political Structures, and Concurrence." *American Political Science Review* 70 (December): 1181–99.

Harrigan, John J. 1985. *Political Change in the Metropolis.* 3rd ed. Boston: Little, Brown.

Harrington, Michael. 1984. *The New American Poverty.* New York: Penguin Books.

Hayes, Samuel P. 1964. "The Politics of Reform in Municipal Governments in the Reform Era." *Pacific Northwest Quarterly* 55 (October): 157–89.

Heclo, Hugh. 1978. "Issue Networks and the Executive Establishment." In Anthony King (ed.). *The New Political System.* Washington, D.C.: American Enterprise Institute.

Hennessy, Tim. 1970. "Problems in Concept Formation: The 'Ethos' Theory and the Comparative Study of Urban Politics." *Midwest Journal of Political Science* 15 (November): 537–64.

Hofstadter, Richard. 1935. *The Age of Reform: From Bryan to FDR.* New York: Knopf.

Hudson, William. 1980. "The New Federalism Paradox." *Policy Studies Journal* 8 (Summer): 900–905.

Jacobs, Jane. 1984. "Cities and the Wealth of Nations." *Atlantic* 253 (March): 41–66.

James, William. 1902. *Pragmatism: A New Name for Some Old Ways of Thinking.* New York: Longmans, Green.

Jones, Bryan. 1983. *Governing Urban America: A Policy Focus.* Boston: Little, Brown.

Jones, Charles O. 1977. *An Introduction to the Study of Public Policy.* 2nd ed. North Scituate, Mass.: Duxbury Press.

Karnig, Albert R. 1976. "Black Representation on City Councils." *Urban Affairs Quarterly* 12 (December): 223–43.

Katznelson, Ira. 1981. *City Trenches: Urban Politics and the Patterning of Class in the United States.* New York: Pantheon.

Kingdom, John. 1984. *Agendas, Alternatives and Public Policies.* Boston: Little, Brown.

Kirp, David L. 1986. "Poverty, Welfare and Workfare: The California Work/Welfare Scheme." *The Public Interest* 83 (Spring): 34–48.

Laverty, Edward B. 1984. "Assessing and Affecting Community Power: A Blueprint for Action." *Municipal Management* 7 (Fall): 55–60.

Lewis, Eugene. 1980. *Public Entrepreneurship: Toward a Theory of Bureaucratic Political Power: The Organizational Lives of Hyman Rickover, J. Edgar Hoover, and Robert Moses.* Bloomington: Indiana University Press.

Lindblom, Charles E. 1959. "The Science of Muddling Through." *Public Administration Review* 19 (Spring): 79–88.

———. 1977. *Politics and Markets.* New York: Basic Books.

———. 1979. "Still Muddling, Not Yet Through." *Public Administration Review* 39 (November/December): 511–16.

———. 1980. *The Policymaking Process.* 2nd ed. Englewood Cliffs, N.J.: Prentice-Hall.

Lineberry, Robert L., and Ira Sharkansky. 1978. *Urban Politics and Public Policy.* 3rd ed. New York: Harper & Row.

Lineberry, Robert L. 1980. *Government in America: People, Politics, and Policy.* Boston: Little, Brown.

Lipsky, Michael. 1970. *Protest in City Politics.* Chicago: Rand McNally.

Lowi, Theodore. 1964. "American Business, Public Policy, Case Studies and Political Theory." *World Politics* 16 (July): 677–725.

———. 1972. "Four Systems of Policy, Politics, and Choice." *Public Administration Review* 32 (July/August): 298–310.

———. 1979. *The End of Liberalism.* 2nd ed. New York: Norton.

Lukas, J. Anthony. 1985. *Common Ground: A Turbulent Decade in the Lives of Three American Families.* New York: Knopf.

Lunch, William. 1987. *The Nationalization of American Politics.* Berkeley: University of California Press.

Marshall, Dale Rogers (ed.). 1979. *Urban Policymaking.* Beverly Hills, Calif.: Sage Publications.

———, and Robert J. Waste. 1977. *Large City Responses to the Community Development Act.* Davis: University of California, Davis—Institute of Governmental Affairs.

Marvick, Dwayne. 1960. "A Quantitative Technique for Analyzing Congressional Alignments." Ph.D. diss., Columbia University.

Matthews, Donald R. 1960. *U.S. Senators and Their World.* New York: Vintage.

Mayhew, David. 1974. *Congress: The Electoral Connection.* New Haven: Yale University Press.

McConnell, Grant. 1966. *Private Power and American Democracy.* New York: Knopf.

Meir, Kenneth J. 1985. *Regulation: Politics, Bureaucracy, and Economics.* New York: St. Martin's.

Miller, Gary. 1981. *Cities by Contract: The Politics of Municipal Incorporation.* Cambridge: MIT Press.

Mladenka, Kenneth. 1980. "The Urban Bureaucracy and the Chicago Political Machine: Who Gets What and the Limits to Political Reform." *American Political Science Review* 74 (December): 991–98.

Moe, Terry M. 1982. "Regulatory Performance and Presidential Administration." *American Journal of Political Science* 26 (May): 197–225.

Mollenkopf, John. 1973. "On the Causes and Consequences of Neighborhood Political Mobilization." A paper presented at the 1973 annual meeting of the American Political Science Association, September 4–8, New Orleans.

———. 1983. *The Contested City.* Princeton: Princeton University Press.

Molotch, Harvey. 1976. "The City as Growth Machine." *American Journal of Sociology* 82 (September): 309–30.

———. 1979. "Capital and Neighborhood in the United States." *Urban Affairs Quarterly* 14 (March): 289–312.

———. 1984. "Romantic Marxism: Love Is Still Not Enough." *Contemporary Sociology* 13 (March): 141–43.

Murray, Charles. 1984. *Losing Ground: American Social Policy, 1950–1980.* New York: Basic Books.

Nathan, Richard. 1986. "The Underclass: Will It Always Be with Us?" A paper presented at the New School for Social Research, November 14, 1986, New York City.

Nordlinger, Eric. 1981. *On the Autonomy of the Democratic State.* Cambridge: Harvard University Press.

Olson, Mancur. 1965. *The Logic of Collective Action.* Cambridge: Harvard University Press.

Orman, Larry. 1984. "Ballot-Box Planning: The Boom in Electoral Land Use Control." Berkeley: Institute of Governmental Studies.

Page, Benjamin. 1983. *Who Gets What from Government.* Berkeley: University of California Press.

Percorella, Robert F. 1986. "Community Input and the City Budget: Geographically Based Budgeting in New York City." *Journal of Urban Affairs* 8 (Winter): 57–70.

Perry, David C., and Alfred J. Watkins (eds.). 1977. *The Rise of Sunbelt Cities.* Vol. 14. Urban Affairs Annual Reviews. Beverly Hills, Calif.: Sage Publications.

Peterson, Iver. 1988. "Land Use Decisions via the Ballot Box." New York *Times,* May 22, 1988, 8-1.

Peterson, Paul. 1976. *School Politics: Chicago Style.* Chicago: University of Chicago Press.

———. 1981. *City Limits.* Chicago: University of Chicago Press.

Phillips, Kevin. 1969. *The Emerging Republican Majority.* New Rochelle, N.Y.: Arlington House.

Polsby, Nelson W. 1960. "How to Study Community Power: The Pluralist Alternative." *Journal of Politics* 22 (August): 474–84.

———. 1980. *Community Power and Political Theory.* 2nd ed. New Haven: Yale University Press.

———. 1984. *Political Innovation in America: The Politics of Policy Innovation.* New Haven: Yale University Press.

Prewitt, Kenneth. 1970. "Political Ambitions, Volunteerism, and Electoral Accountability." *American Political Science Review* 64 (March): 5–17.

Rakove, Milton. 1975. *Don't Make No Waves, Don't Back No Losers.* Bloomington: Indiana University Press.

Reagan, Michael D., and John Sanzone. 1980. *The New Federalism.* 2nd ed. New York: Oxford University Press.

Ripley, Randall, and Grace Franklin. 1984. *Congress, the Bureaucracy and Public Policy.* 3rd ed. Homewood, Ill.: Dorsey Press.

———. 1986. *Policy Implementation in the United States.* 2nd ed. Homewood, Ill.: Dorsey Press.

Ritt, Leonard G. 1974. "Political Culture and Political Reform." *Publius* 4 (Winter): 131–34.

Rubin, Irene S. 1982. *Running in the Red: The Political Dynamics of Urban Fiscal Stress.* Albany: SUNY Press.

Savas, E. S. (ed.). 1978. *Alternatives for Delivering Public Services: Toward Improved Performance.* Boulder, Colo.: Westview Press.

———. 1982. *Privatizing the Public Sector: How to Shrink Government.* Chatham, N.J.: Chatham House.

———. 1987. *Privatization: The Key to Better Government.* Chatham, N.J.: Chatham House.

Schulman, Paul. 1980. *Large-Scale Policymaking.* New York: Elsevier.

Schiller, F.C.S. 1927. "William James and the Making of Pragmatism." *Personalist* 8: 81–93.

Schwartz, John E. 1983. *America's Hidden Success: A Reassessment of Twenty Years of Public Policy.* New York: Norton.

Sears, David O., and Jack Citrin. 1982. *Tax Revolt: Something for Nothing in California.* Cambridge: Harvard University Press.

Sharkansky, Ira. 1969. "The Utility of Elazar's Political Culture." *Polity* 2 (Fall): 6–83.

Simon, Herbert. 1957. *Models of Man.* New York: Wiley.

Sokolow, Alvin D., Priscilla Hanford, Joan Hogan, and Linda Martin (eds). 1981. *Choices for the Unincorporated Community: A Guide to Local Government Alternatives in California.* Davis: University of California, Davis—Institute of Governmental Affairs.

Sternlieb, George. 1971. "The City as Sandbox." *The Public Interest* 25: 14–21.

———, and James W. Hughes (eds.). 1980. *America's Housing: Prospects and Problems.* New Brunswick, N.J.: Center for Urban Policy and Research, Rutgers University.

Stone, Alan. 1982. *Regulation and Its Alternatives.* Washington, D.C.: Congressional Quarterly Press.

Stone, Clarence N. 1976. *Economic Growth and Neighborhood Discontent.* Chapel Hill: University of North Carolina Press.

———. 1986. "Power and Social Complexity." In Robert J. Waste, (ed.). 1986. *Community Power: Directions for Future Research.* Beverly Hills, Calif.: Sage Publications.

———. 1980. "Systemic Power in Community Decision Making." *American Political Science Review* 74 (December): 978–90.

Thompson, Frank J., and L. R. Jones. 1982. *Regulatory Policy and Practices.* New York: Praeger.

Truman, David B. 1951. *The Governmental Process.* New York: Knopf; 2nd ed. with new introd., 1971.

Warren, Robert, Mark S. Rosentraub, and Karen S. Harlow. 1986. "Coproduction, Equity, and the Distribution of Safety," *Urban Affairs Quarterly* 19:447–64.

Waste, Robert J. 1983. "The Early Years in the Life Cycle of City Councils: A Downsian Analysis." *Urban Studies.* 20: 73–81.

———. (ed). 1986. *Community Power: Future Directions in Urban Research.* Beverly Hills, Calif.: Sage Publications.

———. 1987. *Power and Pluralism in American Cities: Researching the Urban Laboratory.* Westport, Conn.: Greenwood Press.

Wildavsky, Aaron. 1984. *The Politics of the Budgetary Process.* Boston: Little, Brown.

———. 1988. *The New Politics of the Budgetary Process.* Boston: Little, Brown.

Williams, Oliver, and Charles Adrian. 1968. "Community Types and Policy Differences." In James Q. Wilson (ed.). *City Politics and Public Policy.* New York: John Wiley.

Wilson, James Q. (ed.). 1968. *City Politics and Public Policy.* New York: John Wiley.

———. 1973. *Political Organizations.* New York: Basic Books.

———. 1980. *The Politics of Regulation.* New York: Basic Books.

————. 1980. *American Government: Institutions and Policies.* Lexington, Mass.: D. C. Heath.

Wilson, William Julius. 1985. "The Urban Underclass in Advanced Industrial Society." In Paul E. Peterson (ed.). *The New Urban Reality.* Washington, D.C.: The Brookings Institution.

————. 1987. *The Truly Disadvantaged.* Chicago: University of Chicago Press.

Wirt, Fred. 1974. *Power in the City: Decision Making in San Francisco.* Berkeley: University of California Press.

Wiseman, Michael. 1985. "Workfare." *California Journal* 16 (July): 289–92.

Wolfinger, Raymond E. 1972. "Why Political Machines Have Not Withered Away and Other Revisionist Thoughts." *Journal of Politics* 34 (May): 365–98.

————, and John Osgood Field. 1966. "Political Ethos and the Structure of Government." *American Political Science Review* 60 (June): 306–26.

Yates, Douglas. 1977. *The Ungovernable City.* Cambridge: MIT Press.

Zeigler, Harmon. 1964. *Interest Groups in American Society.* Englewood Cliffs, N.J.: Prentice Hall.

Index